TELLING

What Remains Hidden Becomes Lethal

A Memoir

CELIA HIRSCH

Gray Productions Publishing
Guttenberg, New Jersey

ISBN 9798992551204
Cover illustration by Celia Hirsch
Cover by Rachel Kirschner
Book Design: Judy Corcoran
www.judycorcoran.com

Printed in the United States

This book is dedicated to my two daughters,
Alex and Jess, my granddaughter, Fiona,
and my best friend, Sharon. It's no coincidence
that they are all women, because this is not
just my story. It's a woman's story.

Acknowledgements

This book would not have been written without these people:

— Ron Hirsch, my patient husband, who wholeheartedly embraced what this project meant to me. He didn't know that, for four years, all my free time, including every Sunday, no matter the weather, would be spent writing. His unconditional support and love allowed me to immerse myself in this journey.

— Alex and Jess Hirsch, my amazing daughters, and Fiona Foster, my exceptional six-year-old granddaughter, all who inspired me to write this book. To them I leave a legacy rather than a black hole. By divulging private and regrettable parts of my life, I hoped to provide them with a handbook as they navigate their own choppy waters. I take solace in knowing that my granddaughter and future grandchildren will know who I am.

— Linda Wade, my therapist since 2012, who created a safe place for me to open doors that had been hermetically sealed. Her validations removed the clamps on my vocal cords. And she guided me to Buddhism, which has become my everlasting inspiration.

— Susan Hodara, my writing mentor, whose thoughtful questions massaged out answers that were trapped inside my tissues. Her generous teaching style allowed the richness of my story to evolve. She has become a treasured friend.

— And finally, Marcel and Irene Bau, my parents. Short of forgiveness, I am grateful for the positive parts of my life that I can attribute only to them. I know with all my heart that I would not be who I am, nor would I be where I am, if it weren't for them.

Table of Contents

Prologue 7

PART 1

1. Van Ness Court I 11
2. Hillside Avenue 14
3. Madison Avenue 20
4. The Meaning of Life 28
5. The Pirate 35
6. Bungalow Colonies 39
7. Dirty Jews 53
8. Fabyan Place 59
9. Running Away 67
10. Mocking Out 70
11. Cheerleading 79
12. Help 87
13. Split 96
14. Sharon 102
15. Fire Island 113
16. Mystic Colossus 126
17. Orgasm 133
18. College 140
19. Ménage à Trois 145
20. The Kiss 149

PART 2

21. Freshman 157
22. Sophomore 165
23. Junior 173
24. Brooklyn Heights 188
25. Gurdjieff 201
26. The Voices 209
27. Woodstock 214

28. VW Beetle 224
29. Infidelity 229
30. The Wheel of Misfortune 236
31. California 243
32. Bearsville 249
33. Broadview Road 255
34. The Health Club 266
35. Charles Street 270
36. The Journals 275
37. Stan 279
38. Van Ness Court II 285
39. Against Protocol 288
Interlude 290

PART 3

40. Phyllis's Funeral 295
41. Abuse 299
42. The Rehab Center 302
43. The Triangle 306
44. Thanksgiving 313
45. Sensations 319
46. Moving 325
47. Bond 330
48. An Exciting Life 335
49. Anger 341
50. Silence 346
51. Sexual Abuse 350
52. Photo Albums 356
53. I Didn't Miss You 364
54. Knowing 371
Epilogue 375

PROLOGUE

I am not a writer. I was led to write this book by a need to chronicle the events of my life with my father. I believed that it would be the source of my healing. I stepped onto this path as clueless as if I were signing onto an expedition into the wildest of jungles. In the jungle, my first steps would have encountered a dense terrain of thick, tangled and unrelenting obstructions. I would have needed a guide to chop and thrash the way through the bramble. Writing my story, my guide turned out to be me.

For seven decades I lived with a deep and granular sense that something was wrong. I was in search of peace and release, but I didn't know from what. Setting off on this journey turned out to be the start of a multi-layered and profound ambition. Each chapter brought me to a new thicket, and often I encountered a dilemma: to turn back or pass through to face the unknown. By choosing the latter, I entered the world of words, and language became my machete.

This memoir began as a record of events and became a powerful and unexpected series of subliminal awakenings. The order of the chapters reflects the course and sequence of my enlightenment. Had I not written this book, I most likely would never have known the truth.

I have reconstructed details and dialogue to reflect the essential truth of my memories.

PART 1

1

VAN NESS COURT I

The door to my parent's bedroom was open. Before stepping over the threshold, I collected my thoughts. But I couldn't control the tightness in my throat, the pounding in my chest or the shaking of my limbs. I told myself, "Whatever you do, don't cry!"

I had come to visit for the weekend. It was early evening, and my mother and father were reclining in their double bed. Mom had her trendy shag haircut, and Dad was beginning to gray at the temples. Their room was almost double the size of my old room, with the same dresser set they'd had since the day I was born, 30 years before. It was a dark wood, maybe mahogany, with three-inch circular brass handles. In front of my parents and to my left, the television was on. I took a few steps forward. "It's now or never," I convinced myself. They acknowledged my entrance but didn't turn off the TV.

My father was nearest to me. It was him I was here to face. I lifted my eyes and said what I'd come to say: "Daddy, I think you know, we have not had a good relationship for a long time. I'm not happy about that, and I think there's a chance we could make it better."

A little of my guard fell, my blood began flowing again, and a small crevice opened to my true feelings. I told him that he didn't listen to me or take any interest in what I wanted for myself. I told him that I felt pressured by him to become his assistant or his partner. Then I took a deep breath. "I don't want to do that," I said. "I want to do my own thing."

I did it! I felt a lightness, unburdened, and a fantasy flashed through my mind: My father's expression would soften. He would leave the bed and approach me with his arms outstretched, wide enough to wrap me in a warm, reassuring embrace. His gentle voice would whisper, "I love you, and I only want what's best for you."

But my father had not moved. He was still lying in bed. His ankles were crossed, his eyes were closed, and his fingers were running through his hair. I knew what that meant. My hand found the doorknob, and I braced myself.

"You're such a moron!" he shouted.

He was sitting upright now, glaring at me with contempt. "I'm doing amazing things, and soon I will be recognized. I'm about to change the world."

He told me he'd soon be making a presentation to "very important people." "They're going to invest a lot of money in me. I'm going to become rich and famous, and you won't!"

As I let go of the doorknob, my knees buckled, and I caught the opposite doorjamb to keep myself upright. I leaned into it and looked down at the floor. Tremors arose from deep within me, and suddenly I was crying. No, I was sobbing. "I don't care that you're going to change the world," I wailed through my tears. Then a guttural sound vibrated my vocal cords: "All I want is for you to be my father!"

Where did those words come from? And now what was going to happen? A sound jolted me back into the room—a loud and evil cackling. It was my father, and he was laughing at me. A force as powerful as a grenade shot my mind backwards. Then a flurry of inner voices launched a barrage of insults: "You're pathetic, stupid, a loser, doomed."

With those words bearing down on me, I peered over toward my mother. She had just witnessed this horrible event, and my demolished figure was standing right in front of her. Surely she would defend me. Surely she'd try and fix this catastrophe. But her face was blank, her body motionless. She was looking at her lap and not at me.

I steadied myself without saying a word, turned around and took the three steps toward my room. I knew I had to leave. As I was gathering my things, my mother appeared at the door. "Where are you going?" she asked. "I thought you were staying over."

How could she be so clueless? I looked up at her and said, "I can't stay here. I have to go home!"

Her head was tilted in a familiar way, her expression apathetic. "Aw, don't be like that. He didn't mean it. Don't leave," she said.

The pull to stay tugged at the pull to go, as it had done all my life. But that night I went.

2

HILLSIDE AVENUE

My parents, Marcel Bau and Irene Landesdorfer, grew up in Krakow, Poland, until both of their young lives were shattered by WWII and the Holocaust. My father was sent to a concentration camp with his parents and two brothers. He and his older brother were the only ones to survive.

My mother and my grandmother Regina had to leave Krakow without my grandfather. Mom explained that early on, rumors had it that women and children were safe. The belief was that the Nazis were after the men. My grandfather was among the many who relocated to Russia.

"Besides," Mom would continue, "everyone thought the war would be over in a matter of months."

While separated from my grandfather, my mother and grandmother settled in a northern town in Poland where they lived as Christians. They both survived, but my grandfather died of typhoid fever while in Russia.

After the war and before they got their papers, my mother and grandmother lived in Germany for several years. That's where my parents met and got married in a civil ceremony. I'd been told by my mother that she was a teenager and my father six years her senior. Not until after she died did I find out that wasn't true. Instead of being 18 when she married my father, she was 21, and he was 26.

They were a striking couple. My mother was a slender, natural beauty, barely five feet tall. Everything about her was soft and elegant. My father was eight inches taller than she was, with a distinctive crop of brown hair. He had piercing hazel eyes and a roguish quality.

When they were finally able to emigrate to the U.S., they came to Newark, N.J., where my grandmother's sister lived. My mother's Aunt Sadie and Uncle Ike had come to America before the war. They were established and affluent, able to take the newly arrived refugees under their wings. At their insistence, my mother and father had an American-style wedding in June of 1949. They were sent off to the renowned Nevele Country Club, in the Catskills, for their honeymoon. I was born in March of 1950.

My mother's uncle had a thriving wholesale housewares business with a big warehouse and showroom. My father was offered a starting position in the company, but he turned my uncle down. He did not want a regular job; he didn't want to work for anyone else. Instead, he became a window decorator for local furniture stores. My mother had no professional ambitions, so my father was the breadwinner.

Our first family home was on Hillside Avenue in Newark, a neighborhood filled with all sorts of ethnicities and nationalities. We lived in a one-bedroom apartment in a small brick building with a grand white marble lobby, which we entered through a heavy glass-and-metal door. There was an elevator, but we often took the wide stone staircase up to the second floor. Our apartment was at the top of the steps and to the right.

The building was known to be a first-stop for refugee families. In no time my parents had a big social circle of other Polish Holocaust survivors and their children. A lot of my parents' enduring friendships were formed in that building, none more significant than with Phyllis and her husband, Leo. They lived down the hall, on the other side of the elevator. Phyllis was a housewife, and Leo worked in the Wonder Bread factory. He'd often stop by our apartment to give me a miniature loaf of the bread in its iconic wrapping. My mother and Phyllis became best friends. Their fateful meeting resulted in a lifelong relationship, which had a profound impact on my life.

I have fond memories of elaborate birthday parties with lots of people crammed into our little apartment. Mom had me in the perfect crisp party dresses, with white ankle socks and brand new shoes. My hair was always impeccably combed with big bows on either side of my head. The adults wore birthday hats and trumpeted their horns as I blew out the candles on my cake.

On my third birthday, during my party, it was not yet springtime, and an unexpected blizzard blew in. It left so much snow on the ground that everyone who didn't live in the building had to stay at our apartment. That is why, even today, I hesitate to celebrate the end of winter until late April.

In those days there was no such thing as a "playdate." My favorite playmate was the superintendent's daughter, who lived in the basement. Whenever we could, we'd play in the enclosed courtyard. If I looked up, I could see my kitchen window. A black family lived across the street, and I played with their daughter, too. Our game of choice was hide-and-seek, and I loved to hide behind the thick drapes in their living room.

Clinton Avenue was the main drag where everyone did their shopping. Strangers would stop my mother and me on the street, point to me and ask, "Where did you get those freckles?" And I would proudly reply, "From my mommy!"

On the weekends we'd get dressed up for strolls in Weequaic Park. I was allowed to play in the playground as long as I didn't get dirty. Across the street was a bakery that made the best coconut custard pie. On those special occasions that we brought one home, I devoured my slice. My tongue lingered in the creamy custard filling, and I savored the awesome crunch of the toasted coconut on top. The sweet buttery taste of the crust was the finale of this sublime treat.

Those were the days of drive-in movies. We'd pull our white Chevrolet sedan up to a pole and hang the speaker from the window. I fell in love with Elvis Presley when we saw *Love Me Tender* at one of those theaters. Often, on the way home, we'd stop at the bagel store for a dozen fresh bagels. If I were still awake, I'd get to eat one. The heat underneath the hard brown shell warmed my little fingers. It took a forceful bite to get to the soft, white dough inside. Once I did, I'd pause to watch the steam rise out of it.

My favorite excursions were to South Mountain Reservation, a sprawling nature preserve minutes from our house. I fed the deer at a small zoo or went sleigh-riding in the winter. The reservation had a good-sized skating arena where I learned to ice skate.

We lived on Hillside Avenue until I was six years old.

I didn't know then but I do know now: These seemingly happy years belied a toxic whirlwind that was inching toward me.

Irene Landesdorfer and
Marcel Bau in Germany
after WWII

Mom and Dad on their
wedding day

From top right: Uncle Ike, Aunt Sadie, Aunt Eda and Aunt Roslyn
From bottom left: Grandma, Mom, Dad and Uncle Victor

3

MADISON AVENUE

In 1956, when I was six years old, Phyllis and Leo bought one of four new two-family houses in Elizabeth, N.J. They were all white cubes with a hip roof. The entry door was smack in the middle, reached by a few concrete steps that led to a cement stoop bordered by black wrought iron handrails. Two small plots of green grass sat on either side of the path that led to the stairs.

Phyllis and Leo's was the fourth one in from the intersection of Madison Avenue and Fanny Street. We became their tenants and moved into the three-bedroom apartment upstairs. It was much more spacious than our apartment in Newark. On one side was a decent-sized living room, a separate dining room and a kitchen. On the other side, the three bedrooms were all in a row.

The other homes in the neighborhood were older, multi-family, three-story houses, almost twice the size of ours. They were painted different colors; I particularly liked the ones that were two-toned: the first floor, say, a cream color and the second, mustard. Some of them had front yards with elaborate fences at the edge of the sidewalk. My friend Christine lived in one of them, several doors down from me. Her house had an enclosed porch on the second floor. I'd never seen a space like that. With the shingled wall on one side and the other three lined with windows, we were outside but inside at the same time. It felt like we were floating in our own ship, private and removed from everything and everybody.

It was there that Christine and I got lost in our paper doll world, spending hours improvising intricate scenarios. But first, we'd place the cardboard figures in their plastic stands and methodically go about cutting out the clothes. I found out the hard way that if I didn't take my time to cut the tabs carefully, I would not be able to hang my favorite outfits on my doll. I became a very precise scissor operator.

Kellogg Park was in the other direction, across Fanny Street. It was the sweetest four-block patch of nature, with lots of paths and a playground. It was packed with trees, and sometimes I would find baby birds that had fallen out of their nests. They were tiny featherless creatures with eyeballs bulging underneath closed eyelids. Their beaks looked like big yellow lips, and their little bodies could hardly hold up their heads. The mama bird was always nearby, chirping frantically. One of my friends told me that if I didn't save the baby, it would not survive, but the mother would reject the chick if I left my scent on it. So I wore my gloves as I carefully lifted the frail baby and placed it in a shoebox that was lined with soft cloth. My mother would help me try and feed it with an eyedropper, but sadly, the fallen chicks always died.

Whenever hurricanes passed through the area, they uprooted the trees in the park. After the storms, my mother and I would walk there with Phyllis and her sons. We'd climb over and under the fallen trunks, just like Peter Pan in Neverland.

I mastered riding my two-wheeler with training wheels in Kellogg

Park. I'd ride up and down the sidewalks until I knew I was balancing on the two big tires. When I was confident that I could sustain it, I asked my father to take the extra wheels off. With my parents by my side, I took a few spills but eventually glided along as though there was never a time that I couldn't pedal without trainers. From that day, I was off, riding on my own.

Then came the time I found my first real pet: a tiny tabby kitten that I cradled in my arms and brought home. I wanted to keep it. My mother was an animal lover, so I assumed she'd say yes. But the decision was not only hers to make. My father disliked animals, and it was Phyllis's house. She had the last word, and it was "No!" I pleaded with my mother, who probably wanted to keep the kitten as much as I did. She changed Phyllis's mind under one condition: "The kitten has to live in the hallway," she said.

Deal! I ran to find a box big enough for a blanket and a small dish for milk. I nestled it into a safe corner on the staircase. Each morning I woke up and ran to get my kitty. I'd play with it in my room when I wasn't in school, and I'd dutifully return it to its bed at night. One morning it was not there, and I desperately looked for it, to no avail. It was gone!

It turned out that when Leo left for work early that morning, he'd let the kitten out. Even though they all said it was an accident, I feared —no, I knew—it was intentional. Either Phyllis had told him to do it, or it was his own volition. Either way, I blamed him.

A short walk to the end of my block and diagonally across the street was a candy store. A bell rang as the door opened, and there before me was a case filled with my favorite treats. With the few pennies my mother sometimes gave me, I purchased Bazooka bubble gum, Tootsie Rolls, Lifesavers or Milky Way candy bars. To the left was the long soda fountain counter, which had stools that spun around. It was there that

I'd order my malted milk shakes or ice cream sodas. When we first arrived in Elizabeth, my mother had to lift me up onto the seats, but by the time we moved away, I was in sixth grade and able to climb onto the stools myself.

One day, on my way back from the store, I was licking my ice cream cone when the tip of my nose collided with a bumble bee. Boy, what a sting! I ran home crying. It hurt; my nose swelled up, and my eye began to close. Mom mixed together baking soda and water, which created a paste that hardened and cooled half of my face. I couldn't very well go to school deformed, so I stayed home until I was back to normal.

When we moved to Elizabeth, I entered the first grade at Madison Monroe Elementary School, a block from our house and across the street. I was old enough to walk there by myself. There were two ways to get to school: One was straight up the block where my mother could watch me from our big picture window. The other was a zigzag route that, within seconds, took me out of her sight and to the school's back entrance. I had a new pair of black patent leather Mary Janes. They had a strap that could swivel to the back of the shoe so it became a pump. My mother wouldn't let me move the strap, so I took the zigzag route, and as soon as I knew she couldn't see me, I'd switch the strap. How clever was I? With my big girl shoes on, I grew an inch, strutted the rest of the way and swung the arm that wasn't carrying my books.

We had one shiny, black telephone. It had a rotary dial in the middle and a curly cord that I liked to stretch. The handle felt big and heavy in my hand. It sat on its own little wooden table, which was tucked in a corner of the dining room. Underneath was a special compartment just for the Yellow Pages—a thick telephone book that I often sat on at the dining room table. Whenever I heard the loud, tinny sound of the bell's ring, I'd dash to answer it. When my mother began letting me use the phone to call my friends, she instructed me, "Never call anyone before 10 o'clock in the morning!"

I watched the clock, and as soon as the big hand was on the 12 and the little hand was on the 10, I'd dial Richie's number. He was one of the many children I played with in the neighborhood. On the phone, we'd arrange to meet, and when I hung up, I'd leave through the back door and run down the big wooden staircase that led to our backyard. I'd walk quickly across the street and almost to the end of the block, where he would be standing in the driveway waiting for me. His house was one of the big ones with a large front yard, but his had a long hedge instead of a fence. Dried leaves that fell from the trees nestled in the delicate branches of the bushes. Richie taught me how to find spiders that had woven tight webs inside the coils of the foliage. We'd gently pick up a leaf and carefully open it until the milky web was exposed. As we continued spreading the edges, the web would break open and the spider would scurry away. It was great fun unless the spider decided to race in my direction.

Sometimes Christine and some other kids would come over to play "make believe." Someone would be the mommy, someone the daddy, and the rest of us would be the kids. I preferred to play a girl who was sleeping or someone who was dead. Lying with my eyes closed, motionless on the ground, was strangely comforting. I listened to the activity going on around me, but I didn't have to participate.

I didn't know then but I do know now: I was playing out and mimicking the way I felt as a member of my family.

When we got tired of play-acting, there was a vast, secret world behind the houses. All the backyards were connected, sometimes delineated by low fences. It was better than any playground and the perfect place to play explorers. There were trees to climb, garages to sneak into, and abandoned spaces to swallow us up. We found old keys, rusted cans and forgotten toys behind the structures. These were treasures that we incorporated into our game. Our imaginations took us way beyond Elizabeth, N.J. Sometimes what brought us back was a shouting woman sticking her head out of a window or a man stepping onto his porch, shaking his fist and gesturing that he was going to chase us. We'd blast off, running and screaming with laughter.

Over the next few years, Nancy became my best friend. We did everything together. I'd ride my bicycle along the Madison Avenue side of the park, to the intersection where our school was. I'd pass the front of the school, peddle to the next intersection, cross the street, and Nancy's house was right there. She'd meet me downstairs, and we'd take off with our transistor radios hanging from the handlebars. "Where the Boys Are," by Connie Francis, and Bobby Vee's "Take Good Care of My Baby" were in the top 20. We both had serious crushes on Ricky Nelson. With our radios tuned to WABC-AM, we'd sing along while we rode, oblivious to the transistors swinging, bouncing and crashing into our knees.

One day, we decided that Kellogg Park was the ideal place for us to experiment with the curse words we'd been learning. We stepped onto the path closest to school, began walking, and as soon as we felt safe we pointed to a rock and declared, "That's a fucking rock!" A spindly bush looked like "shit!" "Let's go to the damn playground" really made us laugh. And when we were ready to leave, we'd say, "Let's get the hell out of here!"

The most radical thing I did in Elizabeth was go to church. Ours was one of only four Jewish families in town, and all my friends were Christian. The church was across the street from the school, and I'd occasionally go there with Nancy. It was a massive, beautiful space that had the rich, dry smell of old books, aged wood and melted wax.

I gazed in awe at majestic stained-glass windows. Nancy showed me how to light a candle and make a cross on my body. I'd bring all the fingertips of my right hand up to my forehead, down to my sternum, across to my left shoulder and over to my right. I can still feel the coolness of the marble as I knelt halfway down the aisle and crossed myself. Upon reaching the front of the church, I knelt again, put my palms together and prayed. I had learned "The Lord's Prayer" at school, and that's what I quietly recited. Sometimes I just sat in the pew and watched Nancy.

I spent quite a bit of time with Nancy and her family. My first Christmas experience was at her house. Our Menorah, eight candles and one gift was no match for their elaborately decorated tree with its tinsel, sparkly lights and mountains of presents below. I was so enamored of their holiday I convinced my mother to, at least, put Christmas stencils on our picture window.

By the fifth grade, Nancy and I started noticing the cute boys at school. Our bicycle routes now included all the places we knew they'd be. We were most likely to find them playing basketball or horsing around on the school playground, where we'd coyly enter, as though it were an accident that we were there. After all, we had to practice basketball, too. But instead of playing ball we'd whip out our Chinese jump rope, which was all the rage. The knotted rubber bands were conveniently rolled up in our pockets. Three girls were needed; two to wrap the jump rope around their ankles and one to do the jumping. We never had a problem finding a third girl. It was the perfect opportunity to show off, and show off we did!

If the boys weren't on the playground, we scouted around until we found them somewhere else. Brief flirtatious meetings happened in driveways and backyards. I liked Dino and heard whispers that he liked me, too. When we saw each other, we could barely contain our little smiles, and I felt the flush that rose to my cheeks. But my true love was Jimmy. He was handsome, with chiseled features. He was very thin so, unlike the other boys, he didn't have any baby fat on his face. His blond hair was always neatly combed in a pompadour. I was so infatuated with him that his sixth-grade photo grew frayed and worn from the number of times I looked at it.

I didn't know then but I do know now: The innocence and normalcy of my life in the outside world contradicted the dysfunction of my family and the life I was living inside my home.

4

THE MEANING OF LIFE

Due to his bodacious style, my father was known as the "whorehouse decorator," which he proudly broadcast to everyone, bragging that he was going to revolutionize the window decorating business. Instead of arranging the furniture in a storefront window to resemble an average room, he used wire to suspend the sofas, chairs and tables at different angles. It gave the appearance of being haphazard and informal. Where other designers created plain rectangular signs, my father's boards were cut asymmetrically. He used stencils and spray paint to fill the spaces up with irregular starbursts in splashy colors. His customers loved it.

Prior to our move into Phyllis's house, my dad rented a space in downtown Newark where he produced his displays. Now, in Elizabeth, Phyllis offered him the use of the basement. My second-story bedroom window was directly over the metal doors that opened to his "shop." I grew accustomed to the banging of his hammer and the buzzing of his bandsaw.

Phyllis also gave him permission to finish part of the basement. He built what he called a bar. There were no right angles. The walls were neither parallel nor perpendicular, and he spray-painted them with circles of different sizes that to me looked like giant chicken pox. He cut out big, arbitrarily positioned holes, which he filled with artificial plants. The only surface that was level was the counter, because it had to be.

Then he started to make lamps, and they began appearing in our apartment. They had quirky sculpted wooden bases that he painted in bright colors with a shiny, lacquered finish. The shades were made from translucent sheets of resin. He punched equally-spaced holes along the edges and wove colored lanyard through the holes.

"No one is making lamps like these," he boasted. "They're going to sell like hotcakes, and soon we'll be rich." The mention of wealth made him puff up with pride and grow taller. It seemed to be a good thing for our family, and I wanted it, too.

I didn't know then but I do know now: These would be the first of many of my father's failed endeavors, which all began with the prediction of untold riches.

My father had turned the third bedroom into his office. I'd see him sitting and writing at the table in the far corner. Often he was shirtless or without pants. His legs would be crossed, his left elbow on the table with his left hand cradling his forehead, his right hand clutching the number-two pencils he used on loose-leaf paper. That was before he had an automatic pencil sharpener, so there were razor blades and wood shavings all over the place. Papers and notebooks were strewn everywhere.

The scene looked very important to me. I moved around quietly so as not to be a disturbance; I dared not interrupt him. So the afternoon when he first called me into his room, I was flattered. He pointed to the twin bed opposite his table and told me to move the papers that covered the mattress. I took my seat at the edge of the bed with my feet dangling halfway down the side. With my hands in my lap, I waited for him to speak. I was eight years old.

"I want you to know what I'm doing," he said. "I'm explaining the meaning of life."

Then he began talking. He named famous scientists and said their work didn't go far enough. He pointed to some drawings he'd made of cells, atoms and molecules. He used words I'd never heard before: plasma, nucleus, protons and neutrons. He talked and talked, and I didn't understand anything that he was saying. Suddenly he stopped, the silence startled me. "So, what do you think?" Caught off guard, I had nothing to say, so I shrugged my shoulders.

"I'm doing the most important work in the world, and you should understand it," he said.

From that day on, whenever he'd ask me to come into the room, I froze. My feet wanted to walk anywhere other than through that doorway. But I had no choice; I had to comply. Each time, he'd start a feverish lecture that made no sense to me. I'd grow fidgety and nervous. But my father didn't seem to care. He just went on and on. There was a window to my left, I tried turning my eyeballs in that direction, hoping that he wouldn't notice and praying that he'd leave me alone. But, again, he'd ask me what I thought, and when I was unable to give him the answer he wanted, he screamed, "You have to use your mind!" Or he'd call me a moron.

I didn't know then but I do know now: This was the beginning of my father's oppressive and predatory behavior.

Skiing had been a popular pastime for my parents in Poland, and here, from New Jersey, we made trips to Belleayre and Hunter Mountain in upstate New York. We packed up the new black-and-gold De-Soto for the two-hour journey. Even if there wasn't any snow on the ground in Elizabeth, I knew mounds would appear the closer we got to the slope. My stomach would flutter with excitement upon first sight of them.

We'd rent the boots, skis and poles. The boots were leather with little metal clips that the laces wrapped around. My father had to tighten mine for me. The skis were made of wood, and in the middle was a metal plate that I'd step into. A thick cable wrapped around the heel of the boot, which was attached to a latch that locked the boot to the ski. I also needed Dad to help me with this. These fatherly acts were so rare that they made me uneasy. I was inured to my father's testy ways, and that was normal to me.

My father refused to send me to ski school; he was confident that he could teach me how to ski. We stayed on the beginners' slope. He and Mom skied in front of me with the tips of their skis together and the backs out to the side. "Keep your skis in a V-shape," they told me. I followed them from one side of the slope to the other and was soon doing the snowplow.

I enjoyed the tug of the rope tow and keeping my skis in the grooves until I got to the top of the slope. But as my fingers got colder, it was harder to keep them wrapped tightly around the line. When I complained to my father, he said, "We're not going to stop until it's time for lunch."

After the first winter season, my skiing ability had improved. Sometimes Dad would point to me and say, "She's got that serpentine motion." I had no idea what "serpentine" meant, but he was praising me, and that was all that mattered.

By the age of 11, I graduated to the intermediate slopes and began taking the chairlift up the mountain. There was a distinct way that the more advanced skiers dismounted from the chair. I was intent on mastering it. As each trip took me to the end of the line and the tips of the skies touched the snow, I zoomed straight ahead, then made a sharp stop, both skis together and to my left. My favorite part was the snowy spray that kicked up behind me.

It was on the open slopes that I mastered my parallel technique. The trail runs were peaceful and quiet. I'd glide past the trees, sometimes skiing between them, gracefully swooshing from one side of the trail to the other.

I'd usually start out skiing with both of my parents, but often I'd be left with just my father. I had to ski the slopes he chose, and that's how I learned to ski the moguls. In no time I picked up the rhythm of hopping from one hump to the next. It was exhilarating, and I moved up to the harder slopes.

But as usual, skiing with my father meant there'd be no break until lunch. We didn't go back to the lodge, even if I complained about being cold. Even if I told him my fingers and toes hurt. His back would stiffen, his brow would furrow, he would look down at me with disdain, and I knew I had to keep skiing.

I'd clench my fingers inside my mittens, but there was nothing I could do about my toes. It got worse on the chairlift. When we finally returned to the lodge, I'd rub my feet or sit by the fire praying that I'd start to feel my toes again. It was the only chance I'd have, because my father would make me ski for the rest of the day, until the resort closed.

I didn't know then but I do know now: My fingers and toes were often brought to the brink of frostbite, and neither my father nor my mother took notice or cared.

We never went skiing with families who had children. At the hotels, on the shuttle buses, in the lodge and at the restaurants, I was the only kid. Their group was young, all in their 30s. They were lively and carried on wherever they were. And then, there was me.

The women orbited the men, giggling and flirting. When they weren't in the ski shop purchasing the latest in ski fashion, they were gossiping in Polish. And then, there was me.

It seemed as though my father was in the middle of everything. He spoke, and the men listened. If their voices got loud, my father's got louder. He had their undivided attention. And then, there was me.

On our trips home, Dad was emboldened and intent on continuing his oration. The car was filled with his provocations, and his now familiar words were rapidly firing as though shot out of a machine gun. At first they were directed toward my mother, but soon he zeroed in on me. Whether I was sitting in the front with my parents or in the back by myself, he just kept flinging words.

"Do you have anything to say?" he'd ask. If I did, it wasn't what he wanted to hear, so I always said, "No."

It happened over and over, trip after trip. He'd unleash a pounding diatribe—demanding and unyielding. His tone was taunting and oppressive. His voice needled me; it felt like a barrage of sharp objects were flying at me. I wanted to melt into the door I was leaning against.

I didn't know then but I do know now: There was no escape from my father's constant harassment. I felt hunted, then captured. My only option was to turn my head from the torment and drift far, far away. It marked the start of a split between my physical and mental world. It was when I began to dissociate.

Mom posing behind
Dad's newly built bar
in the basement in
Elizabeth, NJ

Me, surrounded by nine adults, at
Belleayre Ski Resort, Highmount, NY

5

THE PIRATE

Art was my favorite subject at school. It was 1958, and I was in the second grade at Madison Monroe Elementary. As I descended the staircase that led down to the basement classroom, I breathed in the smell of glue, paint, crayons; even the paper had an odor.

The art room was at the end of the hall—a big shiny room with narrow windows up by the ceiling. All the projects that we did in art interested me, but I particularly loved to draw.

I practiced all the time; I couldn't help myself. At my desk, when I should have been paying attention, I doodled in my notebook. I sketched little houses with flowers, trees, birds and lots of clouds. My mother had been enrolling me in dance classes since I was little, and I had visions of ballerinas up on their tippytoes ready to twirl. I'd draw them over and over again.

I had it down. I started by drawing a big U-shape for the ballerina's head. I figured out that if I added a horizontal line slightly below the top of the U, it looked like bangs. The rest of the hair was drawn as a semi-circle with flips at the bottom: the latest hairstyle. Next came the thin, dainty neck that attached directly to the arms, which went up and encircled the head. I didn't know how to draw hands, so I simply connected all the lines. Where the arms and the armpits met, I made a line down on both sides to a narrow waist. Two horizontal lines formed the waistband. I made the tutu with two diagonal lines down and out from the waist and another horizontal line across the bottom. The legs were like a pedestal with a vertical line down the center. Sometimes the ballerina was on pointe, and other times she was in first position. Then I drew the top of the bodice like two low mountains. I was not good at faces, so I gave her dots for eyes, a vertical line for the nose, and a little smile.

Everyone wanted to learn how to copy my ballerina. During free period, they came over, sat next to me and watched as I went through the steps. If there were extra time, I taught them how to draw tulips, which I also had a formula for.

At home, on the coffee table in my living room, I found a matchbook with a pirate's face drawn on the cover. I couldn't stop staring at it—it looked so real. The lines were all different weights; in some places it seemed like the pencil had been pressed harder than in others. There were parts that were colored in and other parts that weren't. The dimension it produced caused my eyes to dance.

I saved the matchbook in the drawer of my night table, took it out periodically and gazed at it. If I could learn to draw like that, I could improve my ballerina and even draw her face.

Studying it one day, I noticed that the words above the pirate's head mentioned a contest, so I opened the matchbook to find the details. It read, "Copy the drawing, mail it in and win a prize." From that moment on, each time I looked at the matchbook, I pictured myself copying the drawing. I knew exactly how I would do it.

One evening, my parents were getting dressed to go out. It was not unusual for them to leave me alone because Phyllis was downstairs if I needed anything. I was sitting on the sofa in the living room watching television. I couldn't wait for my mother to come out of the bedroom; she was always so pretty. Her slim frame looked great in dresses. Tonight she wore one with cap sleeves, a cinched waist and a full skirt. Her shoes matched perfectly. Her auburn hair was in a soft bouffant, a few strands falling intentionally onto her forehead. Behind her, my father was wearing a short-sleeve button-down shirt with stylish beige slacks and a leather belt. He hated suits, rarely wore them.

As soon as they left, I went to my night table to get the matchbook. With paper and a pencil, I set myself up at the dining room table, which was in the center of our small apartment. Outside, It wasn't dark yet, but inside I needed to switch on the light fixture over the table. I grabbed the telephone book from the stand so I could sit on it to draw my picture.

Bathed by the bright light and surrounded by the silence of an empty apartment I took a moment to collect myself. I'd been waiting for this moment. I studied my pirate's head one last time before putting pencil to paper. At first, all my lines looked the same. Nothing was darker or lighter. I lost track of time as I made one attempt after another. Even if I had to draw 100 pirates that night, I would.

When I finally stopped, I was delighted to see that I couldn't tell the difference between my drawing and the matchbook. Could I really have done this? The lines were the same, soft and hard where they should be. The beard required many lines to resemble hair, and it did. The pirate's hat, which I colored in completely, really looked like a hat. One eye was covered with a patch; the other one, deeply set, stared back at me. It seemed impossible that I'd been able to capture the image so perfectly, yet here it was, right in front of me.

As I was fantasizing about entering the contest and winning a prize, I heard my parents coming up the steps. I quickly gathered the matchbook and my drawing and planted myself by the door so I could show them as soon as they came in. My father was an artist, so I knew he would appreciate what I had done. I wanted him to be as proud of me as I was of myself.

I handed him my drawing and explained that I had copied the matchbook. "Doesn't it look just like the pirate?" I said.

He stood there with the drawing in one hand and the matchbook in the other. His eyes darted back and forth. Inside, I was jumping up and down, anticipating his approval. But when he looked at me, he had a scowl on his face. He tossed both the matchbook and the drawing onto the table and said, "Anybody can copy. A real artist draws from his imagination!" He turned and walked into the bedroom, with my mother right behind him.

CRASH—I was alone. There was no more apartment; the walls were gone. Where seconds before I had been surrounded by color, now it was a desolate wasteland. There was nothing underneath me, nothing to stop whatever was keeping me alive from draining through the soles of my feet.

I wished I could dissolve into a puddle and evaporate. What was I thinking? Where did I ever get the idea that I was an artist?

I didn't know then but I do know now: Before this moment, my artistic expression had been free and without self-judgment. This devastating incident was the first cut of a wound that handicapped my artistic aspirations. From that day forward, I distrusted my inclination and passion for drawing what I saw. I have since heard it said that "imitation precedes innovation," specifically in regard to creative growth. My father's cruel actions put a wedge between me and my instincts that stayed firmly in place into my adulthood.

6

BUNGALOW COLONIES

Each summer, from the age one until I was 15 years old, my parents would pack up our car and drive 45 minutes west to Mount Freedom, a popular New Jersey vacation town. The area was home to hotels and bungalow colonies.

Our first few years in Mount Freedom were spent at Kessler's Hotel. It had a gigantic swimming pool, and I have fond memories of passing through a tile-lined tunnel that echoed our footsteps and voices. The warmth and humidity made my skin tingle, and as my nostrils picked up the scent of chlorine, I knew we were moments away from dipping into the cool, refreshing water.

After the Kessler years, we bounced around from one bungalow colony to another. Once I got older, the drives became more memorable. I'd sit in the back seat with the windows open, anxiously waiting for the swaths of pavement to give way to more and more trees. As the wind hit my face and blew my hair, I anticipated that instant when the congestion in the air disappeared and the fresh, sweet smell of nature took its place. I'd inhale it deeply.

Life in the bungalow colonies was different from life at home. It was a self-contained, communal world filled with children to play with and all forms of summer amusement steps from our cottage. The soundtrack was the slamming of screen doors and the squeaks of rusted latches, punctuating a refrain of birds chirping, adults chatting, kids laughing and water splashing. At night there was a chorus of crickets and other unseen creatures.

The rhythm followed the movement of the dads. They came on the weekends; during the week they went back to their homes for work. From Monday through Friday, life felt idyllic. Our mothers were preoccupied with one another, gossiping and congregating outside on their lawn chairs or sitting around the card tables playing Mahjong. We'd catch sight of them exercising on a grassy knoll, or shopping the vendors that showed up in their trucks. They lounged poolside, chitchatting or reading books and magazines. I rarely saw my mother in the water; she didn't like to swim. Either she never learned how, or she didn't want to get her hair wet. I thought it was a combination of both.

We kids were in camp all day. Immediately after breakfast, I'd join the stream of children moving en masse to the casino. Our camp bags, filled with dry bathing suits and clean towels, were slung over our shoulders. We met at the flagpole, found our groups and recited the "Pledge of Allegiance." Then, off we went to drama, arts and crafts, archery, sports or swimming. Being on the short side, I was always third in line as we marched in single file to our designated activity.

I loved everything about camp, but the most vivid memories are of my arts and crafts projects. Popsicle sticks might be waiting for us on the large picnic tables. Before I started to work with them, I'd slide my fingers up and down the smooth surface of the light wood, and I'd tap them together to hear the sound they made. Elmer's glue, with its distinctive aroma was applied to the tips of the sticks. There was a window of time when the glue was almost dry and I could maneuver the sticks so they lined up perfectly. I admired the strong and sturdy structures. Sometimes we'd make little "stick figures" and use pipe cleaners and felt to fashion their hair, clothes and shoes.

The paper mâché projects were not so satisfying. Soaking the strips of newspaper in the flour-and-water mixture was drippy and messy fun, but I didn't love the way these pieces came out. They were too lumpy, and I couldn't get the paint to cover up all the holes.

The porcelain pieces that we fired in the kilns made up for what the paper mâché lacked. When I was younger, we made bowls, little animals and mugs. One summer, I chose a seated teddy bear that reminded me of the stuffed animals I had as a baby. I painted the head and the body a soft pink, the snout white and inside the ears maroon. The ends of the limbs were like flat plates, so I decorated them with hearts and flowers. Before these pieces were fired, the colors were dull, and the texture was chalky. But once they came out of the hot ovens, it was like magic: They looked like they were store-bought.

When my counselor led us to the chain link fence, I knew it was lanyard time. The box stitch could be done anywhere, but the cobra stitch was another matter, and that's where the fence came in. We'd all line up, attach our hooks and tie on our three strands of the plastic-coated cords. At first it was tricky—it took some time to learn—but eventually I had a keychain.

I didn't care for the competitive nature of sports, so when rain forced us indoors, I was not unhappy. All the groups would crowd into the casino, where we'd have sing-alongs, play all sorts of games and watch movies. Sometimes the counselors treated us to an impromptu performance, where they showcased their talents. In some cases they were silly and I liked seeing that side of them.

I didn't know then but I do know now: Camp and bungalow colony life provided me with a badly needed sense of belonging—the opposite of how I felt in my family.

My biggest summer problem was my extreme allergy to poison ivy. It seemed I would get it just by looking at it. When I found out that I could get it by being downwind of it, the three leaves became an even more insidious foe. I'd get it everywhere—the worst in my eyes and ears, on my lips and in my nose. The unbearable itching could not be treated, and I was not allowed to scratch it. My mother's remedy for the other parts of my body was a bath with brown soap. She'd lather up a washcloth and vigorously scrub the blisters until they broke and were raw. It was a strange confluence of itch and pain— difficult to determine which was worse. Relief came when she dabbed the mess with cotton balls dripping of calamine lotion. I watched and waited as the cool, pink coating soothed and dried out my oozing skin.

The last bungalow colony we went to in Mount Freedom was Sherman Acres. It was different from the rest—bigger and more diversified in terms of the bungalows. Most of the structures were the archetypal wooden clapboard buildings, with cinderblock stoops and screened-in porches. But up on a hill were four new and coveted bungalows that looked more like real houses. I wanted to live in one of those.

The first of the four years we spent at Sherman Acres, I was 12 years old. We shared one of the older bungalows with Mitzi, Max and their son, Henry. Ever since my parents had met them at Kessler's, we'd spent our summers together. Henry was a year older than I, and everyone made a fuss about us. "They're so cute, just like brother and sister!" Or worse, "Boyfriend and girlfriend!" and "I can't wait for the wedding!" As far as I was concerned, Henry was a braggart and unkind. Every chance he got, he beat me up until I cried. I complained to my mother, but she'd always say, "That's what brothers and sisters do."

I'm not sure how she'd have known that because she, too, was an only child. She'd say it with such conviction, then she'd turn on her heels and walk away. And that was that.

Max was a tall, skinny man with a prominent nose. He was my father's sidekick: They carried on boisterously, competing for who could be the most outlandish and who the smartest.

Mitzi was a large, homely woman with a thick Polish accent. She was strict, loud and scary. When she wanted Henry to come home, she'd yodel, "Henrrrrrrrryyy!" Her voice began on a deep note and escalated to a high pitch, when her tongue vibrated the "r" and the "y." She could be heard from one end of the colony to the other.

Each season Mitzi returned with a rattan switch, which she used to threaten and sometimes beat both Henry and me when she felt we'd misbehaved. I knew it was there; I tried to avoid it, and it terrified me.

I didn't know then but I do know now: My mother must have sanctioned Mitzi's disciplinary measures because Mitzi hit me and yelled at me in front of my mother.

The families at Sherman Acres were American Jews from the New York City area. They were more sophisticated than the Eastern European group with whom my parents had surrounded themselves. This marked a dramatic shift in their social circle, and therefore in mine.

These city kids were from the same neighborhood in Brooklyn, and they were already friends. I liked them and had no problem fitting in. From morning until bedtime, we moved from one activity to another, in relative harmony. At the end of one camp day, after dropping off my wet bathing suit, I strolled up the hill to Robin's bungalow. I entered without knocking and found Robin in her room. We spent a little time checking out a new outfit: a red boatneck, button-down, midriff shirt with a geometric pattern. It came with a matching cloth belt that she planned to thread through the loops of her white Bermuda shorts.

The radio was blaring "He's a Rebel" by The Crystals. We turned it up, sang along and practiced our "Loco-motion" moves.

Our plan was to pick up Ellen and Bonnie before heading to the casino, where the boys and older kids hung out. It was a short walk up a dirt road. As we approached, we could hear that a lot of kids were already on the dodgeball court, which was our first stop. We sat at the edge of the blacktop until a new game started. Not good at team sports, I knew I was not going to be picked first, but I didn't want to be left out, so I patiently waited to be chosen.

When dodgeball ended, I spotted one of the boys messing around with the tetherball. I was good at that game, so I strode over and challenged him to a round. Even though I was small, I moved quickly, I was strong, and I could jump high. I slapped that ball as hard as I could and watched it spin wildly around the pole. I won!

As though on cue, we heard the piano being played in the casino. Glenn, one of the older boys, was our very own rock star—our Frankie Avalon or Bobby Vinton. We timidly opened the double doors that led into the massive room. The piano sat caddy-corner to the stage, and there he was, with his slicked-back hair and his wife-beater t-shirt, which displayed his muscular physique. He was playing "Heart and Soul" by the Cleftones. The older girls who surrounded him were swooning, batting their eyelashes and swaying to the music. Anytime we heard the tinkling of the keys we'd make our way to the casino, Glenn was like the Pied Piper, and we'd follow him anywhere. Eventually, I weaseled my way onto the piano bench and he taught me to play "Chopsticks."

Some of those summer kids became my best friends, and because our parents socialized in the winter months I got to go to Brooklyn for weekend sleepovers. So when summer break rolled around, I was 13 and I counted the days until we got in the car to make the trip again. I knew that once we hit Route 10, Sherman Acres was around the corner. My eyes stayed peeled for the Carvel that marked the right turn to the owners' big house at the entrance to the colony. I made a mental note to return to the site for my preferred purchase: the Brown Bonnet, a vanilla ice cream cone dipped in dark chocolate. I could feel my teeth cracking the hardened shell, which released the cold creamy contents onto my tongue.

With the big house in eyeshot, it would be a left turn down a long narrow road before the casino came into view. I craned my neck to see who was already there. Was a dodgeball game in progress?

Finally we reached our bungalow, and I was elated to see it was a modern one on the hill. As soon as I could, I ran down to my friends, whom I spotted at the large pond next to the pool. The previous year, Barry had shown me how to fish off the cement dock. He'd taught me to find the straightest and most pliant branches for my pole. We tied fishing twine onto the thinnest end and fastened a small hook onto the twine. My favorite part was slipping a rolled-up wad of moist white bread onto the hook. My least favorite part was catching and releasing the little sunnies that took the bait. They flopped around on the dock, making it almost impossible to grab their slimy bodies. The hook made a hole in their thin, rubbery lips. I winced while removing the hook, which made the hole bigger. Sometimes I gagged. I was sure I was hurting the fish, but Barry assured me I wasn't. Once they were freed, I was happy to throw them back in and watch them swim away.

At the far end of the colony, another dirt road led to a big field. We'd hiked up there for softball games, bonfires and, at the end of camp, color war. The tree-covered passage was a long and winding adventure full of mysterious plants and insects. We would pick the burrs off the burdock plants that lined the road and make huge balls out of them.

We called them "budji-budjis." Years later, when I found out that those burrs were the inspiration for Velcro, I knocked the side of my head with my palm, lamenting over how rich I could have been had I been the one to make that discovery.

At dusk we would sneak up to the field to watch the lightning bugs put on their light show. We sometimes brought jars and collected the bugs so we could continue watching them flicker. Or we would catch them, pick out their lights and smear them on our faces. I'm not proud of that. It was rumored that the older kids went there to smooch and drink alcohol. As for us younger kids, we played spin the bottle and strip poker. Being a year older, I wondered whom I'd be "making out" with that summer.

I didn't know then but I do know now: That dirt road made a lasting impression on me, and it continues to appear in my dreams. Sometimes it's through the same woods, but it can also morph into majestic mountain passes with snow-covered boulders and sprawling vistas. Or into a thick jungle filled with friendly animals. These are always pleasant dreams, and they speak to a lighter, more peaceful time.

On the weekends, when my father returned, so did the tension, pressure and chaos. On Saturday mornings, when all the families descended on the pool with their tubes, floats and water toys, our family had none. I played volleyball and Marco Polo with the other kids, but the game of choice was the chicken fight. It required at least two fathers and two kids, each on their father's respective shoulders. The winners were the pair who knocked the most kids into the water.

I rarely participated because "this kind of nonsense" didn't appeal to my father. I stood at the edge of the pool watching the other kids laughing, falling sideways or flipping backwards. I told myself, "I don't like to fight," but inside I envied my friends.

I didn't know then but I do know now: My father's vociferous scoffing at anything conventional, anything that "everyone else was doing," left me on the sidelines when he was around. My ache for a father who would play with me was excruciating.

Cocktail hour on Saturdays buzzed with activity. The adults gathered outside the bungalows with their chairs and their booze, and barbecues were fired up. "One Fine Day" by the Chiffons, "Heat Wave" by Martha and the Vandellas, "Walk Like a Man" by the Four Seasons, and other Top 40 hits blasted from transistor radios or record players. This was all in preparation for the evening's festivities at the casino, which was transformed from the hub of camp life into an entertainment venue.

My parents had been adopted by the liveliest group of adults. They were given the nicknames Maurice and Zsa Zsa, which reflected my father's flamboyance and my mother's alluring European beauty. The other women were equally as glamorous, and the men were shameless tricksters who constantly played practical jokes. The most unforgettable was when they stretched Saran Wrap across the toilet bowl underneath the toilet seat. Picturing someone using the toilet like that was disgusting, and for the longest time, I couldn't go to the bathroom without checking before I sat down.

Saturday nights at the casino were a big deal. Sprinkled in among the cabaret-type evenings were musical performances or comedy acts. And then there were the shows that the adults put on. My mother always took part, she fancied herself a dancer and was usually right in the front. We kids attended, and we were allowed to stay when the after-party began.

Chubby Checker's "Twist" was all the rage, and the new movement incited my father's extroverted tendencies. I watched as he danced with abandon, swinging his arms in big flowing movements and shifting his hips in a circular motion. He had no qualms about dancing alone in the middle of the floor, eyes closed, trance-like, at one with the music. It was as though he were part of the entertainment. Of course he'd dance with my mother, but sometimes he'd sashay his way over to another woman and entice her to join him. He drew her in as close as possible and put his hand on her back, just above the buttocks.

If he caught sight of me, Dad would grab me and pull me onto the dance floor with him. At first we'd be dancing separately, but invariably he'd draw me in close and press his hand against my lower back. "Feel the music," he'd say. As my body stiffened, he'd line his mouth up to my ear and tell me to relax. At which point my nerves began to screech. "Let me show you how to move," he'd continue. Then I'd feel a grinding action, which paralyzed me. I was pinned. I had to wait until the song was over, when I could finally dart away. Each time that happened, I was a jumbled mess. And my father always seemed so disappointed in me. Why did I clam up? Why couldn't I surrender to him, give him what he wanted? I never knew what he meant when he called me "inhibited and uptight." But I was getting the message that it was a problem that I needed to correct. I started to hate myself for it.

Our new bungalow on the hill had two bedrooms, one for us and the other for Mitzi, Max and Henry. The rest of the space was an open floor plan, which provided little privacy. One Sunday morning, I slept late and woke up to the muffled sounds of everyone in the common room. Bleary, I emerged from the bedroom, intending to make my way over to the kitchen table. As I took my first step, I saw my father lunging toward me. I couldn't make out what he was saying; all I knew was he was angry. He stepped right in front of me, and while knocking his knuckles into my forehead, he said, "Get it through your head!"

CRASH—A trap door unlatched and opened underneath my feet. All reason vanished as I plunged into a dizzying tumble.

My father had never hit me—I must have done something really bad. But what? I wracked my brain, but there was nothing. He hated when I was "demanding." It must've been that. Why couldn't I control myself?

Somehow I knew I couldn't turn around and crawl back under my covers. Instead, I made it over to the table and took my seat. Everyone sitting there had seen it and heard it, but not a word was spoken. Humiliated, my lower back sunk into the chair, my hands clung to each other, my head bowed, and my eyes cast downward. My favorite dish of farina sprinkled with cocoa and sugar was placed in front of me, but I had no appetite.

I didn't know then but I do know now: This was the point when my father's erratic outbursts and inappropriate behavior began to escalate. I never knew when they were going to happen or why. The only logical explanation was that I was possessed by an evil spirit that made me do bad things.

The coolest bungalow on the hill was the log cabin, and we rented it the following year. I was 14, recently graduated from elementary school and heading into high school. By this point, my parents and I were woven into the social fabric of Sherman Acres.

It was cocktail hour and the typical raucous shenanigans were going on in front of our bungalow. My father was, as usual, holding court, standing in the center of the men, proselytizing and pontificating. Some of the women were seated in lounge chairs, egging their husbands on. Everyone had a drink in hand.

My friends and I knelt behind the chairs and stood behind the trees in order to spy on the adults. Using pantomime, we sent signals to one another that resulted in squelched giggles. I was sure they were undetectable, but as I turned my gaze back toward the circle, I saw my father glaring at me. He charged toward me and clutched me by my upper arm. He was furious that I was laughing at him and his friends.

He reminded me that they were "very important people."

"Either you're in or you're out!" he screamed.

CRASH—My life was over.

My father still had me by the arm. He was squeezing my flesh and yanking me toward the bungalow. My muscles went limp, and I tripped over my feet, missing the first step but managing not to fall. He dragged me through the house and into the bedroom.

As the door slammed behind him, I stood in the center of the room, dazed and demoralized. The evil part of me had snuck out again and gotten me into the worst trouble ever. I found my bed and sat at the edge until I keeled over. It took a second to slide myself into the middle of the mattress, grab my pillow and wail into it.

No one came into the room until much later, when my mother cracked the door and asked me to join everyone for dinner.

"I'm not hungry," I said. All I wanted to do was vanish.

I didn't know then but I do know now: I'd never experienced that level of rage from my father, nor had he ever threatened me in that way. "Either you're in or you're out" confirmed a subliminal message that sat at the bottom of my soul: If I didn't do what he wanted me to do, he'd abandon me, and there was no worse fate

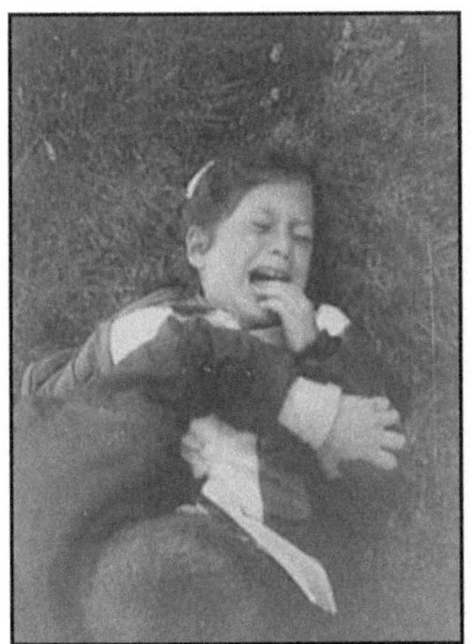

Me getting beaten up
by Henry at one of the
bungalow colonies

First dance at Henry's Bar
Mitzvah

Program from the
adults' annual show
performed at the
casino

Dad dancing
by himself

Dad holding court somewhere on the grounds
of Sherman Acres

Dad, with beer can in
hand, pontificating in
front of the log cabin

7

DIRTY JEWS

Our first summer at Sherman Acres, my father tried to jump out the window in the middle of the night. I was sound asleep in the bedroom that I shared with my parents. When I woke up in the morning, I found that his failed attempt had ripped a gigantic hole in the screen. The adults were already up chattering about it, and I listened. My dad had had a nightmare in which he was escaping from a concentration camp. It wasn't the first time I'd heard reference to these camps, but it was the first time I understood that because my father had been held in such dreadful circumstances, he suffered from violent dreams. I couldn't imagine a terror so ghastly it would cause him to do what he did.

My introduction to the horrors of the Holocaust had come prior to that incident when I was about seven years old. Our apartment in Elizabeth only had one television. My parents, my grandmother, Phyllis and Leo were gathered around it when I was summoned to join them. All the seats were taken, so I had to sit on the floor just inches from the TV.

"Celia, I want you to watch this," my mother said.

It was a black-and-white newsreel from WWII. Dramatic music filled the room, large words flashed on the screen, and a huge airplane soared across the sky. This was followed by scenes of battles, tanks in the street and men signing papers. Fighting made me nervous, military scenes scared me, and I wondered why I was being made to watch. I began to fidget and turned to my mother, but her disapproving look made me stop. She pointed to the screen.

The camera lens was panning across a group of people standing behind a fence. I'd never seen such sad faces in my life. They were all wearing the same dirty, striped clothing, and their emaciated bodies stood huddled together. I wasn't sure what I was seeing, but I felt ashamed to be a spectator.

Cut to a street scene where wheelbarrows were piled high with—what? I craned my neck to get a better view. Something was dangling and scraping on the pavement. I kept looking; a hand and then a foot came into focus. These were dead bodies, pale and limp. A deep shudder ran through me, and I had to fight to sit upright. All the images that followed took me to the brink of nausea. I wanted to put my hand in front of my eyes to block what I was seeing, but I was afraid my parents would chastise me. The urge to leave was so strong that I pleaded with my mother to let me return to my room.

"No," she said. "Stay where you are. You have to know what the Germans did to the Jews and your family."

Then, "This is why your grandfather died and why Grandma and I had to hide."

And then, "When Phyllis was your age, she was living in a barn by herself."

The way my mother said these things made me feel guilty for wanting to leave. There was so much blame in her voice that I almost felt responsible for the horrific events I was viewing.

Each time these newsreels were aired, I was beckoned by my mother to watch. I joined the other viewers and obediently took my seat at the edge of the TV. When the worst scenes appeared on the screen, I tried to avert my vision, but I didn't want to get in trouble. Instead, I glazed over and retreated to the safe place inside my body where I couldn't feel anything.

A couple years later, when I was 11 years old, I heard a commotion downstairs in Phyllis and Leo's apartment. Phyllis was apoplectic, scurrying around and shouting. Then she was crying. Inconsolably. No one told me what was going on. All my mother said to me was, "Stay away from our next-door neighbors."

I'd usually pass by that neighbor's house whenever I met up with my friends. The kids who lived there were older than me, so I'd never been inside. It had always been just another house, but now it was the home of dangerous people. I began walking a little closer to the curb or crossing the street entirely. I wondered what they had done.

Days passed, but Phyllis's hysteria did not. Both our households were in an uproar. Sometimes my mother went downstairs, and all I could hear were muted, agitated sounds. But when Phyllis was in our apartment, I heard the words "Dirty Jews" loud and clear. Apparently there'd been some sort of altercation between Phyllis and the neighbors about a fence and tree. It led to a heated exchange that ended with the neighbors calling all of us "Dirty Jews."

My mother often reminded me that Phyllis carried a tremendous burden from her years in hiding, and that she'd never gotten over the loss of her sister. Anytime the Holocaust was mentioned in Phyllis's presence, her demeanor would change—her eyes would widen, and she seemed to be catching an eerie sight. Then she'd say, "They blame the Jews for everything, and it's going to happen here!"

Prior to these events religion had not played a role in my young life. Most of my friends were Christian, and I was oblivious to any differences between us. But the dark images from the newsreels coupled with the new threat that lived next door shattered my innocence. The ominous prediction that danger lurked began to conjure images of the police coming to our house, dragging us into the street and killing us. The possibility of an American Holocaust haunted me. Even into my adulthood, anytime a major world event did not result in the annihilation of the Jews, I breathed a sigh of relief.

And then there was my father's story, combined with his opinions. He didn't exhibit any outward emotion regarding his ordeal, but I never forgot the nightmare he'd had in the bungalow. Whenever he did speak of himself in the camps, he portrayed himself as an enterprising and resourceful survivor rather than a victim. He'd peeled mounds of potatoes in order to make a few pennies. The tale always culminated with the detailed account of his dramatic escape: "Rumors were circulating that the Americans had won the war and were on their way to liberate us," he explained. The German officers, who were still in charge, began lining up prisoners in the huge courtyard. "It was as big as a football field," he'd say.

As he took in the scene, he calculated that there were more prisoners than captors. He turned to his fellow inmates and made a last-ditch appeal: "We outnumber the guards and could easily overtake them." "But," he'd say to me, "they were cowards."

He knew they were being marched to their certain death. I was riveted at this point in his narrative. What came next was nothing short of a miracle. "Can you imagine that in full view of everyone, including the officers, I ran toward the barracks? No one saw me." The Germans even came back to look for him, but they didn't find him. "I hid there for a few days, and when I knew it was safe, I climbed the fence and ran."

The "Dirty Jew" dispute was the catalyst for our move from Elizabeth back to a "Jewish" neighborhood in Newark. Suddenly, instead of commemorating Communions, Confirmations and holidays such as Good Friday, Easter and Christmas, I was thrust into a culture that celebrated Bar and Bat Mitzvahs, Rosh Hashanah, Yom Kippur and Passover. It was the first time I was faced with how little I knew about my own faith, and I was ashamed. The coming-of-age ceremonies held in synagogues were much more intimidating than the church services I'd gone to with my Christian friend. I did not understand any Hebrew, and I couldn't follow the prayers. Unlike all the other kids, I had no idea what was going on, which made me feel stupid.

I don't recall celebrating the Jewish holidays in Elizabeth. I do remember special dinners to observe Rosh Hashanah and Passover at Phyllis's house in Newark. We'd get dressed up; the men wore yarmulkes; the table was set with fancy plates and silverware. Eastern European delicacies were abundant and delicious. Phyllis's chicken soup with matzo balls was legendary. Grandma made mouth-watering kreplach that was sometimes served with the soup but also with caramelized onions on the side. Gefilte fish was my mother's contribution, and she put enough sugar in the gelatinous sauce that we kids actually ate it. There was brisket, lots of matzo, horse radish and sometimes kasha varnishkes. It all depended on which holiday we were celebrating.

A few of the rituals that were associated with the meals were performed, but they were abridged and out-of-context. I don't remember a Haggadah being passed around. I vaguely recall reference to the Jews walking through the desert. We didn't sing the songs, repeat the legends or learn the meaning behind the holidays.

I didn't know then but I do know now: My Jewish identity was shaped by the insensitive way my parents introduced me to the Holocaust. To me, the Jewish experience started and ended there. It didn't help that our family had no religious affiliation; we didn't belong to a congregation, and I was never afforded the opportunity to learn about Jewish history, heritage and customs. My father used the dinners at Phyllis's as a forum to impose his vehement opposition to organized religion. He challenged, antagonized and ridiculed those who observed, which I suspect might have been why some of the traditions were kept to a minimum. I found the gatherings to be tense, which made me uncomfortable, and I'd tune out. Sadly, it all manifested in an aversion to Judaism.

8

FABYAN PLACE

In the spring of 1962, I was 12 years old and we moved back to Newark. This time my parents bought our own house on Fabyan Place, and Phyllis bought the house next door. They were both two-family structures, similar to the house we left in Elizabeth. Ours was a boxy design with eight concrete steps up to the front door. The first story had a brick veneer, and the second story was clapboard.

The Weequaic section, as it was called, was not just infamous for its Jewish population but also for its affluence. It was where my mother's Aunt Sadie and Uncle Ike lived, but their house was close to Weequaic Park, which was the better side of town. Our house, far from the park, overlooked Valley Fair, the largest convenience store in the neighborhood, with its equally massive parking lot.

The front entrance in our new home led into an L-shaped living room and dining room. The eat-in kitchen sat neatly within the arms of the L, turning the space into a square. In the back of the house, down a hallway, there were three bedrooms. The main bathroom was off the vestibule outside the bedrooms, and the master bedroom had its own bathroom. That was the first time I'd ever seen an en suite bathroom.

My maternal grandmother came to live with us in this house, and my parents gave her the master bedroom. I was too young to understand this new arrangement, but I suspect it was for financial reasons. Even with a tenant, my parents could not have afforded to own the house without Grandma's contribution. She worked in a factory somewhere in Newark, and I later learned that she had been recently divorced from her second husband. She was fiercely independent, a solemn woman with a stoic personality—she had a quiet strength and dignity. We didn't have much of a relationship, and for some reason that I didn't understand, I resented her living with us.

I didn't know then but I do know now: My grandmother might have been the only person who knew the truth about the kind of man my father was. My mother would always conclude the story about how she met my father by saying, "Grandma did not want me to marry him." That was the only hint I had that a member of my family had a negative view of my father.

My new bedroom was painted powder blue, and I got to pick out my furniture. My mother took me to a store owned by one of my father's customers, and I chose a white bedroom set. The dresser with its big mirror was connected to the desk—it was the latest thing. I chose a fancy bookcase headboard for my twin bed, where I kept my clock radio and my Princess phone. For the first time I had my very own full-length mirror, which was hung on my closet door.

By this time I was already a fashionista—I loved clothes. In Elizabeth I'd been voted "Best Dressed," which I took seriously and didn't hesitate to boast about. One of my favorite activities with my mother was shopping for school clothes. Buying the garments and arranging the outfits was quality time that we spent together. And I could count on my mother to get the money I needed to purchase whatever I wanted. Before school started, we hopped onto the bus, headed to downtown Newark and hit Ohrbach's and Bamberger's department stores. My mother knew every nook and cranny of these shops.

I'd be entering the seventh grade at Chancellor Avenue Elementary School. For my first day, I wore a red pleated wraparound kilt with a fringe on the open end. It had a large brass safety pin that kept the skirt closed. A matching red short-sleeve blouse was tucked into the skirt, and I finished the outfit off with red knee socks. Oxblood penny loafers were in, but they couldn't be just any loafers; they had to be G.H. Bass Weejuns.

I was ready! My new notebooks were filled with crisp, blank loose-leaf paper, and my pencil case was loaded with freshly sharpened pencils, a couple of pens and bright Pink Pearl erasers. I jogged down my front steps with my supplies hugged to my chest. I'd only been in this neighborhood a few weeks, and nothing felt familiar, especially the houses I had to pass before getting to Chancellor Avenue, the main drag, aka "the Avenue." On each of the four corners leading up to the school, kids were meeting and walking together. I felt conspicuous walking by myself, so I set a mental goal to find walking partners in the future.

Chancellor Avenue Elementary was huge compared to the intimate Madison Monroe in Elizabeth. Initially, I found the number of children in my class to be formidable, but in no time I was befriended by Sherry, who lived on Wainwright Street, a couple of blocks away from me. Soon I was meeting her on her corner, and we'd set off for school, picking up a few more of her friends. It just so happened that she was part of the "popular crowd," and they began including me.

I didn't know then but I do know now: During this critical period, I began cultivating an external persona. Because I could not face the traumas that had already occurred within my family, I turned my sights outward, where I'd experienced a measure of success. I tapped into my innate ability to study and mimic my friends. Fitting in seemed to be the likeliest path to the stability I yearned for.

Most of these kids had grown up in this neighborhood, where, I was soon to learn, there were many traditions, none more exciting than The Bunny Hop. It was a small restaurant that hosted an overflow of kids all day and night. Whoever couldn't fit inside congregated on the sidewalk outside, rain or shine. I'd never seen anything like it.

At 12 years old, my new friends and I were the youngest in the crowd. It was intimidating, but it was also thrilling. Following my friends' lead, I waited in line in front of the window to the right of the entry door and under the huge awning. Behind the opening sat a jovial guy who kibitzed with us, which put me at ease. He wore the same t-shirt and white boat-like hat that all the guys inside were wearing. The Bunny Hop served hot dogs, hamburgers, knishes and sodas. I placed my order and handed him the money my mother had given me to "eat out."

The parade of cars driving up and down the Avenue added to the party-like atmosphere. No matter what time of year it was, the kids who had licenses piled their friends into their vehicles and blasted their radios. Shouts from the cars to the sidewalks drowned out any other sounds.

It was a spectator sport. Who was driving? What girl was sitting beside him? I knew it would be years before that could happen to me, but that did not stop me from fantasizing about being one of those girls.

I arrived in Newark just in time for the Bar Mitzvah season, and because I was in the popular crowd, I was invited to all of them. This gave Mom and me an excuse to do what we did best. I needed a different dress for each affair and Queen Ann pumps dyed to match. We shopped in the usual stores, and Mom had her sources for the shoes.

She introduced me to girdles and taught me how to attach my stockings to the metal and rubber contraptions that dangled from the weird garment. It was uncomfortable, but all the girls were wearing them, and so did I.

Conte's, Mom's beauty parlor, was on the corner of Fabyan Place and Chancellor Avenue. She was a regular; Conte himself did her hair. Therefore, I had the great honor of having my coif done by him, and I reveled in the fuss he made over me. I never knew if I'd be leaving with a flip or a bouffant or even a French twist. Whatever it was, I stepped out of the salon with the biggest, most perfectly teased and sprayed hairdo. But there was one problem. How was I going to get my party dress on? Mom to the rescue. She showed me how to take a large square kerchief, gently place it on my done hair, tie the corners together under my chin and carefully slip the garment over it.

The evening celebrations were the most extravagant affairs I'd ever attended. Stepping through the grand entryways into the giant ballrooms with their glitzy chandeliers made me feel like a princess at court in a castle. Standing amidst the elegance of women in their satin gowns and elbow-length gloves, the men so debonair in their tuxedos, dazzled me. The dias, which was usually higher than the other tables, felt important and also gave us kids a birds-eye view of all the festivities. When the music started, I felt most at home; I was not shy about getting onto the dance floor. To my surprise, I was often chosen for the first dance with the Bar Mitzvah boys.

I was months away from becoming a bonafide teenager, and I was cultivating my style. I got my inspiration from Seventeen magazine, which I bought at the corner store. With my teasing comb in hand, I created a massive mane and masterfully smoothed it into a perfect flip. I held the can of hairspray at just the right angle, filled the bathroom with clouds of the sticky contents, and voila, I emerged with a brittle, immovable helmet-like thing on my head. I had clip-on bows in every color that I placed strategically above my bangs. Conte himself would have been proud.

My make-up took some ingenuity. The application of the two-tone eyeliner required several tries. Using a fine brush, I would paint on a thick line of white or turquoise. On top of that went the black line, slightly thinner so that a hairline of the first color remained. I deftly handled the tiny brush and lightly touched the point to the inner corner of my eye. As I stroked toward the center, I increased the pressure, and then I lifted it to create a nifty wing at the end of my eyelid. To finish the look, I painted either the white or turquoise right on the lip of my lower eyelid. All the girls were impressed, and soon I was teaching them how to do it.

It was 1963, smack in the middle of the Beatles' invasion. They blew my mind! I was in love with Paul and dreamed that he would marry me someday. I knew all the words to "I Want To Hold Your Hand" and "She Loves You."

Every Friday night our school held a dance in the gym. During the week it was all we talked about and prepared for. Ten of us girls would meet at someone's house so we could enter gang-like through the doors. We were so obsessed with the Beatles that we all went with our hair in a ponytail. The plan was that when a Beatles song came on, at the spot where the Beatles did their iconic hair shake, we'd remove our rubber bands, loosen our hair and shake away. We were the only girls who did that.

Dancing was my thing. I'd watch American Bandstand incessantly, keep my eyes glued to the best dancers and internalize what they were doing. In my room, I'd pile my 45s, insert adaptors in place, on the stacking spindle of my record player. As soon as the first record dropped onto the turntable and the music left the speakers, I'd start.

While standing in front of my full-length mirror, I'd recapture what I'd seen on the TV screen. My inherent understanding of rhythm coupled with the confidence I had in my coordination kept me practicing until I was doing a mean Mashed Potato, Jerk, Pony or Watusi.

At the dances, most of the boys stood on the sidelines until the slow songs came on. Then everything shifted. Where moments earlier we girls were zealously throwing ourselves around, now we scurried like frightened rabbits to the opposite side of the gym. Standing in clumps and whispering to one another, we waited for the boys to make a move. My heart would pound as the first notes of "Blue Velvet" by Bobby Vinton or "The End of the World" by Skeeter Davis came over the loudspeakers. Jay was the most popular boy and Toby the most popular girl; there was no question that they would be the first couple on the floor. For me, I wasn't sure who I liked yet, but I definitely wanted to be chosen, and I usually was.

To the right of the elementary school was the high school, and to the left was a huge stadium where the football games were played. Early Saturday mornings in the fall, I'd lay my casual clothes out on my bed so I could make the critical choice of what outfit to wear. Definitely a pair of ankle-length pants—but with what? A mohair sweater? And did I have a dicky to match? Or should it be a button-down tailored shirt under a tennis sweater? Once I was satisfied, I'd bound down the front steps of my house and head toward the Avenue to meet my friends. I could barely keep up with my feet. The sound of the marching band made me want to fly, and the drums felt like they were beating in my solar plexus. As soon as we arrived at the gate, we'd purchase our tickets and find the seats closest to the center of the bleachers. The air might've been cool and crisp, but the energy sizzled.

I sat on the edge of my bench as the cheerleaders made their entrance through the goal post and down the field. When they arrived in front of the stands, my eyes never left them. Their athleticism, syncopation and spirit mesmerized me. I watched them closely; again I internalized their moves, especially their half-time solos. I imagined myself wearing those uniforms and shaking those pompoms. But I'd have to wait two more years to enter high school.

I didn't know then but I do know now: These were the years when movement became the connective tissue that held me together. When my body was in motion, I transcended all the stressful situations in my life. It was an essential form of creative expression for me.

9

RUNNING AWAY

It was a weekday evening. I'd finished my homework, and before I sat down to watch TV, I strolled into the kitchen. Mom was standing at the stove in her capri pants, a flowery short-sleeve shirt and an apron tied at her waist. She was preparing my favorite meal: pot roast with mashed potatoes.

My mother was not a good cook—she preferred to open cans—but she made the potatoes just the way I liked them. After they got mashed, she left them on the burner long enough for a brown crust to form on the bottom. She'd serve my portion upside-down so the scraped, burnt part was on top.

A half-hour later she called us all to dinner. The table in our small eat-in kitchen was big enough to fit four people. It had a white flecked Formica top with a two-inch chrome edge. The chairs were also chrome, with shiny red plastic seats. In spite of the white rubber stoppers on their feet, they made a lot of noise as they were pulled out and pushed back in.

Grandma and I were the first to sit down, in our regular seats.

She sat against the wall, and I with my back to a window that over-looked our driveway. It was dusk; the weather was mild, and the window was open. I could hear the neighbors' kids still playing in their backyard.

My father emerged from his "shop" in the basement several minutes later and took his seat opposite me. He'd been making signs, so his hands were stained with ink and his clothes were soiled and wrinkled. From across the table, I picked up his sweaty scent. As usual, he was immersed in his own thoughts, and when he finally spoke it was as though he were in the middle of a sentence. The table was not set with placemats, so the plates and stainless steel utensils clicked and clanged while we ate. The only sound above that was my father's voice, and as long as he droned on as he usually did, I was free.

I kept my eyes on my plate and allowed my mind to drift to my girlfriends, the boy I liked and what I was going to wear to an up-coming party. But then I felt an uncomfortable weight bearing down on me.

"Do you hear what I'm saying?" my father was asking. I didn't have time to answer.

"Sex is the most important thing in life. You have to have an orgasm."

My head was still angled downward, and the room became silent. I looked toward my mother and grandmother, but they wouldn't meet my eyes. Then I gingerly shifted my glance toward my father. He had a frightening expression on his face. From across the table he bellowed, "Don't run away!"

How did he know that I hadn't been listening to him? Wrenched out of my refuge, I was caught. Trapped.

"Don't run away!" he yelled, even louder.

Through the slits of my narrowed eyes, I looked toward the hallway to my right. Every muscle in my body wanted to dash in that direction, but I was immobile, as though shackled to the chair.

Then came his rampage. I was shallow, superficial and a moron. My thoughts were boring. My drive to be like everyone else made him sick. If I continued like that, I'd be an "uninteresting person" who would live an "unexciting life." He went on and on, assassinating my character. Nothing was off limits.

Then, "If you don't open your mind, you'll be frigid, like most women."

CRASH—A bull, full of contempt and hostility, came charging at me. Everything shut down. I was no longer in the room.

I didn't know then but I do know now: My father's abuse was in full view of my mother and grandmother, and neither of them came to my defense. The entire episode went unacknowledged, as though it had never happened. I was forced to find a place for it in my psyche, a place where I could not feel its cataclysmic impact.

10

MOCKING OUT

Being a member of the popular crowd at school was proving to be as tumultuous as my 13-year-old life at home. Toby was the leader, and at first I couldn't figure out why. She was cute but not pretty, and she was short and stocky, yet she was in command, and everything passed through her. All the girls vied for her attention. I was to find out that she was the best female athlete, she oozed confidence and was very clever. I soon fell in line.

Toby gossiped about everyone and was a consummate name-caller. I learned the phrase "mocking out" from these girls, and it was the last thing anyone wanted to be on the receiving end of. We were in eighth grade, and pointy-toed shoes were in. I convinced my mother to buy me a pair of the pointiest. Toby's opinion mattered, so I couldn't wait to show up at her house wearing my brown, fake-alligator, lace-up wingtips.

Toby's eyes always scanned everyone from head to toe. When I noticed her scrutinizing my shoes, I assumed she was admiring them until she turned to Bobby, who was standing next to her, and declared,

"Look at Celia's big feet!"

While they were pointing and snickering I looked down at my new shoes and saw clown feet, huge and floppy. "Here comes Big Foot," the girls would say every time they saw me. Those shoes went into the back of my closet, never again to see the light of day. But the humiliation stuck, and from then on I cursed my own enormous appendages.

I didn't know then but I do know now: My friends in Elizabeth and those from the bungalow colonies were kind and inclusive, and our interactions were congenial. I'd never been around kids who were so mean, and I was ill-equipped to stand up to them.

Francine's house had a finished basement, so she hosted many sleepovers. At one such event, we were in our pajamas, frolicking around with our blankets and pillows. Toby was choosing who was going to sleep near her, and it wasn't me. I set up my spot in a corner, at the edge of the group. Feeling excluded, I sat with my back against the wall. Internally, I receded to a quiet place within myself. Toby noticed, pointed at me and said, "Look at Celia, sitting there and sulking!" From that night forward, I was given another nickname: "the Sulker." I didn't want to be viewed that way, but each time I got "mocked out," what I felt inside of me was so powerful that I had to extricate myself. I had to retreat. It was out of my control.

I didn't know then but I do know now: Toby's ridicule attacked and exposed the only place I felt safe.

At the regular "meetings" we had at Toby's house, she'd sit on a chair in her living room as though on a throne. The rest of us sat on the floor. The girls were starting to get their periods, and one by one they'd make their announcements at Toby's feet. She kept a tally, which she shared with the boys. Because I didn't get mine until I was 15, I was called "period-less." Armed with my new nickname, the boys shouted it in the hallways at school, at social gatherings and on the Avenue.

This was the ultimate cruelty; I couldn't bear it. Each time they teased me I disappeared. However, when I finally got my period, I did what all the other girls had done. I groveled at Toby's feet and shared my "good" news, secretly hoping that the heckling might stop.

I didn't know then but I do know now: I had no way of discerning that these kids were bullies. What I was encountering as a member of this group mirrored the dynamics within my family. There, I was a target, and I'd never learned how to defend myself. I only knew how to withdraw or shut down.

As our interest in the boys grew, animosities in this competitive group flared. A rift arose between the "pretty" girls whom the boys pursued and the ones they did not. Dressing up, wearing make-up and flirting was frowned upon. And accusations of betrayal, being a "traitor to your girlfriends," flew like bullets from the less desirable girls. It reached such a fever-pitch that it required Toby, our undisputed leader, to come up with a solution. She identified two separate factions: the "impressers" and the "babies." She was going to decide which group each of us belonged to. It was a nail-biter—I was never sure of my place in this clique, and waiting for my assignment was intense. I was shocked and reassured when Toby chose me to be an impresser.

Pretty soon we started having parties—"make-out" parties. They were usually held at someone's house when their parents were not at home. We'd begin by gathering in the living room; the girls stuck together in one area and the boys in another. It was awkward and titillating at the same time. When everyone had arrived, the host put on the first record, which was always a fast song. Just like at the Friday night dances at school, the girls danced together until the first slow song came on. Then the pairing off would begin. The braver boys were the first to ask their chosen girls to dance. There were always more girls than boys, so the unchosen found an inconspicuous corner to wallow in self-pity or trash the girls who got picked. The lights would dim as couples found their way to a spot on the couch or elsewhere to smooch.

Meanwhile, at home, my father was redecorating our living room. It was not going to be an ordinary remodel; it was going to be "outrageous." The wall to the left of the entry door, which included a large picture window, was entirely covered by a gaudy floor-to-ceiling curtain. In the corner across from the door, he installed a tree with artificial leaves that mimicked a weeping willow. From the branches, which protruded into the room, he hung a golden spherical light fixture, two feet in diameter. The far wall was draped in a burnt orange suede-like fabric. A huge semicircular sectional sofa, upholstered in an exotic gold and orange brocade, sat under the tree. An ornate brass statue of some divinity soared four feet high on top of a round wooden coffee table.

When the living room was finished, he turned his attention to the basement. The back portion served as his shop, and now the front part became a full-scale nightclub. In his usual flashy style, he built two long banquets on either side of the room, each with recessed lighting that could be dimmed. He installed projectors that produced a light show on the walls above the seats. On the back wall, which separated his shop from the party space, was one of his iconic bars, complete with little round tables for snacks and drinks. He even constructed a control room that housed an early sound system with a large stereo, an amplifier and multiple speakers.

No sooner had the last nail been hammered in, my parents began hosting "chip-in" parties, where couples paid a small sum of money to cover the expenses. Some of the guests were local friends, but the bulk were my parents' Sherman Acres crowd from New York.

This was the start of what felt to me like monthly happenings. I was usually still awake when their friends arrived, at that point sober. I said my hellos and then was relegated to my room. As the festivities began, I'd hear the first tunes my father chose. He loved "Wipe Out" by the Surfaris, "Wild Weekend" by The Rebels and "Pipeline" by The Chantays. I knew the party was in high gear when I heard "Sugar Shack" by Jimmy Gilmer and the Fireballs. When I thought it was safe to do so, I'd tiptoe to the door off the kitchen that led down to the basement and listen to what was going on. It sounded like a rowdy and wild affair. Eventually I fell asleep and when I woke up in the morning, the whole house smelled like cigarettes and booze.

I didn't know then but I do know now: My parents had strippers at these parties. I'd blocked it out of my mind until one of Phyllis's sons recently reminded me. When I pictured it happening in my house with my parents, it was too much.

My father's faux nightclub gave me an idea. It was the perfect venue for our teenage parties, and, no surprise, I got my parents' permission to host them. One night, an hour before such an event, Nancy and Sherry came over. We were going to get ready together. We each had a mirror: I was doing my hair in the bathroom, Sherry was putting on her make-up at my bureau, and Nancy stood in front of the full-length mirror on my closet door. I walked a tightrope when it came to my looks and always compared myself to my friends. In my opinion, they were slimmer and taller than me, which was preferable. They had long waistlines where I was short-waisted. And worst of all, they were already wearing real bras, while I was I still in a training bra. I'd been planning my outfit all week: a teal jumper, which made me look longer, a white blouse and my new black t-strap flats that made my feet look smaller.

Sherry was beginning to get a reputation for being "easy." Nancy and I had talked about her behind her back, but there was no mention of it that night. Jay, who used to be Toby's boyfriend, became unavailable: he and Nancy were now an item. Next on my list was Jay's cousin, Arnold. He wasn't as cute as Jay, but he was equally as popular, and we'd danced together at school and Bar Mitzvahs.

While the girls gathered up the refreshments and took them down to the basement, I organized the records for the start of the party. I set the lights to be semi-dimmed until everyone arrived. The rest of our girlfriends showed up first, inciting a flurry of loud, anxious jabbering, with plenty of showing off and checking one another out. As the boys dribbled in, they gathered on the other side of the room, disguising their uneasiness by horsing around. I checked to see if Arnold had arrived and got goose-bumps when he walked through the door.

When it came to the boys, I was pretty shy and not as self-assured as I would have liked. Thankfully I had to manage the stack of records, so I disappeared into the control room, which settled my nerves. I chose the best dancing music to mark the start of the party: "Dancing in the Streets" by Martha and the Vandellas, "Love Me Do" by the Beatles, "Where Did Our Love Go" by the Supremes, and "My Guy" by Mary Wells.

I dimmed the lights a little more before stepping onto the dance floor. As soon as I flung myself into the circle of my gyrating girlfriends, my social clumsiness disappeared and my confidence returned.

I knew exactly when it was time for the first slow dance. I made my way back into the music room, removed the stack of dance records and replaced them with the slow-dance vinyls. I lowered the lights to almost off and returned to face my fate.

"You Belong To Me" by The Duprees was up first; it was so romantic, and I yearned to "belong" to someone. We all stood around with jittery anticipation until Jay made the first move. He strolled over and asked Nancy to dance, which was the signal for the other boys to choose their make-out partners. My eyes were on the floor; my heart was fluttering so loudly I was thankful the music drowned it out. I felt like I could faint at any moment. I knew where Arnold was standing, and as his figure emerged through the darkness, I took a deep breath, ready to accept. But he stepped to my left and asked Sherry to dance. It took every ounce of strength to hold back my tears.

Suddenly Gary was standing in front of me asking me to dance. In those days boys like him were consider "fags," which was the equivalent of "lame," "dork" or "loser" today. He had buck teeth and bad breath. Oh no, what a letdown! Was I going to have to kiss him? What a dreadful thought. I made it through the song but excused myself and went back to the control room before anything else could happen.

Many parties ended with me in a puddle on the music room floor, sobbing and mumbling the words to "It's My Party" by Leslie Gore.

I didn't know then but I do know now: All the taunting and name-calling had stigmatized me, so the more popular boys steered clear. Even though the parties were often at my house, they ate away at my already-weakened self-esteem, and they tested my early teen-age years.

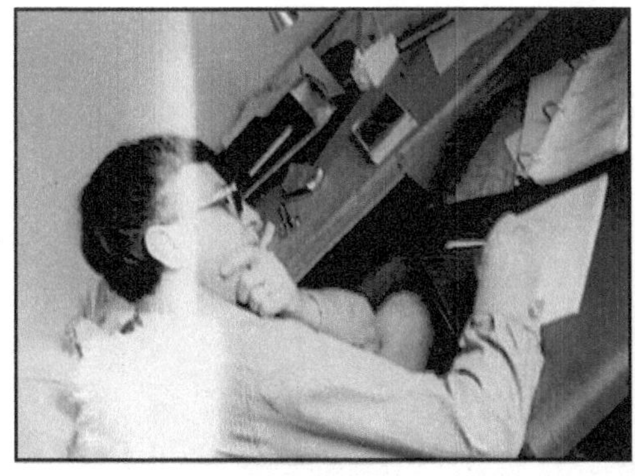

Dad, half-dressed, writing and
posing at his card table

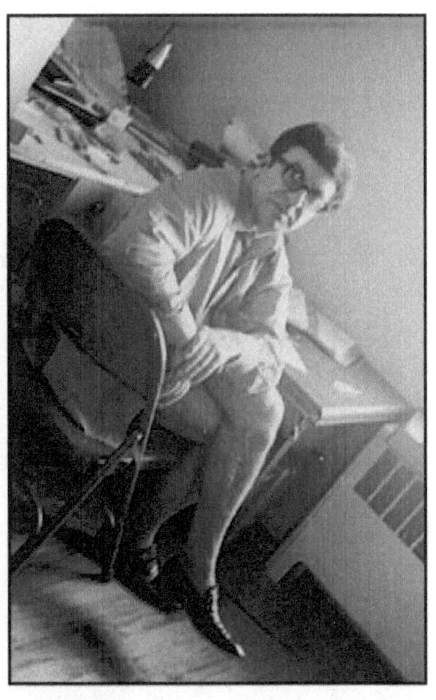

Me having fun with Dad's
mysterious deity and dancing in
our renovated living room on
Fabian Place in Newark, NJ

From left to right:
Sharon, Grandma, Phyllis and Mom

11

CHEERLEADING

Everything changed when I graduated from elementary school to high school. Toby's family had moved away, and our group dissolved. Those eighth-grade boys who'd rejected me didn't matter anymore. It was customary for the high school senior boys to date the freshman girls, and I was on board with that.

I found high school enthralling, from the bustle of the crowded hallways, to the social politics of the massive cafeteria. Homeroom, different classes, different teachers and new friends blew my world wide open. Stylishly decorating the interior of my assigned locker was like having a home away from home. The clicking of the turning locks and the slamming of the metal doors was melodic.

I'd been planning to try out for cheerleading ever since the first football game I attended. My dream was about to come true. The first fliers began appearing all over school. When Wednesday afternoon arrived, I joined all the other girls in the gym where we were briefed on what to expect going forward. We had to learn all the words to the cheers and the movements that accompanied them. We'd have several practice sessions and then the actual competition for available spots. I had my mimeographed copies of the words with me wherever I went. I spent all my free time stretching and strengthening my body until I was able to do the jumps, cartwheels, round-offs, splits and lifts. I wanted this more than anything I'd ever wanted in my life.

It was cheerleading every day, all the time. I ran the drills through my head at school, and I mastered the motions in my room. Weequaic cheerleaders had a signature move—a jump with a complicated arm movement. It had to be synchronized, and it required extra coordination. I got it before my girlfriends, who were also trying out, so I taught it to them.

On the day of tryouts, I waited impatiently for the hours to pass. After school, we girls met in the gym, and the air was electric. The gym teachers and the current cheering squad were there to judge us. As the group spread out across the floor, I took in the sea of kids to the right and left of me. I wondered how on earth I'd ever make it. My nerves were pulsating as they gave out the first cheer. I knew it, so I performed it confidently.

It was an elimination process. The girls who did not make the cut were politely asked to leave. I was not among them—I was still standing. Round after round I prevailed, and finally it was announced that I made the squad. I'd truly worried about my ability to project enthusiasm and motivate the crowd, but the teachers and squad members hailed me for "embodying the Weequaic spirit!" Nothing surprised me more.

Toward the end of my freshman year, I began dating a senior. Arie was tall, with dark, exotic features; his family was from Israel. He had a license, and I'd be that girl sitting next to him when we drove down the Avenue. I was living the freshman girl's dream.

But then Arie took me to the senior prom, and while we were dancing a slow dance, he burped loudly in my ear. He thought it was funny, but I didn't get the joke. I broke up with him the next day.

Before school ended that summer, we were measured for our first cheerleading uniforms, which we'd be wearing in the fall. We were the Weequaic Indians, and the school colors were brown and orange. Everyone but the two captains wore matching brown vests and culottes. Captains wore orange. We supplied the white turtleneck that went under the vest, the brown-and-white saddle shoes and the white woolen socks. For the colder football games, we received a thick white cable sweater, which had an appliqué of a megaphone superimposed over a "W" on the back.

For me, the most exciting garment was a brown satin jacket with my name embroidered in front and another large appliqué of an Indian on the back. I wore that jacket everywhere: It screamed clout. Everyone would know I was a cheerleader. My sophomore year was going to be spectacular.

When school opened in September, practice started immediately so we'd be ready for the first football game. That Saturday couldn't come fast enough. We gathered on the field, and I took my place with the rest of the squad behind the goalpost. I stood in the crisp fall air, with the grass under my feet, incredulous that I was there. I had chills as the marching band played their first notes and began the procession. The majorettes followed, and when they got about 10 feet in front of us, we joined the parade. We had a distinctive strut, which was coordinated with a synchronized shake of our white, brown and orange pompoms. The roar of the crowd caught my attention. They were applauding us. Standing in front of them at the foot of the bleachers, firing them up with our carefully choreographed cheers, was as close as I'd ever come to a transcendental experience.

Halftime was the signal for each girl to perform a solo cheer. I wanted to stand out, so I chose to do a flying split. I'd jump as high in the air as I could with my legs outstretched from right to left, and as I came down, I'd turn my torso to the right in order to land in a split with my right leg in front. The fans went wild!

I didn't know then but I do know now: I was so inured to my parents' indifference that I didn't notice that they never came to any of the games. They showed no interest in what was important to me. I don't remember them recognizing or acknowledging my achievements.

With winter came basketball season, which brought us indoors to the gym. We waited in the locker room while spectators filled the seats and the players warmed up on the court. It was a symphony of bouncing basketballs, squeaky sneakers and the crowd's noisy anticipation. Before the game started, we stood in the hallway as revved up as racehorses at their starting gate. With pompoms in hand and fists on our hips, we burst through the doors and ran onto the shiny wooden floor. We lined up at the base of the bleachers, and as the captains gave their nod, we were off cheering our boys.

Not only was I cheering for the team, I was cheering for my new boyfriend Larry. Nancy, from elementary school, was now my best friend, and she, too, had made the squad. She was dating Kenny, a junior who was co-captain of the basketball team along with Larry. Larry and I began flirting and then sitting together on the busses going to the away games. Soon we were dating. Larry and Kenny were also the co-captains of the YM-YWHA basketball team, and I became the captain of that cheering squad. My two passions, cheering and boys, had become intertwined.

Larry would pick me up at my house, escort me to the car door and open it for me. I'd slip in right next to him and wait for his arm to land on my shoulder. It was less than a 15-minute ride to the date-night diner on Springfield Avenue, but to me it was a heavenly eternity. When he dropped me off back home, he kissed me at the front door.

A tingly shiver ran down my spine, and I thought, "So this is what it's supposed to feel like."

We were all negotiating how far to go with our boyfriends. Larry and I were moving at a comfortable pace. We had innocent, flirtatious meetings in the school halls, formal dates and lots of making out. One evening, Larry invited me to his house when his parents were not home. I knew what that meant; my feelings were mixed, but I was curious. We were on a sofa in the downstairs study when I felt his hand going under my shirt. I held my breath as he made his way to my back. He fumbled to undo my bra. I wasn't sure what to do, so I didn't do anything. He finally succeeded, but for some reason his awkwardness gave me the courage to tell him that was as far as I wanted to go, and he did not pressure me. Having Larry as my boyfriend was a sweet experience. It came to a natural end when we were both ready to move on.

For the summer of 1965, my parents and two other families decided it was time to try a new bungalow colony. They chose Quaker Hill, in upstate New York, about 45 minutes southeast of the Borscht Belt in the Catskills. It was much bigger than Sherman Acres, and everyone except for us was from New York.

At 15 years old, I was no longer a camper, but a CIT (Counselor In Training). I was assigned the five-year-old group; they were all adorable, but Seth was my favorite. He had sea-blue eyes and the straightest blond hair, cut in a mop-top.

The casino, which was located opposite the entrance to the colony, was huge. It made all those I'd been in before seem quaint. It was the center of everything, and it housed a canteen that was like a mini-convenience store. I never saw money being exchanged, just the words, "Put it on my parents charge account." What was that? I asked my parents and was thrilled to find out we had one, and I, too could make my purchases that way. Boy, did I feel rich.

The center of the rec hall, where the pinball machines were, was *the* place to meet up with the other kids, most of whom had returned to the colony summer after summer. They were friendly and welcoming and super cool, up on the latest fashion and music. We'd spend hours deciphering the messages we thought were hidden in the Beatles' lyrics on the *Sgt. Pepper's Lonely Hearts Club Band* album. When they played "Light My Fire" by The Doors, my heart stopped. I'd never heard music like that. It sounded mysterious and dangerous.

Allen, who was part of our gang, was the youngest son of the owner's family. Allen's older brother had a lot of local friends—a wild bunch that took great pleasure in corrupting us. On Saturday nights, while the adults were occupied at the casino, we hopped into the back of their pick-up trucks and drove off the colony grounds. We turned down a dark, bumpy dirt road until we came to a clearing, a secret place that they called the "quarry."

The headlights stayed on, and the truck radios blasted Jimi Hendrix, The Rolling Stones, The Young Rascals, Sam & Dave and The Association. Everything outside the lights was pitch black, making it seem as though we were the only people on earth. We were like a tribe of feral kids, singing at the top of our lungs and bopping around with moves that could not be identified.

The older guys brought coolers filled with pre-mixed whisky sours. The first time I tasted the tangy blend of the drink, it was so good that I helped myself to several until the world began to spin and my stomach started flipping upside-down. I stumbled into the darkness outside the perimeter of the lights, found a bush and vomited my guts out. I'd gotten way too drunk, but that didn't stop me from doing the same thing the next time.

That summer, Lenny and I fell madly in love. He was a year older than I but not much taller. His hair was very dark, and his eyes were a light shade of hazel. We were crazy for each other. Hand-in-hand we'd walk around the grounds; we'd kiss in the back of the field trip bus, at the bowling alley and in the movie theater. I'd never felt like that before, and I surrendered completely. Or almost. Our sexual exploits included everything but intercourse because I was still not ready.

We tried to continue our love affair through the winter. I didn't have my license, so I commuted to Queens by bus or train. He drove to New Jersey, but ultimately the distance caused us to break up.

I didn't know then but I do know now: This was a special time in my "love" life. Sex was still an innocent and tender exploration. I never felt pressured, I had command of my integrity, and I felt in control.

Back in Newark, the outgoing cheerleading squad had to choose the two new captains. To my amazement, I was the unanimous choice for one of the spots. Wow! I was humbled and empowered by the team's confidence in me. But they were undecided about who would be my co-captain. It was a suspenseful affair, full of intrigue. Nancy, who was still my best friend and the most popular girl in our class, was considered a shoo-in, so when they passed over her for Susan, it was scandalous. We considered a boycott before reluctantly accepting the decision. In time I warmed up to Susan, and it ended up being a great partnership.

As captain, I turned in my brown uniform for an orange vest and culottes set, and my jacket had to be re-embroidered to include "Captain" above my name. I loved cheerleading so much that when asked what my major might be in college, I'd say, without irony, "If I could, I would major in cheerleading!"

I didn't know then but I do know now: Socially, I was growing. This part of my life was functioning on its own track, separate and uncontaminated by my father's influence at home.

An early candid shot of me, exhibiting the Weequaic spirit in my brown cheerleading uniform

One of my yearbook photos as Captain of the cheerleaders in my orange uniform

12

HELP

"Why don't you get Ds and Fs instead of As and Bs?"

My father was standing in the living room holding my report card between his grimy fingers. I'd worked hard the past semester, and I'd gotten good grades. But after hearing his absurd words, I wished I could press rewind, snatch back my report card, and retreat to my room. Except "running away" was forbidden, so I stayed put as he launched into a tirade about traditional education, inferior teachers and independent thinking. He berated me for "wanting to fit in." My ambition to do well in school suddenly seemed trite. Just moments before, I'd been bursting with pride, and now I stood inside a swirling and shameful tornado.

At this time the counterculture was in full swing; Norms were under scrutiny, and formalities were being relaxed. Some kids were embracing the "revolution," taking up social causes and pushing against authority.

My own transformation, though, was still a year away. I was comfortable in the world as it was, and I wasn't ready to move on from my conventional life. Getting good grades was gratifying; nothing filled me up more than cheerleading; formal dating was fine by me, and so was conforming.

I didn't know then but I do know now: My father's attacks on my conservative values were the start of a profound inner conflict, causing me to question my personal preferences rather than his irrational proposals and contradictions.

After moving from Elizabeth back to Newark, my father set up a corner of his and my mother's bedroom with a table and chair, where he'd do his writing. It was the same cluttered and messy affair as it had always been. My bedroom door was catty-corner to theirs, and I'd see him half-dressed, bent over the table, engrossed in what he was doing. I tiptoed by that room as though it were occupied by an unrestrained and vicious tiger.

As writing began occupying more and more of my dad's time, he relocated to the dining room table, right in the middle of the apartment. Now, when he wasn't in the basement working on displays, he sat there consumed with converting his thoughts into the written word. There he'd be, hour after hour, concentrating intently, deeply pensive, as though nothing and no one else mattered. It sent me the unspoken message: "I'm important, and you're not."

One Sunday afternoon, I was in my room doing schoolwork when my father walked in. There was no knocking in our house, and his intrusion was a common occurrence. He took a seat at the foot of my bed, across from my desk chair. "What kind of stupidity are they teaching you now?" he said.

I knew where this was going. "I'm studying for a social studies test tomorrow," I replied. I braced for a blow.

He launched into a lofty lecture degrading my education and lauding his intellectual prowess. "I'm the only man alive who understands the real meaning of life. You see me sitting at that dining room table, don't you?" I nodded my head. "I'm writing a book that will change the world."

I had to suppress a dithery energy rising from the soles of my feet; the door was inches away, yet that option was not available to me. I wanted to get back to my studying, but I sat there until he finished. "I want you to help me," he said. "I need you to correct my spelling."

"I can't," I said. "My test tomorrow is a final exam. I have to do well to keep up my average."

Then came the onslaught: School was "irrelevant," "meaningless," "a waste of time," "useless garbage." "What I'm doing is brilliant," he declared, "and you should want to be a part of it."

But I didn't want to—I needed to study. I wanted to study. And I didn't want to help him. Even though I managed to get rid of him, an ominous cloud lingered. Several days later, I left my room and headed down the hall. I knew my father was sitting at the dining room table, so as quietly as I could, I turned left into the kitchen. Then, with my hand already on the doorknob that led to my exit, I heard him call, "Celia, come here."

Wincing, my grip tightened, my teeth clenched, and my shoulders pinched up to my ears. I turned the knob without making a sound. Maybe I could still slip out and make believe I hadn't heard him, but he peered around the corner.

"Where are you going?"

"To meet my friends," I muttered softly.

'Your stupid friends can wait," he said. "Come sit down. I need your help."

This was not a negotiation. Defeated, I followed him. He was seated at the head of the table, with his back to a window. I removed my brown satin cheering jacket, hung it on the back of the chair to his right and sat down. In front of me was an unruly ocean of papers that obscured the surface of the tabletop. The light from the window caught my attention, but I dared not look in that direction. I was frozen, my mind ricocheting inside my brain. I wanted to be anywhere but in that room. Perhaps if I didn't move, he'd forget I was there, and I could sneak away. Instead, he handed me a sheet of loose-leaf paper covered with handwritten words, scrawled in pencil, all in capital letters.

Before that day, I'd never read one word of what my father had written. I glanced at the paper in my hand. "What do you want me to do with this?" I asked.

"Correct the spelling," he said.

The page was almost indecipherable: "THIS IS A MOST SIRIOUS ATEMPT TO INFORM YOU ABOUT GRAVE DANGER TO YOUR LIFE. IT IS A WARNING THAT CAN SAFE YOU, AT THE SAME TIME HELPING YOU TO TRANSFORM AND EVOLVE OUT OF THIS DYING WORLD INTO A NEW KIND INDEPEND AND EX-ISTANCE."

Nothing made sense. There were words feverishly crossed out with dark squiggles; other words were crammed into the margins. The only consistency was the uniformity of the letters, all uppercase. Paragraphs were delineated by two horizontal lines, above and below, and he'd scribbled over the chunks of copy that he wanted deleted. My throat was swelling from the scream I wanted to let out, and I had to squeeze my eyelids to keep the tears from flowing. I dared not meet my father's gaze.

I forced my sight to focus on the writing he'd put in front of me. It was barely a language. He wrote the way he spoke—in broken English.

"THE NATURAL FUNCTION OF SOLITAN PULSES IS TO TRANSFORM INORGANIC MATER INTO ORGANIC STATE. IN-ORGANIC IS DEATH MATER AND ORGANIC IS LIVING MATER

COMMUNICATING THROUGH DECOMPRESSION AND COM-PRESSION OF ENERGY WAVES. THIS IS WHY SIMMERTRICAL ALGORITHM CAUSES LIFE AND ASIMMETRICAL ALGORITHM CAUSES DEATH.

I pointed out that practically every word was misspelled in the hopes that he'd see how ludicrous his request was,

"That's exactly why I need you," he replied. "You know English. You learned spelling in school, didn't you?"

I didn't know then but I do know now: On the one hand, my father denigrated my education. On the other, he exploited it.

Clearly I was not going to be allowed to get up. I thought about my friends who were meeting at the schoolyard. They'd be deciding where to go, and if they left before I got there, I'd have no idea where they'd be. An aperture closed, and the afternoon I had planned vanished. And with it went a part of myself. The part that was left was disappointed, hollow and crushed.

I didn't know then but I do know now: The definition of a hostage is "a person taken by force to secure the taker's demands." My father was holding me hostage.

"Just erase the wrong words and replace them with the right ones," he instructed, handing me an eraser and a number 2 pencil. Then he pulled out a stapled set of four pages from the mounds in front of me. "Start with these," he said.

Under the table my right foot began to twitch uncontrollably. I looked for the letters that resembled a word and began erasing and replacing. I went sentence by sentence, paragraph by paragraph. After an hour had passed, my section of the table was covered with tiny pink flakes. When I handed the pages back to him, he was pleased. "See?" he said. "You can be a big help to me."

"Can I go now?" I asked. He nodded his consent, and I left.

As I trudged toward Chancellor Avenue, my mind twisted and turned, looking for some way out of this preposterous circumstance. My father couldn't possibly expect me to do this on a regular basis, could he? That dreadful thought accelerated my pace, and my fingernails practically pieced my clutched palms. I hovered on the edge of darkness when a light suddenly appeared. If I appealed to my mother, she'd surely intervene, and he'd finally leave me alone. Consoled by that thought, I set out to find my friends.

The next day, while my father was at a meeting in the city, I found my mother in the bathroom putting on her make-up. "Daddy wants me to help him with his writing, but I can't," I explained. "I have schoolwork, cheerleading and being with my friends." She was listening, so I continued. "Can you talk to him and tell him that I'm too busy?"

She took a moment to ponder what I'd said and returned to applying her mascara. I waited, and then she said, "Your father is all by himself. He doesn't speak good English, he doesn't know how to spell, and he's trying to write a book."

"Mommy, I don't want to help him!"

"It wouldn't kill you to help him every once in a while," she said as she turned back to the mirror. "You're the only one who can do it."

I didn't know then but I do know now: In prior years, I had heard my parents arguing because my father wanted my mother to do the same editing he was now asking of me. This was her way out from under the pressure my father put on her. She sacrificed me for her own peace of mind.

So my father was free to hijack me whenever he wanted. And he did it often. School and cheering were my only acceptable excuses; anything else was fair game for him. The word "help" became a drill bit that whirred its way deep into my skull. Each time I heard it, a part of me died.

I took the pages I was given, erased and replaced the words and waited to be liberated. But my father wanted more.

"Do you understand the meaning of what I'm trying to say?" he asked one day.

If I gave him an honest answer, perhaps he'd set me free. "No, Daddy, I don't."

"Well, you should!" he barked. "I'll explain it to you, and then you can put it into words that other people will understand." He handed over a set of pages that were fastened by a large paper clip. As though in slow motion, I picked up the papers. A queasiness rose from my stomach as I gulped back panic. What was scrawled in front of me was mind-bending.

"WHAT IS THE NEW ORDER: IN SEARCH FOR ORDER IT IS A GOOD IDEA TO KNOW WHAT NATURAL ORDER IS BECAUSE IF ONE DOES NOT KNOW WHAT ORDER IS, ONE MIGHT DESTROY IT IN ATEMPT TO FIND IT. IF ORDER IS WHAT CAUSES A HEART BEAT AND IF ONE DO NOT KNOW HOW THE BEAT IS GENERATED THEN ONE CAN INTERFERE WITH IT IN AN ATEMPT TO UNDERSTAND IT."

Staring at my father's cryptic marks, I ran my eyes from line to line. I might as well have been reading Swahili, but somehow I had to make sense of his abstract concepts. Mentally, I tried to pull out the words I understood, then string them together in the hopes they'd give me a clue, but it didn't work. As much as I was loathe to engage with him, I had to ask him questions. He loved that. His answers did help me get the gist of what he was trying to say. As I reflected back to him what I understood, his face slackened, his expression softened, and a smile replaced his usual scowl.

"See? I knew you were a genius!" he said.

I didn't know then but I do know now: I was slowly being en-

trapped. I was so starved for my father's love that the slightest praise from him turned my defiance into compliance. He had succeeded in detaining me physically, and now his tentacles were slithering toward my emotions.

My father's demand was insatiable, and his oppression was like dense quicksand—it closed in on me and sucked me down. Before it smothered me, I appealed to my mother one more time. "Mommy, please talk to Daddy and tell him to leave me alone."

"Your father is doing very important work," she said. "Who knows? He might actually change the world." Her eyes looked into the distance as she added, "You know, he's right about a lot of things."

My mother—my only hope—was siding with him. But it was more complicated than that: She was endorsing and normalizing his craziness, which caused me to question: Why was helping my father so objectionable to me? Didn't I want to be part of history? The quicksand was devouring me.

Approaching the end of my sophomore year, I continued to live my life on two tracks, but the gulf between my home life and my life in the world was narrowing. Although cheerleading remained outside the scope of my father's influence, his constant pressure for me to prioritize him over my friends was exhausting. But it was my academic life that was taking the brunt of his intrusions. Like a chisel, my father's cynicism and slandering of my education chipped away at my aspirations and principles. I began to settle for Cs rather than As and Bs.

I didn't know then but I do know now: I was at a pivotal juncture in my young life. My father's verbal abuse had already caused me to compartmentalize. His preying on my most vital need for love and acceptance was taking the emotional abuse to a new height. Yet even more insidious was his determination to empty out my brain and replace it with his. His intellectual abuse was underway.

Back at the table, I faced a dilemma. My logical brain was being coerced to translate my father's manic rantings into coherent ideas. The only option I had was to reboot my own brain to think like my father's.

When my father approved of what I did, he'd say, "Your brain is working."

"No," I wanted to say, "my brain is hurting."

I didn't know then but I do know now: At home, my father was brainwashing me.

13

SPLIT

1966 marked my transition from the conventions of the 1950s to the emerging counterculture. For me, everything started with fashion. The tight, preppy conservative look gave way to a loose and casual bohemian style. Moccasins replaced my penny-loafers; love beads replaced my gold nameplate necklace. Out went the teasing comb and hairspray; in came long, natural and flowing hair with the part in the middle.

My friends and I spent hours listening to the radio. We still liked to dance, but now lyrics and messages began to shape our ideologies. "The Letter" by The Box Tops, "San Francisco" by Scott McKenzie, Buffalo Springfield's "For What It's Worth," "Respect" by Aretha Franklin and "White Rabbit" by Jefferson Airplane became our anthems.

The customs we'd grown up with were disappearing. Being bourgeois and "uptight" was frowned upon. It was no longer cool to follow the rules or be materialistic. Self-expression trumped formality; being "real" trumped being "phony." Outspokeness, cynicism and dissidence were the new currencies for popularity.

I didn't know then but I do know now: The changing times would complicate my already precarious life. All the words used to define and represent the new culture were the same words my father had been firing at me since I was old enough to understand him.

Newark was a microcosm of the racial turmoil that was exploding all over the country. The demographics of our neighborhood had gradually shifted from predominantly white to primarily black. I watched as Newark burned during the riots and was alarmed to see such violence and destruction so close to home. Tensions even ran high in the halls of Weequaic High.

Television and radio broadcasts were flooded with news of the Vietnam War, including the anti-war movement and accompanying social unrest. I'd been oblivious to the role of government in my life, but my eyes were opening. "Peace" and "Make Love, Not War" seemed reasonable to me.

A lot of the boys I associated with were about to turn 18, and debate about the draft was a hot topic. College students not much older than I were occupying administration buildings and disrupting campus activity. I followed the development of SDS (Students for a Democratic Society) with great curiosity. These students were bucking the system and challenging the establishment. They were demanding that society change and old values be replaced by a new morality.

None of this went unnoticed by my father, and he was invigorated. "Society is aligning with my principles!" he said. "We are in the middle of a revolution, and I am at the forefront of the new order!"

When my father would say, "I am a visionary, a prophet and the smartest man in the world!" my mother would add, "It's amazing. Your father is truly ahead of his time."

The dining room was now the headquarters for Dad's crusade. An obsessive and urgent energy emanated from the center of our home.

He directed all conversation toward current events, especially as it related to his work. According to him, the world was sanctioning his efforts, and it was imperative that "we" get his theories out there as soon as possible. "The world is waiting for what I have to say. You're the only who can 'help' me," was the way he tightened the clamps on me.

And back to the table I would go. Each time, I'd have to zip myself out of my own skin and replace it with another.

The more successful I was in making sense of my father's maddening scribbles, the more he'd shower me with accolades. When he told me, "You might even be smarter than me," it worked like a narcotic. It lulled me into a dream-like state where I was finally my father's equal and he adored me the way I imagined a father should. When he'd say, "You will become the voice of the new generation," I thought of the young, inspired activists I'd seen on TV and wanted to be among them.

"He's my father, and he should know!" I'd tell myself. I remembered my father's declaration at the bungalow colony years earlier: "Either you're in or you're out." Maybe now I would be "in" and not "out."

I didn't know then but I do know now: My father was masterfully manipulating me.

I was peripherally aware that Dad went to meetings in the city, and now he began talking about them with me. He raved about the people who attended and described them as "very connected and influential." He'd say, "These kinds of people make things happen." It sounded exciting, and I actually began to believe that my father was on the cusp of success. "With your help, we will become rich and famous. You will get in on the ground floor, and I'll share the credit with you."

Like a horse to a carrot he drew me in. So when he proposed I accompany him to one of his gatherings, I was eager to go.

In preparation for the meeting, I helped him create a 22"x28" presentation board. The headline, in big, thick, capital letters at the top, read, "THE LIVING ENVIRONMENT FOUNDATION." Below, with a thinner pen, he wrote the subtitle "EMERGENCY CONFERENCE to integrate scientific & religious knowledge." Around that copy he drew a dramatic halo of lines radiating outward. The words "Confucianism," "Buddhism," "Christianity," "Judaism," "Split Brain," "Interfaith," "Sociobiology" were inscribed inside big arrows. Boxes with smaller, dense type were placed at angles around the headlines.

He had gotten my mother to type up some of my correctly spelled and edited pages, and he put them into loose-leaf notebooks. He placed the board and the binders in the back of our red Pontiac station wagon, I got into the passenger's seat, and we drove toward the Lincoln Tunnel. He bloviated all the way to the city.

Once we parked in midtown, he handed me the binders, and we set off in the direction of Fifth Avenue. The city was overcast, and everything felt grey. As we approached our destination, I noticed the building we were heading toward was similarly gloomy and grungy. Entering through a set of revolving doors, my father fumbled with his board.

Inside, the hotel looked and smelled old. As we waited in the dingy lobby, my father kept checking his watch, becoming increasingly agitated. Finally a man emerged from the elevator and walked in our direction. He looked as disheveled and unkempt as the lobby we were standing in. He shook my father's hand, excused his tardiness and glanced over at me. His eyes passed over my entire body. I shivered. My father introduced me, and the man offered me his hand, which I reluctantly shook.

I wondered what I was doing there.

I didn't know then but I do know now: The subtle alarms that were going off within me were trying to send an alert that my father was putting me in an inappropriate situation at best, and in harm's way at worst.

The man led us toward the elevator bank, and we traveled up to a high floor and into some sort of conference room where a few people were gathered. There was a desk at the front and several chairs set up for the audience. Across the space, a pair of windows overlooked the backs of other buildings. I stood awkwardly right inside the door, with no idea of where to go or what to do with the books I was holding.

My father was introduced and shown to the desk. I followed and obediently placed the books in front of him. Then, not sure what to do next, I walked past the mostly empty rows toward the back of the room and took a seat at the end of the last one. At first I wanted to disappear, but then I heard my father's voice. Peering over the few heads in front of me, I saw him—arms gesturing, eyes half closed and head thrown back. He delivered his stream-of-consciousness lecture with his usual fervor.

I had no way of knowing how he had been received, but my father had a lot to say about it on the way home. According to him, he "dazzled" them; they "marveled" at his presentation; they'd never seen such "original" ideas. The fictitious script in his mind had him all revved up. His frenzy convinced him that "these people" were going to become his financial backers as well as his disciples. He was certain that it all hinged on his writing and his presentations, which required my "help." He was invigorated, myopic, relentless and sure that I was the only one "who could put his ideas into words that these people could understand." He must have known that phrase had power over me because he repeated it whenever I tried to pull away. There was no arguing that without my help, no one could have made sense of his scribbling.

"Soon I'll be recognized," he predicted. For so many reasons I wanted that to be true. Perhaps he'd be happy and he wouldn't need me. Perhaps his prophecy of riches would come to fruition and I'd be like all my friends. All our troubles would be over. Once again, I got swept into his hallucination.

I didn't know then but I do know now: My father suffered from delusions of grandeur.

Nonetheless, his constant encroachments left me feeling robbed and trapped. When I felt pushed to a brink, when I could no longer tolerate it, I'd make feeble attempts to get out from under the oppression. "Daddy, I can't help you with everything," I'd say. "I have my own life to live."

He didn't like it. One day he spun toward me, his face distorted by a new degree of fury. "If you don't help me, we will SPLIT!" he bellowed.

CRASH—A vast nothingness bowled me over.

The words "You're either in or you're out" reverberated from earlier years. Every cell of me, then and now, understood what he meant. If I were to hold my ground, he would cut me out of his life. I had no choice but to concede, and all the fight within me died.

I didn't know then but I do know now: My father saved his most heartless weapons for when he sensed I was close to slipping out of his clutches. Not only was he stealing my time, he was stealing my soul. Each victory for him left vital parts of me splintered into tiny pieces. That was the real "splitting" that was underway.

14

SHARON

Mid-way through high school, I had found my best friend for life. Sharon had not been part of the mean girls clique in elementary school. Back then I'd barely noticed her, and I don't remember how our relationship started. All I knew was that Sharon was different from the other kids I'd befriended. Like me, she was the only child of Polish Holocaust survivors, and that was just one of the many unspoken bonds we shared. Ours was a friendship based on kindness, respect, fun and most importantly, trust.

Outwardly, we couldn't have been more different: Sharon was tall and lanky, with cropped blond hair. I was petite, falsely thought of myself as stocky, and my brunette hair was halfway down my back.

Our personalities were different as well. Where she was cynical, I was idealistic. She leaned toward the ironic, while I toward the romantic. I didn't have much of a sense of humor, but Sharon's wit had no bounds. She was the mastermind of most of the antics that galvanized us, and I was happy to be her sidekick.

But the biggest difference was that her family was rich and mine was not. Her father was a builder, and they lived in one of his newly built single-family homes close to the park. The house was the fanciest and most modern on the block. Stepping inside her front door was like entering the interior of the sophisticated Bar Mitzvah venues from earlier years.

The vestibule walls were covered with shiny white marble, and a sparkly chandelier hung from the two-story ceiling. A carpeted stairway led to an extravagantly decorated living room. Sharon's bedroom had the trendiest furnishings, and floating above her bed was a princess crown with opulent satin fabric draped all the way down to the floor.

As impressive as all this was, I was not comfortable being there. The furniture was covered in plastic, and we were not permitted to be in the living room. Sharon had to keep her bedroom door opened, and the oddest thing was that she would not allow anyone—including me—to sit on her bed.

Like mine, Sharon's family life was complex. Her parents were strict and controlling: She was not allowed to do a lot of the things that the rest of us could do, like date or go to parties. Her mother was never friendly or welcoming. She seemed bitter; her tone was sharp and sarcastic, and she judged everyone. When I told Sharon that her mother intimidated me, Sharon shared that she herself was the target of her mother's most severe criticism.

In contrast, Sharon's father was charming and gregarious. Sharon and I would laugh hysterically when she'd imitate his favorite phrase. In a heavy Polish accent, she'd roll her Rs, and say, "RRRules are rrrules, not to be brrroken!" He doted on Sharon; he was generous with both money and attention, which I envied.

Sharon and I were both crazy for fashion. Sharon's mother took her shopping in Manhattan, and she always showed up at school in what I thought were the coolest, most stylish clothes—none of which could be found in Newark. When our parents finally allowed us to go to the city alone, we boarded the bus to Port Authority and headed straight to the Village.

I'd never been in the city without my parents. Going with Sharon was the biggest adventure I'd ever had. We scoped out all the best places to find the edgiest clothes. Our first stop was a head shop on Bleeker Street. The funky lava lamps and water pipes in the window previewed the provocative interior, which reeked of incense. After we passed the glass counters filled with pot apparatus, geodes, silver jewelry and buddhas, we entered a dark section. Pausing inside the narrow, tunnel-like hallway, we took in the posters that were plastered on the ceiling and from top to bottom on the walls. The only illumination came from the purple blacklights, which made the psychedelic images glow. At the end of the space was a portiere of wooden beads. The clicking sound they made as we parted them epitomized this new bohemian world.

The clothing section was packed with garments, some hung on racks, others in piles on the floor. We'd come for bell-bottoms, which were in one of the heaps. Nothing was sized, and there were no mirrors. As we rummaged, I grabbed a pair, held it up to my body, turned to Sharon and waited for her thumbs-up or thumbs-down. I did the same for her before we headed to a makeshift dressing room, which was essentially a shower curtain on a U-shaped metal rod. If a pair were too big, instead of taking them right off, we pulled them up past our waists, stuck our stomachs out and rounded our shoulders, nerd-style. We yucked it up as though we were the only ones in the store.

With our treasures slung over our arms, we made our way back to the glass counters in the front of the shop. The guy standing behind the cases had long, scraggly hair and multiple piercings in his ears; he wore a colorful tie-dye t-shirt and dirty jeans. We were also looking for safari jackets and asked him where he thought we might buy them. "There's an Army-Navy store on Canal Street," he said as he pointed south.

There was nothing like walking through the Village, past crowds of colorful people. We took our time getting to Canal Street, found the store and purchased our jackets. On our way out, we spotted vintage wool GI Navy pants and P-coats. Our eyes met, and we made a plan to come back for those.

The Mod trend had taken over all the magazines. Sharon knew exactly where to shop for the hippest threads. On another excursion, instead of going south we went north to an uptown boutique called Paraphernalia. It was a happening, with go-go dancers in the windows grooving to "Let's Spend the Night Together" by the Rolling Stones, which was blasting through the shop's loudspeakers. Our heads whipped from each other to the unbelievable scene. Where were we? Once inside the store, we were transfixed by the equally mind-blowing sea of bright colors, flowing fabrics and bold patterns. After trying on numerous outfits, I left with a yellow and gray gingham wool mini-dress. It had a broad yellow Peter Pan collar and a panel down the front, both with gray embroidery on the edges. Six large pearly buttons on the panel made the dress.

Another trip took us to Fred Braun's, a shoe store on West 8th Street in the Village. Choosing just one chunky style would prove to be a daunting task. Yet I was able to settle on a multi-colored, thick-heeled and round-toed pair. Pantyhose had recently replaced girdles and garters, and they came in lots of colors and patterns. At home I already had several textured black pairs, but they didn't go with my new purchase. So of course I found the perfect matching stockings.

The British Invasion had already infiltrated the airwaves, but it was on the verge of transforming my way of getting music. My AM clock radio had been my main source of new tunes. But FM was beginning to broadcast to a wider audience, and FM radios were becoming more affordable. Sharon got one before me, so when I finally had my own, she turned me on to WOR-FM, with Scott Muni, Murray "the K" and Rosko. We started listening to artists like Laura Nyro and Richie Havens, learning all the words so we could sing along.

When we weren't singing, we found other ways to entertain ourselves. Sharon was fluent in Yiddish because it was the only way she could communicate with her maternal grandparents, who lived in a separate, downstairs apartment. She had a keen sense of the ludicrous. When we were out and about, she kept her eye peeled for unsuspecting pedestrians. With our mark in our sights, we'd approach them, and Sharon would begin speaking in Yiddish. As the strangers stood agape, waiting for this adorable teenager to flash a smile revealing the joke, Sharon stayed deadpan and kept on speaking. I remained quiet at her side as though nothing was unusual. Timing was everything: We'd wait a second, turn on our heels and quickly dash away. As soon as we rounded a corner, we'd double over with laughter.

When we got our licenses, we drove our parents' cars when we could. Mine was an old station wagon, but Sharon's father had a brand new Lincoln Continental, with leather seats and automatic windows. She'd pick me up, and we'd drive around until we spotted another innocent passerby. Sharon would pull up beside them, glide her window down, stick her pretty head out, and beckon to the stranger. "Eh, pliz cen you hep me?" she'd say in her thickest Polish accent. Their perplexed expression was enough to send us into hysterics, but we kept it straight in order to freak them out some more. If we were on Lyons Avenue, she'd say, "Eh, cen you tell me? Were is Lyons Evenue?" And then she'd zoom off, leaving our victim dumbfounded.

During the week, we spoke on the phone every evening. After

dinner I'd go to my room, close the door and lie on my bed with my Princess receiver to my ear. Once the usual school gossip was out of the way, we'd start in with our silliness. We invented all sorts of voices, which led to concocting different ways to laugh. We had a special one—a deep, loud yucking chuckle that we'd do over and over again. My father hated it and would barge into my room demanding that I stop. "You sound like an idiot!" he'd say.

It was worse at Sharon's house, where her mother would often walk around in her bathrobe. She always appeared angry, muttering things I didn't understand. Then, sometimes she'd join us in Sharon's room and act like she was one of the girls. She'd chime into our conversation and even make absurd faces or weird sounds along with us. It was strange, and I could tell it made Sharon uncomfortable. Soon she and I spent all of our time together at my house.

On the weekends we'd make "phony phone calls." I'd be on the extension in the kitchen, Sharon on my phone in my bedroom. "Excuse me," one of us would say. "Is your refrigerator running?" When they replied, "Yes," we'd say, "Better go catch it!"

When we discovered that kids couldn't tell our voices apart on the phone, we made up situations where we could impersonate each other. Heads close together, we'd hold the earpiece between our ears, and I'd call a classmate, making believe I was Sharon. I'd bait the person on the other end to talk about me, which they always did. Instead of laughing, we'd affectionately punch each other or hold the receiver away from our heads so we could pantomime or silently mouth a reply. We began calling ourselves "The Deadly Duo."

I didn't know then but I do know now: We each lived in an abusive household. The safety and support our friendship provided served as a refuge.

One day Sharon showed up at my house with one of the first

Polaroid cameras, the kind that spit out the photos as soon as they were taken. Not only was it a miracle, it inspired us to think of ways to use it. We began collecting odd pieces of clothing and random items from around my house. We put them together, creating kooky outfits and bizarre scenes. Each photograph that slid out of the camera led to another funnier idea. We ended up with so many 2.5" x 3.5" pictures that we started putting them into tiny albums that we found at the drugstore.

Among our earliest pictures is one of us standing together in my room, between my bed and the bureau. Sharon, to my left, wears a terrycloth, sleeveless turtleneck jumpsuit, with my cheering pom-poms on her head and a cigarette dangling from her lips. I have on a black woolen sock cap and gigantic sunglasses. Over a black top and pants is a knee-length tan jacket, with pin-back buttons all over it. I am holding a bladder-shaped wine bag to my mouth.

Turn the page and there are two photos of Sharon standing to the right of my huge Paul Newman poster. In the first she wears a black ski hat and a stocking over her face, which has pushed in her features. She is dressed in one of my father's sports jackets, with a white, bedraggled necktie. In the second photo she has taken the hat off and pulled the stocking up, so her features are even more distorted, and the inside of her nose is exposed.

We took turns doing the same thing, so I'd have photos of her and she'd have them of me. I still have the tiny albums. Several of the clear plastic sleeves are torn, and some of the mostly black-and-white pictures are faded and frayed, but they remain relics of a pure and loving friendship.

At first we created our photo scenarios in the house, but then we took the camera and our creativity outdoors. We wandered around the neighborhood looking for places to use as a stage. We found an abandoned railyard where we would lay across the three metal tracks. Our mouths were wide open, depicting a scream, with an arm extended as if to stop an approaching train. Very dramatic. We found a junkyard and posed sitting on an old, broken toilet like Rodin's "The Thinker." We took photos pouring buckets of water over our heads, jumping out of trees, running and camouflaging ourselves in bushes.

When we noticed that a "B" appeared in both our initials, we invented a new acronym: SCB^2. It was the perfect symbol for our exclusive club, summing up the closeness of our union. No one knew what it stood for, and when we were asked to decode it, we did so with pride.

Sharon was like the sister I never had, and when she was over, her presence dissipated the dense atmosphere, like soap disperses oil. My parents welcomed her, and I reveled in their acceptance of my best friend. My mother got a kick out of Sharon, especially when she spoke with a Polish accent. Phyllis conversed with her in Yiddish. They appreciated Sharon's practical joker side, and they even helped us with our photo shoots. My father suddenly took an interest in our shenanigans. Then I began to notice that when Sharon wasn't around, my mother and Phyllis praised her in front of me. "She's so tall, thin and beautiful," they'd say. "And that amazing personality!"

I didn't know then but I do know now: My parents and Phyllis were infatuated by Sharon. Since they rarely paid me such lavish compliments, their blatant adoration of my best friend shook the tiny bit of bedrock that sat at my core.

Now that Sharon was "part of the family," my father began intruding on her and my time together. Wherever we were, he would barge in, sit himself down and begin his grandiose rhetoric. He was sure to sprinkle in all the latest catchphrases; "radical," "new morality," "anti-establishment," "existentialism," and "psychedelics."

When he first started showing up, I wondered if Sharon was

squirming with the same discomfort as I was. When she didn't meet my glance or roll her eyes, I was concerned. Instead I noticed that she was paying attention; it seemed he resonated with her. And worse, she was easily engaging in an exchange of ideas. His oratory was not overwhelming her; she seemed to welcome it. I knew Sharon was facetious and took pleasure in putting people on. Any second I expected her to signal that's exactly what she was up to. But she didn't.

Instead, she'd say, "Your father's so cool."

And he'd gush, "Sharon is quite a character; she's so smart. And she thinks just like me."

It caused my mind to whip between relief that my father wasn't focused solely on me and alarm that he was paying an inordinate amount of attention to Sharon.

It got even worse when he started telling me, "You should be more like Sharon!" That was code that he approved of her bold and sharp wit. Her confidence was so much more appealing than my shyness, cautiousness and insecurity. But what finally crucified me was his admiration of her intelligence.

The more Sharon interacted with my parents, the more tangled it became for me. It felt as though my already fragile standing within my family was eroding. Now, when my father asked me to "help" him, I imagined that if he were to ask Sharon, she'd enthusiastically comply. It amplified the already loud admonishments I'd fire at myself whenever I was reticent and resistant to my father's requests. I'd ask myself, "Why can't I be more like Sharon?"

I didn't know then but I do know now: My friendship with Sharon was being poisoned by my parents' insensitive behaviors. And my father's flagrant disrespect for boundaries and malicious comparisons added to the casualties that were mounting up within me.

Another yearbook shot of me
in my gingham mini-dress
from Paraphernalia

Me and Sharon in one of our first
silly photos in my bedroom

The photo on the left is Sharon with a stocking over her face in
front of my Paul Newman poster. The shot on the right is her
pulling the stocking up to distort her features even more

Sharon on the abandoned
railroad tracks

The thinker, on the toilet,
in a junkyard

The deadly duo

SCB²

15

FIRE ISLAND

All my life I'd spent my summers in the "country," as I called it. I was accustomed to dirt and grass under my feet. But in the summer of my 17th year, my parents informed me that instead of returning to the bungalow colony, we'd be renting a weekend house on Fire Island.

Three childless couples would be sharing the house with us, and we'd alternate weekends because there were only three bedrooms. Sometimes we'd be there with Stanley and Marilyn, other times with Tom and his wife or Conrad and his wife. No children. All those summers at the bungalow colonies had been teeming with kids. What would it be like to be there with only adults?

I'd never heard of Fire Island and had no idea of what to expect. The first trip out there we sat in bumper-to-bumper traffic, which made the ride feel endless. But as soon as we exited to Bay Shore, parked the car, and approached the ferry terminal, it was a world unlike any other.

This was my first nautical experience. I stood on the dock watching the boats rock in their slips, and I listened intently as my parents explained that the ferries were the only way to get on and off the island—

another layer of this mysterious adventure. I spotted the open-air upper deck, and all I wanted to do was sit up there, which we did. I slid all the way to the end of the bench so I could look over the boat's edge and see into the water. The waves lapping against the vessel and the shimmering light soothed any trepidation. The hum of the boat's accelerating engine roused me. The ferry backed out, turned and slowly made its way through a narrow waterway. On either side were massive rocks where people stood and waved at us, so I waved back.

As soon as the boat got past the rocks, the engine revved and we took off. The speed left my stomach back at the dock. I closed my eyes as the wind caressed my face and the warm morning sun drew the last bit of chill from my body. The sky seemed to span to eternity.

Behind me, the smaller boats were jostled by the waves from the speeding ferry. In front, I watched the sliver of land grow larger and more distinct. We disembarked at the dock in Seaview to crowds of people meeting friends and family. Everyone wore bathing suits, cover-ups, shorts and tank tops. There were no cars, but bicycles and wagons were everywhere. We found the wagon designated for our house, threw our belongings in and began the lengthy walk toward the beach. We passed single-story cottages with items from marine life draped across doorways and porches. The vegetation was low, scruffy and windblown. The air buzzed with music, and every which way my nose turned I picked up the pungent scent of pot.

Another Fire Island first was the tiny boardwalk we had to cross in order to get to the screened-in porch of our little white house. But before I stepped onto it I glanced to my right and spotted a wooden staircase that appeared to lead to the sky. I had to see what was on the other side, so I ran up to it, ascended to the top, and there in front of me was the ocean! We were three houses away.

The novelty of the island unfolded over that first weekend. I'd only been to the seashore a handful of times with my friends, and I didn't dare go in the water. The power of the sea scared me, and I didn't know how to get in and out of the waves. The beach seemed like the safest place for me, and that's where I'd stay.

But a full weekend in the baking sun made it impossible to avoid the ocean. My father and the other men had no problem. They ran down past the water's edge and dove right into the crashing waves. There was no way I was going to do that. My mother, who rarely went into a pool, had the approach that appealed to me. She'd gracefully tiptoe right up to where the water hit the sand and go in ankle-deep. And there she'd bend down and splash her exposed limbs. Then, with the water cupped in her hands, she'd gently wash it over her face. That was doable, so I copied her.

It took some time to get used to the salty film that the damp wind left on my face, and I eventually resigned myself to sand in every nook and cranny. But I found the air with its seaweed smell unique and intoxicating. I loved being barefoot from morning till night.

The best weekends were when Sharon's parents allowed her to come with me to Fire Island. With her, sitting in traffic was fun. We'd make faces at our fellow travelers in the cars inching alongside us. They were bored, too, so most of them reciprocated with similar silliness, which gave rise to our goofiest giggles—the kind that would provoke my father's demeaning tongue-lashing at home. But here, with Sharon next to me, he said, "Very funny, you stupid idiots," with whimsy and irony in his voice.

On the ferry, my buddy by my side, we'd find a spot away from my parents. Once the boat was moving at a steady clip, we'd check out all the other people on the deck. Fire Islanders seemed to be a breed unto themselves—eccentric, sophisticated, intellectual, freethinkers. We found their mannerisms, dialects and attitudes perfect for parody.

Even though we remained discreet, we couldn't curb our amusement.

As soon as we unloaded our things and changed into our bathing suits, we headed for the magic stairway that led to the beach. Sharon, who was not afraid of the ocean, ran straight in, leaving me to face my fears. She was unsuccessful in convincing me to join her, but I did venture deeper than my ankles, and although I never made it far enough to swim, I did learn how to dunk in waist-high water. When satiated we'd leave our little patch of sand to walk farther down the shoreline to see what was going on in different "neighborhoods." Some areas were mellow; others had kids frolicking, swimming and making sandcastles. We followed the sound of the merrymakers and found the "action." People a few years older than us were blasting music, playing bongo drums and dancing. Some sipped cocktails at the beach bar, while others passed around joints.

Another island feature that every house had were rusted bicycles with big wire baskets and bells on the handlebars. They were the only mode of transportation other than our two feet. After unchaining ours from their rickety, weathered rack, we swung our bodies onto the hard seat and peddled away. We never had a plan; we just caroused around on our chariots. Sometimes we'd ride until we were stopped by a fence or a sidewalk's abrupt end. Sometimes we made our way to Ocean Beach, the center of the island's universe. The town was great for perusing shops and people-watching, and it had the best ice cream cones.

As the sun made its way toward the horizon, we disappeared into my room and lounged on the twin beds until the adults told us the outdoor shower was free. Being naked outside was another island anomaly and another challenge to my provincial modesty. After I reasoned that no one could see me over the seven-foot wooden wall, I stepped inside the little enclosure, disrobed and looked up toward the open sky. How cool was that? Letting the hot water wash over my sun-kissed body was a special kind of clean.

An evening's escapade lay ahead. But first we needed to choose our attire. Sharon's pixie cut was now mod-style, a little longer and straighter than it used to be. She modeled a pair of shorts with a midriff blouse, which we both agreed was superb. For me we chose a flower print ensemble with a matching headband. My hair, always long, cascaded down my back. With my usual expertise I painted on Twiggy lashes for both of us. Perfectly put together, we grabbed something to eat from the kitchen and headed out.

Independence was through the screen door, over the boardwalk and down the pavement. Fire Island had the same communal feel as the bungalow colonies, with people ostensibly living outdoors. Our passage took us by one crazy group after another: the same young people we watched on the beach. Now they congregated outside of their rentals, still drinking, getting high and dancing to the funky tunes emanating from radios or stereo speakers. The whole island was one big party. Our chosen route into town took us along the bay, where the vast blackness on our right was broken only by the twinkling of the lights from boats and the distant mainland. At that time of night, thumping sounds could be heard from farther down Bay Walk. The first time we heard them, we turned to each other and almost in unison said, "This is going to be a scene!"

As we approached the Sea Turtle's doors, the line went around the block. We found the end and stood shoulder to shoulder. "We'll never get in," I whispered. "There are too many people, and we're too young."

"Remember, we look older than we are," Sharon said. "Just pretend we're supposed to be here, and they won't stop us."

I rarely underestimated Sharon's audacity, so as we got closer to the bouncer, I kept a hard stare on my face, squared off my shoulders and strutted toward the door. She was correct, and we stepped right into the dark, narrow bar. It was packed with the coolest people I'd ever seen. We had to slither past them to get to the pulsating strobe lights beyond. My nostrils filled with the familiar cocktail of cigarettes and booze. The pounding of the music overtook the beating of my heart and the soles of my feet floated to the dance floor. Sharon and I had perfected all the latest moves, and as usual, the vibrations of the music unleashed my confidence. The dimly lit space and the strobe lights eliminated any vestige of my usual reserve. Catching sight of each other between the strobes was so funny that we began flailing and jumping around with abandon. The thought crossed my mind: "Is this how uninhibited my father always told me to be?"

Future outings to the Sea Turtle were less about dancing with each other and more about meeting boys. My go-to MO back home was to visually sweep the room to find the guy who was the best dancer. I'd put myself in his line of sight in the hopes that he'd notice me. I did it at the Sea Turtle, and it worked. Still naive and oblivious to the pick-up scene, I accepted drinks and toked on the weed from my dance partners. That usually led to an invitation out of the club and behind some buildings. In the warm summer air we'd make out, but no more than that.

Sharon and I had a favorite spot: It was a low wall that encircled a big house at an intersection. We'd often sit on it to watch and yenta about all the people passing by. And now, when our hook-ups took us in different directions, it served as our late-night meeting place. Reunited, often intoxicated, stoned or both, we'd stagger home.

As long as Sharon was with me, Fire Island was a blast. It was on the weekends when she didn't come that everything felt different. I was alone, thrust into the company of my parents' friends, adults I didn't know. It felt treacherous.

I didn't know then but I do know now: My parents did not take my wellbeing into account when making their plans. My loneliness and discomfort did not concern them.

From my vantage point, it seemed like Stanley and Marilyn became my parents' best friends overnight. Suddenly all I heard about was what a savvy businessman Stanley was, and that he loved all my father's ideas. Marilyn was a glamorous blond whom my mother adored. It was Stanley, Stanley, Stanley and Marilyn, Marilyn, Marilyn all the time.

Tom was the most gorgeous man I'd ever seen—tall, tanned, with an impressive physique. He had a full-time job, but he was also a model, and he shamelessly flashed his photos every chance he got. The way everyone spoke of him, I thought he was famous. He and his wife, another blond beauty, lived in Manhattan. I had the impression that they were wealthy, and references were made to him being an investor, whatever that meant.

Conrad was the oddest of the bunch, even more flamboyant than my father. He was a slight fellow and was unabashedly effeminate, even though he was married to a woman. He was a conundrum. I thought he was an Indian from India because his complexion was dark and he wore kaftans and Nehru jackets. On one of our drives home, I overheard my mother talking about Conrad, and I learned that he wore make-up.

Conrad was the only adult in the group who paid attention to me, which was unnerving in some ways but flattering in others. He was an amateur photographer and told me he wanted to take photos of me in a bathing suit on the beach. The date was arranged for a Sunday when my parents were giving Conrad and his wife a ride home. On the way, we stopped at a private beach somewhere on Long Island. We all got out of the car and walked onto the sand. Conrad and I continued to the water's edge where he told me to face him while he took his first shots.

I had dressed for the shoot, in a pink-and-white striped bikini with three white plastic rings: one in the middle of the top and the other two on either side of my hips. In the best of circumstances I was self-conscious, and the situation made it worse. I scanned the beach for my parents, whom I spotted sitting on a nearby dune, talking to Conrad's wife. "See if you can relax a little," I heard Conrad say. "Turn slightly to the right, put one hand on your hip and look to the left." I complied. "That looks good. Keep doing that!"

The clicking of his camera grew frantic, as did his enthusiasm. "Keep walking backwards into the water," he said.

I froze. First of all, I would only enter the ocean if it were calm—and never backwards! That day, the waves were already hitting my ankles at a rapid and rough pace. I wanted to say no, but my father's words—"inhibited," "party-pooper," "sourpuss," "boring," "downer"—began attacking me. I was no match for them, so I took one tentative step back after another. I ignored the many times I almost lost my balance.

When the water was midway up my thighs, suddenly the sand under my feet made a dramatic shift, and I lost my footing. My body was swept sideways then sucked below the surface. I was being tossed, tumbled and rolled by a force so strong I didn't know where I was. A riptide had caught me, and I was dragged by the undertow. Somehow I was able to lift my head from the water and scream for help.

Conrad dropped the camera. It was he, not my parents, who ran into the water to pull me to safety. Back on the beach, my breath returned and my nerves settled, but my fear of the ocean has never left me.

I didn't know then but I do know now: There was no one looking out for me, and I was consistently put into risky and harmful situations.

My father and his Fire Island friends had hedonistic leanings, and the atmosphere in our house was sexually charged. The women were flirtatious and the men blatantly salacious. Stanley introduced pot, and suddenly my father began saying, "Marijuana is the answer to everything."

Wilhelm Reich, an Austrian-born medical doctor and psychoanalyst, was my father's new hero. Reich was known as "the man who invented free love," the one who claimed that "better orgasms could cure society's ills." Everything Reich espoused fit neatly into my father's philosophies, and he steered most conversations toward sex. This crowd was more than happy to oblige, engaging in vigorous discussions of everything from nudity to swinging—the lewder and more perverse the dialogue, the better. When I could, I sequestered myself in my room.

I didn't know then but I do know now: This was no place for an impressionable teenager. It wasn't as though I hadn't been hearing references to sex on a regular basis, but my father was taking his fanaticism to a new level, never considering the repercussions it was having on me. I was on the cusp of confronting my own sexuality, and the environment my parents were callously exposing me to was compounding an already challenging situation.

One afternoon on one of those weekends when Sharon wasn't there, I didn't want to go to the beach, so I set myself up on a sandy patch outside the house. I spread out on a lounge chair with my transistor radio perched to one side and Seventeen magazine in my lap. "Monday, Monday" by the Mamas and Papas was playing, and I was trying to read an article about Dustin Hoffman, whom I'd just seen in The Graduate. I heard my father talking to Stanley, Conrad and some neighbors on our screen porch. I didn't hear my mom, so I figured she was with the other women somewhere in the house.

Unfortunately, I had to use the bathroom. This was going to be tricky because I would have to pass by my dad, and I wanted to be inconspicuous. I held my breath as I quietly opened the screen door. With my gaze on the floor, I took my first step, then my second. I heard my father stop talking, and a familiar weight bore down on me. "Come here and sit down," he said.

"I have to go to the bathroom," I said.

I stayed in the bathroom as long as I could. In the mirror I saw two deep creases between my eyebrows. I rubbed my index finger over them, hoping they would disappear. When they didn't I added my middle finger and pressed harder, going sideways across the lumps— no luck. I gave up, opened the door and made my way back to the porch. I sat down and nervously took in the scene. It was me in the chair closest to the door, my father across from me and the other men over to my left. My father had already launched into a pounding ser-mon: "The sexual revolution is here!" "Uptight society will soon be gone." "Sexual experimentation is the new order." "Anything goes, and the only thing that matters is having an orgasm!" Then with laser-like precision he focused his sight on me and said, "Your generation will be responsible for bringing about this new utopia. What do you have to say about that?"

I was on the spot in front of these male strangers. I had no answer. I felt like I was in the jaws of a vicious dog whose fangs were tearing at my flesh.

He must have noticed that I was drifting away. "Don't be a prude," he barked, "and don't be afraid of sex."

My father thought nothing of putting me on display. Like the after-noon when I awoke from a nap after spending the day on the beach.

My room was filled with bright sunlight streaming in from the west and casting an orange glow on the wall over my bed. My skin felt hot and sensitive; I'd gotten too much sun. I needed to drink something, but that meant I had to walk into the main room where the adults were gathered. My parched mouth won. I smoothed my clothing and stepped out of the bedroom.

I hesitantly glanced to my right, where everyone was lounging, talking and listening to the radio. I heard Murray the K announcing "Shot Gun" by Junior Walker and the All-Stars, one of my father's favorite Motown groups. Without looking, I knew he'd gotten up and was dancing with his arms flung over his head and his hips gyrating seductively. Maybe they won't notice me, I thought. I made it to the refrigerator and poured myself some grapefruit juice, but before I could get the glass to my lips, I heard my father calling me: "Celia, come here and dance with me."

Caught, caged, frantic! I put the glass down and walked into the living room. My teeth were clenched, every muscle constricted, and my arms stiffly hugged my waist. I felt like each part of me was going to crack. This was not the Sea Turtle, where I enjoyed dancing, where the music overtook my body. Here, I was in the clutches of a stone-cold rigidity. I had to perform. As my feet reluctantly tapped out the beat, I could only get my hips to sway slightly. I bent my elbows, which were still stuck to my body, and snapped my fingers. The smile I was trying to put on my face was met by the heat of my blushing cheeks. The only thoughts in my head were: Why am I cringing? Why am I so introverted? Why can't I be free and please my father?

I didn't know then but I do know now: It was becoming more difficult for me to distinguish between my own innate impulses and the outlandish demands of my father. I was convinced that any other way was better than the way I was.

After that first summer, there was talk of going to a nudist colony. The whole idea spooked me; I couldn't imagine what I'd do if that were to happen. So when I heard we were going back to Fire Island, I breathed a sigh of relief.

This time my parents rented a house in the Pines, one of the wildest and raunchiest parts of Fire Island. Some of their friends from the previous summer joined them, but now their housemates included some creepy characters whom I instinctively dodged. We only spent a few weekends there, and Sharon never joined me.

The house was one of the few things I remember about that season. It was a big, modern structure with a lawn that led to the bay. Inside it had large public spaces and a spiral staircase to the second story. My room was on the ground floor behind the stairs. It was small, with a bed to the left and a closet to the right. There was a double window opposite the entry door, where ghostly shadows began passing by whenever I was changing my clothes. I'd snap my head in the window's direction, and a chill would pass through me. I felt I was being watched. Then one day, I spotted a man standing outside leering at me. It was one of the strangers with whom my parents shared the house.

Horrified, I ran to tell my mother. Tremors emanated from every part of me. With my knees ready to give out, I stood directly in front of her, parted my trembling lips and said, "One of your friends was standing outside my window watching me get dressed."

I expected to see alarm on her face. Surely I'd have her full attention. I was certain that she'd grab me, wrap me in her arms and tell me she'd take care of it. Instead, she said, "Are you sure?"

I was sure, and I pleaded with her: "Tell him to stop!"

A second passed before she said, "I think you imagined it." She turned to walk away, and over her shoulder she added, "Don't be like that!"

The blades of a blender began mashing me up. I replayed the Peeping Tom incident over and over for the next few hours until I convinced myself that I had, indeed, made it up.

I didn't know then but I do know now: The lines between truth and fiction were beginning to blur. The slightest intimation of doubt from anyone could steer me toward self-sabotage. This, too, marked a critical turn: the point where I started to mistrust what I knew was real—an obstacle that would become almost insurmountable in the future.

16

MYSTIC COLOSSUS

"My father owns a disco!" I'd brag to my friends. Then, on cue, they'd reply, "Wow, that's so cool," or "Amazing," which I soaked up.

My parents, along with Stanley and Marilyn, had become obsessed with the disco craze and went to all the clubs in the city. One club where patrons removed their street clothes and put on togas was getting a lot of attention on the evening news. When my mother told me that they had gone, I had to suppress my gag reflex as I pictured my parents disrobing and partaking in what sounded like an orgy. She also told me it was there that she'd finally tried pot. "Pot makes me nervous," she confessed. "I don't like it."

One night, Mom and Dad took me, Sharon and a couple of our male friends to the Electric Circus, a discotheque on St. Mark's Place in Manhattan. At night the East Village was ablaze with lights and activity. All the shops were open and the streets were alive with performers and vendors. Artists were lined up with their chairs and easels doing portraits and caricatures. It was a carnival-like ambiance with guys who looked like girls, and girls who dressed like guys—a hippie haven, with absurd hats, rainbow-colored granny glasses, headgear and scarves of all kinds. I was dizzy from darting my head in a million directions.

We ascended a grand staircase to get to the front door of the Electric Circus. Inside, a light show was projected onto the wall of the stairwell. It was so packed that we stood on one step for at least a minute before moving on to the next. We finally entered a massive, dreamlike space with psychedelic images undulating around us. My senses were on overload; my ears heard nothing but the roar of the music, and the shoulder-to-shoulder crowd kept me dancing in one spot. For sure, it was a "happening," one that my friends and I would never forget.

After that heady experience I was to find out that Stanley and my dad were planning to open their own disco. Suddenly, like a new weather pattern, the climate in my house changed. Foggy molecules dispersed, the air was lightened by a cleansing current, and my dad's disposition seemed sunnier. "Stanley's the person I've been waiting for," he said. "He's a businessman, and he's going to finance and market my brilliant ideas." It seemed that my father's fortunes were improving, and I noted that my mother fully sanctioned the enterprise. Better days had to be ahead.

I got swept up in the frenzy. My father becoming a business owner felt like a significant development. A lot of the kids I hung out with in Weequaic had fathers who owned businesses. They wore suits and ties, which connoted wealth to me. Plus, my father repeated with certainly, "We're going to be rich and live on Park Avenue." I pictured a big, beautiful penthouse atop the fanciest building in Manhattan.

I didn't know then but I do know now: The financial disparity between me and most of my friends carried more weight than I realized. Besides wanting to be like everyone else, I also felt inferior. And my father's incessant and bordering-on-pathological references to wealth led me to deduce that his happiness—and mine—depended on it.

I'd often tag along on my parents' trips in search of a location for their club. They eventually landed on Cross Bay Blvd., in Howard Beach, Queens. It was an hour-long odyssey through N.J., over the Goethals Bridge to Staten Island. We had to cross the new Verrazano-Narrows Bridge, at the time the highest and longest structure in America. Once on the other side, we merged onto the congested Belt Parkway. This part of the trip was boring, but I passed the time staring out over the sparkling water and the vast sky to my right. After rounding a certain bend in the road, the Coney Island Ferris wheel came into view. It was the landmark that indicated to me that we were almost there.

The architecture in Queens was different from what I'd seen in Manhattan. The buildings were lower and more densely packed. Most unusual were the overhead train tracks that shook our car when we stopped at a red light beneath them. With my hands over my ears I'd block out the loud rumbling of the subway cars. The high-pitched squeaking of their metal brakes made my teeth hurt.

The building they'd found was in an industrial part of Queens. It was a one-story, standalone structure surrounded by a parking lot. The interior was a blank slate, which my dad announced would be a full-blown, commercial version of his basement nightclub—"a design like no one has ever seen before," he said.

My father pointed to the busy boulevard, where cars raced by all night, "Do you see that traffic?" he said. "Our club will be where it's at, and anyone who doesn't come here will be square."

The club needed a name, and in typical Marcel style, he came up with Mystic Colossus. To my ear it sounded a bit corny and over-the-top. But my dad's obsessions burned like an inferno, and the name was adopted. Blueprints, architectural plans, interior design drawings were strewn all over our house. Mystic Colossus logos appeared on letterheads, posters and advertising proposals. Behind the scenes, dealings that I didn't understand—building permits, business and liquor licenses, health and signage forms—held up the opening. But that was Stanley's department, and nothing was going to stop my father's train from barreling forward.

My parents brought me along on their frequent visits to check on the building's progress. Now, the door to the club was to the right of a ticket booth, which was inside the entrance. Beyond that, the space sprawled and the ceiling soared. They built a DJ tower, and all the walls were painted black, with black lights hung to accommodate the light show that my father and a technician were designing. Everyone said it was going to be the "grooviest," "most spectacular" and "mind-blowing" show around.

The tables surrounding the massive dance floor were placed in front of my father's distinctive asymmetrical structures, which were also designed for the light show. The bar, in the back of the club, was still under construction, but I recognized his signature holes and artificial plants. The edge of the bar, where people would be standing or seated, was going to ripple like a wave finished in shiny black Formica.

On one of our visits, closer to the club's completion, Sharon came with me. At that point, Stanley and Marilyn were hiring bartenders and waitresses, and later that day they'd be interviewing disc jockeys, bouncers and other security personnel. Meanwhile, the workmen were putting the finishing touches on two small stages for the go-go dancers. During the workmen's lunch break, Sharon and I got up on the platforms, making believe we were the dancers. Out of the corner of my eye, I caught sight of my father watching us. He walked over and said, "Why don't you two be our go-go girls?"

Our heads snapped, and a lightning bolt passed between us. "Yes-sssss!" we shrieked back at him.

On the ride home, Sharon and I plotted how we'd get her parents' permission. We arranged for them to speak to my parents, who must have made a good case, because we were going to be the Mystic Colossus go-go dancers!

We scoured the city until we found the perfect outfits: electric blue bellbottoms in a shiny, flowing polyester fabric; halter tops whose vertical stripes were red, white, blue and gold; and, of course, white patent leather boots. I couldn't help but recall the scene we'd encountered at the Paraphernalia boutique. Sharon got her hair cut in the newest Vidal Sassoon geometric bob, and I planned to wear mine in a high ponytail.

On opening night, we arrived at the club with our costumes in garment bags. Stepping into the locker room in my casual clothes and emerging all made up, hair done and dressed in my jazzy getup, made me feel like a celebrity. And the whole giddy experience was topped off by being the owner's daughter.

Sharon and I mounted our separate boxes and waited for the music to start. We hadn't practiced, but once up on the stages, we had only to look at each other to synchronize our movements. Standing heads above the lilting and bouncing mass caused my body to surge with supernatural energy. I lost all sense of time and stopped dancing only when the music stopped. Soaked from sweat, Sharon and I jumped off our respective podiums and strode over to the crowded bar where everyone, including the bartender, complimented us. He slid us a couple of beers, which cooled us off so we were ready for the next set.

Our run as go-go girls lasted only a few weeks. We still had school, and I had cheerleading, and we couldn't commit to a schedule that required two late nights each weekend.

On those occasions when I went to Mystic Colossus without Sharon, I'd spend most of my time in the DJ's booth with the guy Stanley had hired. He was a lot older than I, dark, swarthy and heavyset, with a close-cropped beard. I'd dash up the steep, ladder-like staircase to the booth and take my seat next to him. I watched as he chose the records and nimbly managed the turntables. High above the bobbing crowd of people, he was like a puppeteer manipulating them with tunes.

On breaks, we'd find a quiet spot outside the club and lean against the wall with our cigarettes and beer, and he'd tell me about his life in Queens. But I was more entranced back in the control tower by his passion for music. It was he who introduced me to some of the most important groups of the time: Pink Floyd, The Foundations, Jimi Hendrix, Traffic, Linda Ronstadt, The Soul Survivors, Buffalo Springfield, The Who and Sly & the Family Stone.

Stanley didn't trust anyone to handle the front door, so it was decided that my mother or Marilyn would man the ticket booth. One night when neither my mother nor I was there, armed men approached the booth, and at gunpoint Marilyn had to turn over all the proceeds from the evening. I learned about it the day after, when my father was telling my mother. It sounded shocking and frightening. Days passed, and they were still talking about it, but now I heard words like mobsters, Mafia, payoff and shakedown. I didn't know what it meant, but I could tell that it was a serious matter.

My mother and Marilyn stopped manning the ticket booth, and I was no longer allowed to go to the club. I continued to catch snippets of my parents' heated conversations and picked up that it was a dire situation. As quickly as the disco had materialized, it vanished. Along with it went my vision of living in a Park Avenue penthouse.

I didn't know then but I do know now: The short period that my father was preoccupied with Mystic Colossus was a reprieve for me. He didn't pressure me to "help" him, and I believed I was making him proud with my "uninhibited" performance on the go-go platform.

17

ORGASM

I was still a high school junior, 17 years old. The Mystic Colossus extravaganza was in progress, and my social life was evolving. Allan, a senior, started showing up at my locker at school. He was tall, slender and clean-cut, with straight hair that fell across his forehead. He lived two blocks from me, so we'd walk home together, and soon we were meeting up on the Avenue to walk to school in the morning.

For a guy, Allan was unusually conversational and didn't shy away from gossip. I enjoyed talking to him, so I didn't find it odd when he asked a lot of questions about my girlfriends.

Eventually Allan and I shifted from being friends to dating—weekend movie nights and out for a bite at the popular diners. He drove his car with the self-assurance of a grown-up, sitting back in his seat with only one hand on the steering wheel. To me, he looked suave and sophisticated. I'd slide close to him, but, unlike Larry, Allan's arm never fell onto my shoulder. I noticed, and it made me wonder if he liked me. But later, when he pulled into a dark spot at the "lover's lane" in South Mountain Reservation, I thought, "He must like me."

I didn't know then but I do know now: I was confusing sexual attention with love.

As my feelings for Allan grew stronger, so did my desire to be his girlfriend. That was about the time when he started breaking dates with me and calling me last-minute to see if I was still available. I didn't know any better; I'd say yes.

Then Allan stopped making plans to see me altogether, but he continued calling at late hours to say he'd pick me up. Many a Saturday night I passed excruciating hours sitting on the living room sofa or peering out the window to see if he was there. Sometimes he came, and sometimes he didn't. When he did show up, we'd drive somewhere, park and make out. Soon he began pressuring me to have sex. I was 17, and most of my friends were "going all the way," but I was still conflicted.

At school, rumors started flying about Allan and Francine. I was stunned, until I remembered that she had been among the girls he'd asked me about, and I'd thought nothing of it. In elementary school, Francine had been a member of our clique. When we were divided into the "impressers" and the "babies," she was a baby. I still thought of her that way. How could Allan choose her over me? But then, I suddenly saw that she, too, had matured. She was actually pretty, and her majorette status gave her as much clout as I had.

Mental pictures began torturing me: Allan and Francine together, standing arm in arm, he looking down at her adoringly. Me, tossed off to the side, diminished and dejected. "I'm such a fool," I thought.

The pain felt insurmountable, and desperation consumed me. It took all my courage to ask him about what I'd been hearing. He didn't deny it, admitted he was dating both of us and assured me of his affection. All I had to hear was that he liked me and the raging storm inside me subsided. I would do anything to be with him.

I didn't know then but I do know now: Allan was using me, and it plunged me into the pit of despair, the same pit that swallowed me each time my father rejected me. That cavernous space echoed with degradation, unworthiness and persecution; it convinced me that I deserved the treatment I was getting.

Again and again, I waited for Allan to call, and whenever he did, it was late and last-minute. Finally, one night he picked me up, but he didn't put the car in drive. We sat there for a tense moment before he turned to me and said: "Francine had sex with me. What are you waiting for?"

Caught, caged, frantic! If I don't have sex with him, he'll stop seeing me rattled my brain. So I agreed.

Allan told me his parents were out and he was taking me to his house. My heart began throbbing. He pulled up to the curb in front of his stoop. I got out and followed him up the steps and into the entry vestibule. The front door opened into a pitch-black living room, and he didn't turn on a light. It felt illicit, plus I was banging into furniture. I wished he'd at least grab my hand, but he didn't. When we reached his bedroom, in the rear of the apartment, he finally switched on the bright overhead light. It startled me. I stood glued inside the door frame until I found the doorjamb for support. He strode over to his bureau, where he turned on a softer table lamp. Pivoting toward me, he asked that I shut off the ceiling light and gestured that I come sit next to him on the edge of his bed.

Rigidly, I stepped into the room and lowered myself down next to him. As my hip brushed his, my nerves settled a bit. I leaned into him, and he kissed me. "Maybe this will be okay," I thought.

But then everything began to move at lightning speed. He carelessly removed my clothes and pressed me back onto the bed. There was no tenderness, no quiet conversation, no inquiry into how I was doing.

He was silent and rough. My horrified mind whisked me out of the room. From a million miles away, I felt a sharp pain, and then, without warning, he bolted upright, darted to the overhead light switch and rushed back to look at something on the mattress. On the sheet to my left was a blood stain. Where did that come from?

Allan was now standing over me beside the bed and shouting, "You have to get out of here!"

Numb and dazed, I fumbled to get my clothes back on. He was tearing the sheet off the bed. He grabbed my wrist, dragged me out of the house and loaded me into his car. He sped the two blocks to my house, pulled up to the curb and practically threw me onto the sidewalk. He kept saying, "I have to clean my room before my parents get home!"

I watched as his taillights faded. A terrible thing had just happened. What did I do? He'll never call me again.

Somehow I made it up the steps to my front door and let myself into an empty apartment. As usual, my parents were at the club. I don't know what I would have done if they had been there. I passed through another dark living room, found the bathroom and turned on the shower to wash my filthy self. I slipped under my covers, curled up in a ball and lay there with my eyes wide open until hot tears spilled over my lids.

For the next several days, I returned to my bed whenever I was home. At school, I told some of my girlfriends what had happened, which was how I learned where the blood came from. But that did nothing to ease my anguished state. I found out a week later that Allan was taking Francine to the prom.

I didn't know then but I do know now: I had no one in my life to help me differentiate good behavior from bad. Holding other people accountable for their actions was a concept that did not exist for me.

Alone in the center of a world that lay flattened and demolished, I replayed the events of that night. Shame burned my soul. I couldn't bear to look at the ugly, pathetic girl I saw in the mirror.

I didn't know then but I do know now: What happened between Allan and me was a form of date-rape. First he duped me into having sex with him, and then he brutally discarded me. The trauma erased the innocent and respectful experiences I'd had with my younger boyfriends, and it contributed to the difficulties I encountered in my future "love" relationships.

I was lost and in need of guidance. It never occurred to me to confide in my mother; she'd hardly ever spoken to me about sex. But my father had, and one day I approached him. "Can I talk to you?" I asked.

I didn't know then but I do know now: A decade of my father's depravity and humiliating incitements left my fragile sexuality pulverized, as though put through a meat grinder. Mixed into that concoction was my unfulfilled need for a normal father. A twisted part of me thought that by entrusting him with this most delicate issue—the loss of my virginity—I'd get what I always wanted: his love.

He followed me into my room and reclined on my bed. He was wearing a fitted shirt, almost too small, so the buttons looked like they were going to pop. His bell-bottoms were short, exposing socks that were scrunched down by his crossed ankles. His hands were behind his head.

My joints felt brittle. Somehow I managed to take a seat at the foot of the bed. My right palm found its way over my left, which was already on my lap. I stared into them before gathering my breath. "I'm not a virgin anymore," I said. The words sounded like they came out of someone else's mouth. My eyes had lifted toward my father.

"Did you have an orgasm?" he was asking.

I could feel the uncontrollable blinking of my eyes. All the other times he'd lobbed that word at me I'd been able to swat it away like an annoying fly. But now he was injecting it into my fragile life, in the context of one of the most devastating events that had ever happened to me. I'm not sure what I was expecting, but it wasn't that.

An undamaged person might've known that this outrageous and inappropriate question did not merit an answer, but I was the one he was asking. From what he'd already planted in my brain, an orgasm was "beautiful and the most important thing in life." The experience that I'd had was anything but that, which meant that I had failed. I made my confession. I sat and waited for the rebuke I knew was coming, but instead my father started to cry. I'd never seen him cry. Why was he crying?

This strange man in front of me was now sitting upright on my bed, with my pillows behind him, and leaning against my headboard. Through the time-warp that I was in, I heard him say, "I've been waiting for this day all my life."

This wasn't a stranger before me; it was my father saying the most hideous thing I'd ever heard. And he was still talking. "I should have been the first one. Who better than a father to introduce his daughter to sex?"

CRASH—The meteor that entered my room smashed everything to shreds. The blast left a blinding light that obliterated my sight. The violent NO! that wanted to erupt from my depths did not have a means of expression. The impossible images generated by my father's deranged proposal shut me down.

From the farthest corner of my room, I heard him say, "If you let me, I'll show you what an orgasm is."

CRASH—I was gone.

I didn't know then but I do know now: My father was a sexual predator, and what he was proposing was incest. It was another mon-strous trauma to pile onto all the other traumas that preceded it. Up until that point I'd been able to evade his sexualizing. But now he was fixated on me, grooming me to become his sexual partner. In that context, my unfortunate experience with Allan was inevitable.

18

COLLEGE

Higher education was not discussed in my home. It was in my junior year that I began hearing my friends talk about it. I felt as though I'd been dropped on Earth from another planet and I had to learn an alien custom.

I attended my first meeting with my guidance counselor without my parents' knowledge, which is where I discovered that I needed their permission to apply. I was determined. My mother was my best bet, but when I asked her, she said, "You have to ask your father."

"College is for morons," he said. "I can teach you anything you need to know."

The notion of being my father's student drove me, once again, to broach the subject with my mother. This time, surprisingly, she didn't discourage me. She even intimated that when the time came, she'd deal with him.

Hopeful, I attended more meetings. I learned there were "good" and "bad" schools, and colleges that were local and those that were far from home. When the counselor asked if I knew what I wanted to study, I didn't have to think about my answer. "Yes!" I said.

From as far back as I could remember, when anyone asked me what I wanted to be when I grew up, I'd say, "An artist." If my father heard me say that, he'd correct me, saying, "No, you're going to be a commercial artist." His reasoning was that fine artists don't make money and commercial artists do. As I got older, that made sense to me, and I changed my answer.

"I want to study commercial art," I told my guidance counselor. She was pleased and said that would help to narrow my choices.

Then came the meeting where we reviewed my grades. It was a terrible letdown. I'd be completing high school with a C average, and that would limit the schools I could apply to.

I didn't know then but I do know now: Since college had not been a part of my upbringing, I had no idea that my grades could have a bearing on my future. The more my father's values erased my own and the more he debased my efforts, the less I tried to do well in school. I remember the moment that it hit me: I'd ruined my chances of getting into a good college.

The next blow was when I found out that in order to get into a school with an art program, I'd have to submit a "portfolio." What was a portfolio? It was a book that would showcase my artwork. But I had no artwork. My counselor suggested I consult the school's art teacher, whose only advice was to take a private class to produce some pieces.

Years earlier, when I was 14, I'd asked my parents if I could enroll in a privately taught art class. My father said no. "True artists don't have to be taught how to draw!"

I begged my mother, and somehow she convinced him. I was allowed to enroll in a pastel drawing class, for which a set of pastels had to purchased. They came in a small wooden box with a little brass latch. When I opened the box, a thin spongy sheet sat on top of the most wonderful colored chalks I'd ever seen. In the first few classes, we learned how to use them, smudging with our fingers or with a blending stump. Rubbing the dry substance to produce a smooth transition from dark to light, adding volume and dimension, lit my creative pilot light.

For the final project, the teacher set up a still life: a copper kettle and a teacup on a table. She positioned a light to one side that brought the whole scene to life. I carefully followed her instructions and ended up with a pastel drawing that I loved. When I brought it home and showed my father, he barely looked at it, and under his breath he said, "Moron!"

Now, at 17, I knew there'd be no private class for me. I'd have to figure it out myself. I gathered up any projects I could find and assembled them into what I thought a portfolio should be.

My guidance counselor had compiled a short list of third- and fourth-tier colleges I could apply to. The University of Hartford was the only one that required a portfolio, and I would have to present it at my interview.

I had no idea what my mother told my father, but there I was, on I-95, driving to Hartford with her. I glanced at my portfolio in the backseat and pictured myself sitting in front of a stranger who would be judging my work. I let the wave of dread pass through me.

When we arrived, there was something about the 20 or so wind-blown flags lining the entrance to the campus that calmed my nerves. Once on the grounds of the school, amidst the kids congregating and rushing to class, I could imagine myself there. Maybe it won't be that bad, I thought.

We found the administration building, and I waited to be called for my interview. Inside the office, there were big windows across from the entry door. The interviewer's desk was to the right, facing into the center of the room. I took my seat across from her and leaned my portfolio against my legs.

The interview portion went well: I answered the woman's questions, and she seemed satisfied. Then it was time to present my artwork, and I timidly handed her my book.

The silence was agonizing as she flipped through my few, pitiful pieces. As her eyes scanned my work, I was dying to know what she was thinking. If I were to guess, she hated them. And then I got my answer: "I'm sorry," she said, "but I don't see a body of work here." She explained that the separate pieces didn't relate to one another. "The inconsistency makes it difficult for us to see what you're capable of."

I knew she was right, and I begrudged and regretted the effort I had made to put the portfolio together. Back in the car, when my mother asked me how it went, I told her, "I don't like Hartford." And then with a sharpness I was not used to, I said, "I wouldn't go to that school even if they accepted me!"

The University of Hartford rejected me. But the University of Bridgeport and Fairleigh Dickinson did not. Neither required a portfolio, and neither was recognized for its art program. I chose UB because it was farther from home and I could live on campus.

My parents had not set aside a college fund for me. When my counselor advised me to get a student loan, my mother agreed to apply, and we went to the bank together. She stood nervously beside me. The transaction was impossible to follow, and my mother was no help. As I wrote my name on the lines where the bank officer instructed me to sign, I did not grasp the hefty responsibility I was taking on. All I knew was that this was the only way I was going to college.

I didn't know then but I do know now: I've always been embarrassed that my only two college choices were ranked so low. Had I understood how destructive the environment at home was and how little support I had, I would've known it was a miracle that I went to college at all.

My first and favorite pastel drawing done in
the only outside class I was allowed to take

19

MÉNAGE À TROIS

As a high school senior, with college less than a year away, I threw myself into cheerleading, where I was captain of the team. My friendship with Sharon occupied all my extra time. Allan had graduated and left for college, and the wounds from that relationship caused me to pull back from any other romantic prospects. Plus I was not interested in the senior boys.

This was not so with Sharon: She was in a hot and heavy relationship with the most controversial boy in our class. Jerry was the only child of a single mother who lived at the very edge of the Weequaic section. We all considered him the "bad boy," which was exactly what appealed to Sharon.

Her parents were horrified, and the only way she could see him was by lying to them. She and I had a system: She'd tell her parents she was going out with me whenever she met up with Jerry. Then she'd come back to my house and usually sleep over. That was the case the night before our excursion to South Mountain Reservation.

When Sharon slept over, we'd put my twin mattress on the floor.

She slept there, and I on the box spring against the wall. That night we'd talked until 3AM. She and Jerry were in love and having sex. Sharon was enthusiastic and graphic about their sexual exploits. After the atrocious experience I'd had with Allan, I was transfixed by her descriptions of the affection and passion that accompanied their lovemaking.

We were woken up in the late morning by the light sneaking around the roll-up shades on my windows. It was Sunday; there was no reason to get out of bed, so we dawdled, continued talking and devolved into our usual wackiness.

My father must have heard us laughing. Soon the door opened, and he sauntered into my room. There was nowhere to sit, so he just stood there. His hair was longer, combed forward, and his greying sideburns were trimmed even with his earlobes. He was wearing baggy jeans, and the top four buttons of his tight shirt were undone, revealing his chest hair. With most of his weight resting on his left foot, he placed his arms behind his back and cocked his head to one side. "What are you two idiots laughing about?" he said.

This was the teasing and playful Marcel who always showed up when Sharon was around.

"What are your plans today?" my father wanted to know. I was ready to make up fake plans, but Sharon quickly blurted out the truth: We had none. He suggested that we take a ride to the Reservation. I was dubious, but Sharon said she was game, and we agreed to go.

I didn't know then but I do know now: My father's presence sucked everything out of me, leaving only passivity, compliance and deference.

On the drive over, my father was effusive about communing with nature, and he told us he had brought a joint. I knew that my father smoked pot, but I'd never smoked with him. Sharon was in the backseat, so I couldn't look at her to see what her reaction was. We pulled up to the bottom of the hill, which had very few people on it. The weather was warm, the trees were in bloom, and the grass was like a bright green carpet. Birds were chirping, and the air was sweet with spring fragrances. When we got about three-quarters up the incline, Dad sat down. He patted his hands on the ground, indicating that we sit on either side of him. He lit the joint and passed it around.

The pot and this mellow version of my father unnerved me, and I failed to control the shaking that was emanating from my solar plexus. Casually he leaned back, propped himself up on his elbows and crossed his ankles. "Look at this beauty all around us," he said. He launched into a treatise about how "the new liberal philosophies" were colliding with "the old, antiquated traditions about sex." I tuned him out as he continued throwing out tropes: "Free love." "Anything goes." "Women must get pleasure, too." "A man's potency is his power."

Then I heard: "The three of us have a beautiful relationship. I love both of you, and you love each other."

He had my attention. I needed to catch Sharon's eyes, but my father was sitting between us. What was he up to?

Then: "It would be an amazing thing if all three of us could have sex together." And then, "It would be a happening." And, "I could teach you both so much."

CRASH—The birds stopped singing. The bright blue sky turned dark. Over this landlocked hillside a tsunami appeared on the distant horizon. In an instant it sucked me in, jerking and slamming me with its wild force.

Through the tumult I was able to catch sight of Sharon, but she seemed bemused and distant. My father was still talking; he was urging us to consider his proposition. When neither of us responded, he lashed out: "Don't be prudes! Don't be squares!"

I have no recollection of what might've transpired next. I don't remember standing up, walking down the hill, taking my seat in the car. After that day, I can't recall Sharon and I ever speaking of it. The only words relating to the incident that I do remember passing through my father's lips were, "Don't tell your mother."

I didn't know then but I do know now: My father was a pedophile. He saw himself as a Svengali and us as his sexual disciples. His unspeakable behavior was coming at me with such frequency and velocity, yet I couldn't tell anyone. It happened, and I shut it down. If ever the memory began to smolder, I smothered it.

20

THE KISS

Dance was the thread to my soul, It was my means of escape, and it kept me sane. By 1968, the racial balance at Weequaic High School had shifted, and now, the majority of students were black. There were a couple of black girls on my cheerleading squad, and I was friendly with several others, including Amelia, my closest black girlfriend. She was tall and pretty, with big eyes and delicate features. She used to wear her hair in a shoulder length bouffant, but lately it was straight and long.

We spoke on the phone often. "I love watching you and your friends dance," I said during one of our calls. "You're so much cooler than the white kids." We were still doing the stiff and lame Jerk and Hitchhiker. I asked if she'd teach me how to dance like her. "Of course," she said.

We decided to meet at the gym after school, where I turned the dial of my transistor radio to the soul music station. The DJ played "I Heard it Through the Grapevine" by Marvin Gaye, and "Chain of Fools" by Aretha Franklin, and "The Dock of the Bay" by Otis Redding, and "I Thank You," by Sam and Dave, all of which were the ideal tempo. Amelia eased into a smooth and loose motion that started at her feet and waved through her body, all the way to the top of her head. I watched and attempted to imitate her, but at first I was awkward: My timing was completely off, and I couldn't find the rhythm. Seeing my frustration, she slowed it down, but to no avail. It didn't work.

After some thought, she said, "I'm dancing to a different beat." Where she was going down, I was going up. She gently took my hand, stood next to me and showed me how her knees were bending while mine were straightening.

"It's a down beat," she said. I stood still with my feet plastered to the floor and bobbed up and down with her until my rigid, staccato action was replaced by her fluid, wavy movement.

I was obsessed with learning this freestyle dance. At home I'd grab my albums and take them to the basement. I played them one by one, searching for a record that had that distinctive beat. It took some time, but I found the perfect group and the perfect song: "Born on the Bayou," by Creedence Clearwater Revival. I kept the album downstairs, next to the stereo, and any chance I got, I played that one song over and over again. Then one day, the magic happened: I got it! My feet, hips and head synchronized perfectly, and I was doing the boogaloo, just like the black kids.

With my new dance moves mastered, I wanted to try them out with all my records. One afternoon, I was downstairs dancing to "Stoned Soul Picnic," by The 5th Dimension. Suddenly, I heard the high-pitched sound of my father's bandsaw coming from the other side of the wall behind the bar. My father must have come into his shop through the back entrance of the basement. I tried to block the noise out. I figured he was busy so he'd leave me alone. I was wrong.

The door opened, and my father stuck his head out. "Celia, can you come here for a second?"

"Can I just finish listening to this song?" I asked.

"Okay," he said.

Hoping he'd forget, I continued my dancing.

But again, "Celia, come here."

I entered his shop. He was standing at his worktable, banging and sawing, constructing a display for one of his customers. I stayed by the threshold, which was next to the bandsaw. He walked over with a piece of plywood and started the machine up.

The room smelled like dirt, paint and ink. The shelves were stacked with rolls of fabric, Styrofoam forms and other supplies. Wood shavings were all over the floor. I watched as his short, soiled fingers skillfully maneuvered the piece of wood.

When the buzz of the saw stopped, he gestured for me to come farther in. There was barely any space to move, so I shimmied my way to the only empty spot, in front of the open metal basement doors, the doors he must've come in through. The sun was moving toward the horizon, and warm beams streamed down the cement steps.

"What do you want, Daddy?" I asked.

He turned to face me and started his usual chatter. I stood with my arms crossed, leaning on my left foot, right foot turned out. It took all my willpower to keep from tapping my toes impatiently. I was also attempting to keep my jitters at bay when an abrupt silence snapped me to attention. My father was staring at me in a way I'd never seen before. He stepped closer to me, unusually close. There wasn't any room to get away, and besides, he'd already grabbed me by the shoulders and was drawing me toward him. His arms were now embracing me, squeezing me like a boa constrictor. My nostrils burned from his odious smell. And then I felt his lips pressing into mine. I could taste his saliva. I wanted to vomit. I shoved him so hard that he hit the bandsaw.

CRASH—A blast decimated my eardrums. A cannon had gone off and shards of glass were piercing my skin. I felt myself crumbling, collapsing, imploding.

I had to get out of there. My only escape route was behind me. I turned toward the bright light coming from outside. That first cement step seemed miles away, but I made a dash for it. With my foot ready to take the second step, my father yelled, "Don't tell your mother!"

The top step led out into the parking area where our family car sat. I still had the keys in my pocket from an errand I'd run earlier. My hands were shaking so badly that I fumbled to get a firm grip and then to put the key into the ignition. The sound of the engine turning over was the signal to shift the car in reverse. I did a K-turn so I could head down the narrow driveway and onto the street.

I had no idea where I was going. I barely noticed the lights or the stop signs. Houses, trees and pedestrians sailed by as tears streamed down my face. I drove and drove aimlessly, wishing never to return home.

But where was I going and whom was I going to tell? Nowhere and no one. I'd never felt this kind of anguish. All I could do was stare beyond the windshield and keep driving. After what could have been an hour, my weariness turned the steering wheel to go back.

I slipped quietly through the side door, through the hall and into my room. It was imperative that I be undetected—no, invisible. I shut the door behind me and crawled under my covers, again.

Apparently my father had been waiting for me. I heard the knob turn and the door creak open, and, in a soft, deferential voice, he asked my permission to enter. I'd never heard that tone before.

I didn't say anything. I didn't move. I wanted him to leave. But he didn't. As he came closer to my bed, I shrunk into the blanket wrapped around me. I wanted to recede from the outer layers of my flesh and retreat as far away from consciousness as I could.

My father was talking. "It was a stupid thing that I did. I think it would be good if you forget about it." Then he repeated, "Don't tell your mother."

I didn't know then but I do know now: Even though I don't remember, there's a very deep part of me that suspects that, when I was around nine years old, my father touched me inappropriately while I slept. I believe that it happened multiple times. Before he left my room, he'd whisper "Don't tell your mother." I also suspect that those four words exacerbated an already mangled dynamic between me and my mother.

I prayed for him to go away. He did.

Life did not stop, and eventually I had to emerge from my room. Passing through my house was like slogging through a viscous substance that clung to my skin, impeding my stride and blurring my vision. Danger was inches away. Dodging interactions with both my mother and my father was the only way I found to stabilize myself.

Undeterred, my father continued haranguing me to help him. Zapping me like a taser gun over and over again. When I pushed back or objected, he'd say, "It's because of that stupid kiss, isn't it?" He didn't wait for an answer. "I told you to forget about it."

Just the mention of it seared my ears. I couldn't bear the sound of it. Couldn't face that it happened. Maybe he was right and I should put it out of my mind. So I stuffed it into the drawer where all the other junk was stored, and I returned to what felt like normal.

I didn't know then but I do know now: This incident was the last of four sexual abuses that happened to me within one year. I'd adopted many ways of coping with the dysfunction in my family, but the challenges posed by these episodes pushed me over a line. Dissociation from reality, which was already in progress, became my go-to survival mechanism. I now believe that had I acknowledged my anger, it would have meant that I knew my father had done something wrong, and that would have been worse than the actual trauma.

PART 2

21

FRESHMAN

And so I headed off to college. Move-in day arrived in August of 1968. We packed our red station wagon with my new bedding, school supplies and clothes. We sat in our usual seats for the drive to Bridgeport—my parents in front, me in the back. I couldn't imagine the adventure that lay before me.

I'd been assigned to Bodine Hall, the newest and tallest building on campus. Before we could unload, we had to wait in a long line of cars similarly packed to the brim. One by one, families transferred their stuff from the car to the curb, into the building and through the lobby, where another line was waiting for the elevators. It was noisy, rousing and exciting. I coasted with the mayhem, tried to listen to all the conversations and checked out my future schoolmates. Some of them looked like my friends from Weequaic, and some looked entirely different.

Eventually we found my room, on the sixth floor. I got there before my roommate and chose the bed and desk right underneath the big picture window. Dropping my belongings in the middle of the space,

I shot over to take in the view. A large part of the campus was spread out in front of me. There were unremarkable brick buildings and old Victorian mansions. Beyond them I saw the Long Island Sound. Students were roaming around everywhere. If my parents had not been with me, I'd have hastened to be among them.

My mother was urging me to do some unpacking before they left. Mention of them leaving brought me back to reality. As we said our good-byes, and they disappeared down the hall, an unexpected wave of sadness passed through me. I had no idea what living away from my parents would be like.

I didn't know then but I do know now: Within the cinderblock walls of my dorm room, I carried the dark burden of a rough past and the promise of a bright future.

The melancholic moment was disrupted by the arrival of my room-mate. I don't remember much about her other than that she was one of a myriad of firsts. I'd never shared a room with another person, and it was something I'd have to get used to.

A few days after I moved in, I found a spot on the cement steps in front of Bodine Hall and took in my new life. It was a clear and warm late summer day when I was approached by Mitch, the most stereotypical hippie I'd ever seen. His hair was long and disheveled, and he had a full beard, love beads, tie-dye shirt and ripped, baggy jeans held at the waist with a rope. When he found out I was a freshman, he offered to fill me in about UB life. He knew a lot about the art department because he was an art major, a couple of years ahead of me.

I'd run into Mitch often. He had a sketch pad and ink pen with him at all times, which he'd whip out whenever he needed to record a visual idea. I'd never seen anyone do that, nor had I ever watched someone draw with such self-assurance. He must be the "real" artist that my father was talking about.

Inspired, I found my way to the local art store and purchased my own Cachet Classic Black hardcover sketchbook. Several times in the past, I'd attempted to "draw from my imagination," to no avail. I was ready to try again.

Sitting at my desk in my dorm room, I turned to the first white page. It stared back at me, as if taunting me to come up with something ingenious. But nothing arose through the blankness of my mind. The harder I tried, the emptier my imagination was. I scratched a few tentative lines, but they were lame, so I turned the page. The second page was even more unforgiving as I tried to pull an image from my brain. All that came to me was the ballerina that I used to draw when I was seven years old. That was childish, unacceptable. I slammed the book shut. My father's loud and accusatory message ripped into me: "You're not a real artist."

I didn't know then but I do know now: At seven years old, my creative process had not yet been corrupted. I had direct access to my imagination, and I effortlessly drew what I saw in my mind: ballerinas, landscapes with houses, trees, blue skies, butterflies, birds and tulips. I intuitively knew that by copying the pirate on the matchbook, I'd improve my skills. But when my father so savagely slashed that drawing, it was a wound that arrested my artistic growth.

I didn't know then but I do know now: At seven years old, when I had drawn the pirate my imagination was free. My father's savage slashing of that drawing arrested my artistic growth.

In the first semester of my freshman year, I signed up for as many art classes as I could. For one, "The Art of Color," I had to purchase a special box at the UB bookstore. It was approximately 6" wide by 8" high and 1.5" thick and filled with sheets of vibrantly colored paper. Each ink-coated sheet had a chalky feel that left an invisible residue on my fingertips. The sharp smell singed my nostrils and sat in the back of my throat for an instant. Soon after I bought it, I pulled the pages out of the box to flip through them. I saw shades of color I'd never seen before.

The first few classes were devoted to theory, but finally we were instructed to open our boxes and start working with the sheets. We'd cut out a small square of one color and place it on a larger square of another color, and the small square looked blue. Then we took the same small square and placed it on another larger color, and it looked purple. This was color interaction. It was magic!

But it was the complementary colors that blew my mind. When they were put side by side or one on top of the other, they shimmered. They made my eyeballs wobble in their sockets. And the color wheel— I had no idea there was so much science behind color.

My first painting course introduced me to oil paints, canvases and palette knives. We all arrived at class with brand new shiny wooden paintboxes. Mine was filled with a few brushes of different sizes, tubes of essential colors and a palette. This was no ordinary classroom. Instead of desks there were easels arranged around a simple still life that the professor had assembled. The smell of paint, turpentine and linseed oil was as fragrant to me as a field of flowers.

The second week was when she demonstrated how to start a painting. I watched intently as she squeezed a small amount of paint from each tube onto her palette. With her long, flat brush, she began mixing the colors and applying them to the blank gessoed surface on the easel. Within seconds, a basic image of the pre-arranged scene appeared on the canvas. My hands were itching to begin. Holding the brush's long handle and swirling the tight bristles in the thick creamy paint felt natural. Seeing shades and tones of the colors change was a thrill. Once the paint was on the canvas, it could be pushed, slid and blended right there. I couldn't make a mistake because it didn't dry.

During most of the classes, our professor would walk around and offer suggestions to us students. One day, as I was working on a landscape, she came up behind me and pointed to a spot on my canvas that I hadn't even noticed. "It takes talent to know when to stop!" she said. Was she talking about me? Yes, she was standing by my easel, pointing to my painting.

I didn't know then but I do know now: My father's merciless attacks on my talent left me so jaded that it was unfathomable to me that this teacher was validating my artistic instincts. I knew she was referring to me and my painting, yet I convinced myself that her judgment was meaningless and had no value. It wasn't until many years later, when I started painting again, that I recalled her comment and took ownership of what she had observed.

A few months after I started at UB, I got a job at the art store in downtown Bridgeport. It was a great opportunity for me to learn about the different materials that related to all the creative arts. I got discounts on my art supplies, and I had extra money in my pocket.

I was more interested in making art than studying its origins, so art history was not my favorite class. I did enjoy the large lecture hall where I could stare off into space and disappear in the darkness. Watching slides on the huge screen was entertaining, but the course required more reading than I wanted to do. When test time rolled around, I was unprepared and in a panic. There was too much to catch up on and not enough hours. I learned from the older girls on my floor that drinking coffee, a stimulant, would keep me awake. I tried it, and it worked. I also got a kick out of watching the nighttime turn into daylight. From then on I "pulled all-nighters" all semester and passed the course.

From day one, the student center became the hub of my social life. Each morning I started out there with a cup of coffee, and between classes it was my pit stop. Upstairs was a quiet space where I'd catch up on my work. If I didn't eat at the dining hall, I'd grab my meals in the cafeteria. That's where I'd hooked up with a group of new friends who always met at the same table: the third from the front and the second row in. All of them majored in the creative arts, and they were a dynamic, opinionated and colorful bunch. No matter who was sitting there, I could count on an endless stream of social commentary or just plain gossip.

I didn't know then but I do know now: I was thriving. My mind was opening, my artistic inclinations were finding expression, and my social life was flourishing. Being outside of my father's gravitational pull allowed me to spin freely in my new orbit. It was as though I could relegate the horrible things that had happened to another galaxy.

Drugs were everywhere, and everyone, including me, was experimenting. I preferred hash over weed, and I tried uppers and downers. Pot made me paranoid, amphetamines made me nervous, and barbiturates put me to sleep. LSD just plain scared me. Most of the guys liked to brag about how "fucked up" they got. They'd go into great detail about their trips, or they'd count off how many nights they'd stayed up or how quaaludes gave them the best "head."

Right before Christmas break, rumors were circulating. "If you think you're fucked up, wait till you see Bob McGraw!" So many people were talking about him that I wondered who this phantom druggy was.

It wasn't until after spring break that I was introduced to a tall guy with the most beautiful mane of light brown hair. He looked like a cross between Jim Morrison and Michelangelo's David. He was Bob, and he didn't seem fucked up to me. It turned out he'd been suspended between Christmas and spring break because of his drug use and had stopped getting high.

Whenever I could, I'd put myself in his path. He was often at the student center at the same time I was, and I began to suspect the attraction was mutual. The only problem was, he had a girlfriend. I'd see them together, and then, suddenly, I didn't. He and I began dating at the end of my freshman year. While we were sharing confidences, he admitted that he'd broken up with his girlfriend to go out with me. He also told me that during his hiatus, he'd spent ample time contemplating his future and was now focused on a degree in industrial design. This was getting interesting.

We made a handsome couple. Bob wore Frye boots with jeans that were just the right length. He had a tan, corduroy jacket with elbow patches that gave him a hip and scholarly look. I wore everything from ankle-length flowered dresses with intricate beading, to bandanas, lots of denim and peasant blouses. No makeup, no bras; my hair was long, wavy and full. Sometimes I'd braid it. Strangers would say, "I can't wait to see your babies," which made both of us blush.

When school came to an end that summer, I had no choice but to go home to Newark, and Bob returned to Floral Park, Long Island. I'd found a job at Aetna Casualty and Surety in downtown Newark. Turned out I did not like clerical work, and I hated sitting at a desk. When five o'clock on Friday rolled around, I shot out of the office and took the train from Newark to Penn Station, where I'd meet Bob. Nor only were these rendezvous enjoyable, they kept me away from my father.

When we weren't exploring the city together, we stayed at his parents' modest home, feet away from The Belmont racetrack. Like me, Bob was an only child. His father, Twiller, had grown up poor in North Carolina. He'd often talk about not having plumbing or long pants and walking to school barefoot, which I couldn't imagine. Bob's mother, Pauline, was a homemaker who cooked the most delicious braciole and other Italian meals. She was always crocheting while she watched TV.

They were old-fashioned, so we dared not stay together in his room.

Several of my friends were falling in love and committing to their partnerships. I wanted that. At this point, Bob and I had only been dating for a few months. In spite of him not being emotionally demonstrative, I overlooked it because I was ready for a long-term relationship. Plus, I liked him.

I didn't know then but I do know now: I was not clear about what "love" meant. Was I in love with Bob? It didn't matter. I wanted to have a boyfriend, and I was determined that it was going to be him.

22

SOPHOMORE

In the fall of 1969 I was returning to college with much to look forward to. I'd be moving into Barnum Hall, a dorm at the opposite end of the campus. It was an older building, but the rooms were twice the size as they were in Bodine.

Lynn was going to be my new roommate. We'd met the semester before; she was a member of my student center clique, and we'd struck up an immediate friendship. Lynn was tall and slim, with long, straight blond hair; she was often told she resembled Joni Mitchell. She was a psych major, interested in the workings of the mind. We had intense conversations exploring our emotions, personalities and the intricacies of relationships.

Nothing was official with Bob, but it seemed to me that we were boyfriend and girlfriend. He was renting an off-campus house on Milford beach with his friend Steve. A lot of students lived in the funky, rundown homes right on the Long Island Sound; Bob's was called "La Maisonette." His back deck led onto the sand, and when it was quiet, we could hear the waves washing onto the shore. We'd often watch the sun rise where the Sound kissed the sky to the east.

Whenever I was there, we spent hours in his room listening to music. Bob was obsessed with Bob Dylan. After hearing "Lay, Lady, Lay" on a continual loop, I also became a fan. Soon my musical repertoire expanded to include Cream, the Band, Janis Joplin and the Holding Company, James Taylor, Eric Clapton and Crosby, Stills, Nash and Young.

Bob was an amateur photographer. I'd only used a Brownie or Sharon's Instamatic, and as far as I knew Kodak was the sole manufacturer of cameras. Bob introduced me to the world of Nikon and Canon, with their standard, wide angle and telephoto lenses. He didn't drop his film off at the drugstore; he used the darkroom on campus, which was lit with a red light bulb. I stood next to him, breathing in the acrid chemicals, watching as his white photo paper came alive with his black-and-white images.

I learned the delicate process of loading the film from Bob, and he warned me, if not done properly, the whole roll would be exposed and ruined. When it was my turn to try, I nervously dropped the roll into its compartment, grabbed the thin tab of film, pulled it across to the take-up reel and inserted it into place. The advance lever tightened it, and I was able to close the camera back. I did it! As for the manual steps of setting the aperture, using a light meter and determining the shutter speed, it was too much work for me. I preferred to point and shoot.

One weekend, after Bob had gone home, he returned with a broken-down motorcycle, which he mounted on concrete bricks on the rear deck. A mechanical tinkerer, he enjoyed fixing things. To me it looked unsalvageable, but he had another vision. He was going to bring it back to life, part by part. He'd take a pipe that was almost rotted out with rust, drop it off at some shop and pick it up a week later fully restored and chromed to perfection.

His pride and joy, his new, red VW Beetle, was meticulously washed, vacuumed, waxed and repaired by him. That car sparkled and hummed. It played a pivotal role in our romance. When we weren't together and I spotted it on campus, I knew we'd meet up at the student center at the end of the day. When we had a date, I'd patiently wait in my dorm lobby for it to round the corner.

Off campus excursions took us all over that part of Connecticut. When the weather was warm, the sunroof slid open, the windows were cranked down, and the radio blasted Procol Harum's "Whiter Shade of Pale," or Led Zeppelin's "Whole Lotta Love," or Jefferson Airplane's "White Rabbit." We'd cruise the country roads of Redding and Wilton, finding hidden treasures in remote shops. Our favorite spot was outside of Westport, on a narrow road where the trees were thick and a river raged. We parked the car, climbed down to a crop of big rocks, got naked and jumped into a deep, cool pool of water. I needed quite a bit of reassurance from Bob the first time I took my clothes off. Once convinced, I felt so bold and liberated I never needed coaxing again.

That year I had to declare my major, but I was so ambivalent that I procrastinated. At the last minute, I ran to the registrar's office and perused my choices. There was no commercial art option, just fine art or graphic design. I reluctantly selected the latter without knowing what it entailed. When the time came for me to pick my classes, nothing appealed to me. Most were geared toward creating a visual representation of an idea for publishing and advertising purposes, which I had no interest in. The painting and drawing classes that I coveted were now considered electives.

I didn't know then but I do know now: My passion was in the fine arts. Creatively, I preferred to produce beautiful pictures, which had less to do with what I thought and everything to do with what I saw. Had my father not circumvented my natural tendencies, I would have pursued a career as a fine artist.

I was to find that graphic design was too rigid and linear for me. Conceptualizing and brainstorming did not come naturally. Balancing shape and color with text bored me. I labored and agonized over the assignments, and I loathed presenting my work.

There was just one assignment that I was enthusiastic about. We were asked to use flat colors to graphically represent our astrological signs. I was an Aries, and the zodiac symbol was the ram. The shape of its head and the prominent spiral of its horn inspired a strong and beautiful image. It was the only piece for which I received praise from my fellow students.

Being that Bob was also studying to be a designer, we'd do our projects together at the beach house. He worked at a drafting table with T-squares, triangles, compasses and templates. He used Plasticine to build his models, transforming a grey, shapeless blob into a bottle or a wrench or a telephone. We'd often have substantive discussions about our different design paths. His work was for functional and utilitarian purposes, whereas mine was abstract and theoretical. We'd bounce ideas off each other, which made me feel like we were truly partners and meant to be together.

One of my electives was Mr. Novack's figure drawing class. It was my introduction to nude models. Initially I was embarrassed to be gazing at an unclothed person, but as soon as Mr. Novack did his first drawing demonstration, my modesty disappeared.

He drew on the largest newsprint pad I'd ever seen. To get the basic form of the figure on the page, he used a flat, soft lead pencil about a quarter of an inch wide. With huge, flowing arm movements, a beautiful line that was both thick and thin appeared on the paper. Standing behind him, darting my eyes from the model to the sheet, I took in this most amazing sight.

He'd strategically illuminated the model by placing a light at an extreme angle. One side of her body caught the bright glare from the bulb, while the other receded into a pronounced shadow. The dramatic effect sparked a dynamic optic reaction within me similar to standing before a spellbinding view.

Mr. Novack picked up a piece of compressed charcoal, turned it on one of its flat sides and ran it all over the page. He pressed softly where there was less light and harder to emphasize the darkness. He was like a maestro waving his baton to elicit soft notes and loud notes. Before me was the most graceful and elegant representation of a human body I'd ever seen.

I found the pencil and the charcoal easy to handle. I understood the concept behind the pressure, and after much practice my lines began to look like his. The large sketch pad encouraged me to be loose and unrestrained. In every other class, I dreaded the critiques that followed a presentation, but not in this one. My classmates and Mr. Novack were generous with their compliments.

I didn't know then but I do know now: Mr. Novack's lighting and his technique inspired me as nothing had before. From that point on, light and shadow has played the leading role in all my artwork.

I was so proud of my drawings that I begged my father to come for Parents Weekend that spring. I knew he hated such gatherings, but he reluctantly agreed. In preparation, I mounted all my best drawings on poster board so I could set up an exhibition in my dorm room. Lynn helped me rearrange the furniture to free up one unobstructed wall. Because she knew how excited I was, she agreed to be elsewhere with her parents.

I sat on my bed facing my artwork and admired my curation. I was so sure of what I saw in front of me that the doubt and uncertainty that normally plagued me wasn't there. Waiting for my parents was torture, and as soon as I heard the knock I ran to let them in. After greeting them with quick kisses, I pointed toward the wall. "Look at my drawings!" I said.

My mother walked over, took a look and said, "These are very nice!"

Then I turned to my father, who was still standing by the door and began telling him about the great figure drawing class I was taking. I described how I'd used the flat pencil to get the initial drawing and then the unusual way I'd learned to use the charcoal. I thought he'd be impressed when I told him that Mr. Novak really liked my work.

But he just stood there. He didn't step into the room or make his way over to the wall. Instead he glared at me and said, "You're wasting your time at this stupid school."

His chest puffed up, his head cocked back and his nostrils flared. "Anybody can do this," he went on. "You're learning nothing in these classes."

He walked toward the wall, and with a sweep of his hand and disgust in his voice he said, "These drawings have no commercial value. I want you to come home and work with me."

He spun on his heels, stormed toward the door and strode down the hallway. My mother was right behind him.

CRASH—Seconds before I was alive, my life's purpose before me with endless possibility. Now it was gone, lost and dead.

Catatonic and listless, I followed my parents out of the dorm. We stepped into the same daylight I always saw. The same Long Island Sound shimmered in the distance. But, as though shades had been drawn, the light went out, darkness fell, and the campus dissipated. Every step I took felt like I had a 100-pound weight on each ankle. I had to keep my focus on the ground so I wouldn't fall down.

I don't remember what we did after that. I probably took my parents to the dining hall, where I ate nothing, and then lifelessly said goodbye.

Back at my dorm room, the drawings were still leaning against the wall, but I couldn't look at them. I was an untethered vessel on the verge of sinking. I had no sense of place. I felt the edge of my bed pressing into the back of my knees. They buckled. I sat and dropped my head into my hands. How could I have been so foolish?

There were a few weeks of the semester remaining, and I was miserable. Everywhere I went, my failings followed me. I compared myself to Bob: He was clear and driven and never faltered from his path. I compared myself to my other artistic friends: They were prolific, talented and authentic. I was a fraud. One friend was the epitome of an artist: He'd draw endless caricatures of students in the student center. I'd sit next to him and watch as his magical images appeared out of thin air. Where once I'd appreciated his skill, now it reflected everything I was not. Where did I ever get the idea that I was an artist?

I didn't know then but I do know now: I was already fragmented, fractured and broken. Everything hinged on my father's approval, and when I didn't get it, the few flimsy bricks that I'd managed to get under my feet turned to dust. The groundlessness terrorized me, and my only option was to give up on myself.

Bob in front of "La Maisonette" on Milford Beach, CT

Bob resurrecting his motorcycle on the back porch of the beach house

My hippie days in Bridgeport, CT, with a Jane Fonda shag

23

JUNIOR

When UB closed for summer break, I returned home. My college experience had been ambushed by my father, and I was derailed.

I intended to resume my studies in the fall, which I did. I showed up to my classes, and I did my assignments, but I was present in body only. The ambition, aspiration and idealism that had driven me the previous semesters was gone. In its place was an interminable echo chamber that reverberated with my father's words. There was no volume knob nor switch to turn them off. They dogged me morning, noon and night.

I had no more fight left. I told myself that college was useless, teachers were failed professionals, and fine arts was a dead end. I said good-bye to my friends, and even though my relationship with Bob would continue, it wasn't strong enough to keep me at school. I did not return for the second semester of my junior year. I dropped out of UB and moved back home to New Jersey.

I didn't know then but I do know now: My father had toyed with the purest and most impassioned part of me: my creativity. I was lost and dislodged from my purpose.

My parents had moved to a garden apartment in the nearby suburb of Maplewood. This apartment was as compact as any of the ones we'd previously lived in. The living room flowed into the dining room, and the adjoining kitchen was tiny but efficient. There were two bedrooms upstairs; mine was the smaller one.

Stepping into that room and seeing it filled with my childhood furniture exacerbated my sense of displacement. I was 21 years old, without a plan. Now what?

I knew one thing: I wanted a job, but under no circumstances could it be a 9 to 5. It had to be something unconventional, where I could choose my own hours. I scanned the want ads in our local newspaper and spotted one for a taxi driver. Hum, this could be it, I thought. Women are becoming taxi drivers in NYC, so why not in Maplewood, N.J.?

I was so tickled by the idea that I immediately called the Loop Cab Company. I spoke to a man with a heavy accent and made an appointment for an interview. The next day I used my parents' car and pulled up to a building on a busy street. The office was dark and smoke-filled. The overweight dispatcher sat behind a desk to the right, and the drivers lounged on mixed-and-matched chairs on the left. The owner came out of a back office, stepped through the cloud of smoke and greeted me with a big smile and a warm handshake. He was small and round. He was the man I had spoken to on the phone, and he told me he was Israeli. I didn't mind that he conducted the interview right there, with all the other men listening. He offered me the job on the spot. Then he turned to the others and said, "We're going to be the only cab company with a woman driver." They welcomed me aboard.

I needed a way to get to and from work, so I bought a brown Raleigh 10-speed bicycle. The last bike I'd had was a standard one-speed with pedal brakes. The multi-speed features of my new bicycle made it effortless to ascend the inclines, and the handlebar brakes managed the declines. When I cruised the nine blocks, which meandered through the hilly, tree-lined neighborhood, a smidge of the freedom and independence I'd once felt returned.

Everyone at the company got a kick out of me, and I easily found my place in this new community. I had a good sense of direction, so learning all the routes was not a problem. My handle was "Maple 7," and each time it came over the walkie-talkie, I chuckled.

The rhythm of the business was based on the housekeepers coming to their suburban jobs from more urban areas. They arrived on buses that pulled up in front of the office. Out marched about a dozen black women, who made their way to the pack of drivers standing at the ready. They knew one another by name and engaged in jovial commiseration before they piled into their respective cars. At the end of the day, we'd pick them up, and they'd catch their buses home.

I was such an anomaly that the local paper featured a picture of me with the caption "CABBIE LASSIE." The article described me as "Maplewood's first and only woman cab driver," and I was quoted as saying, "The idea of driving a cab appealed to me more than the alternative of working in an office."

In between rides I hung out with the eclectic bunch of guys who sat around the office in their broken-down vinyl chairs, talking, eating, smoking and telling jokes. I felt like their mascot. They generously gave me extra rides, and they'd frequently offer me the most lucrative charges, which were to Newark Airport. The tip was always $10 or more.

I didn't know then but I do know now: Being adopted by this ragtag group of congenial people was a first step toward stitching me back together.

It turned out that the owner's son was Arie, one of my first boy-friends from high school. Arie was the one who had taken me to the senior prom when I was a freshman. He was the one I'd broken up with when he burped in my ear. Now he was graduating from college and would be working for the cab company until he got a real job. We started flirting over the radios. Then we tried to schedule our rides so we could have lunch together. With Bob still in Bridgeport, I didn't see anything wrong with going out on a few dates.

But it didn't take long for me to realize that it wasn't the belching that had made me break up with Arie. It was his mediocrity. He was a regular guy with conventional interests; he wanted to do something in the refrigeration business. He talked too much about settling down. The probability of that happening with me was next to zero, and our fling petered out.

Meanwhile, Bob and I spoke on the phone regularly, and on the weekends I'd commute to Trumbull, Connecticut, where he now lived with his childhood friend Donnie. Bob had half a semester left before he graduated from UB. When he was inundated with schoolwork, I hung out with Donnie, who was also a photography enthusiast. When Bob was free, we continued taking our drives to local destinations. If time allowed, we'd venture farther north to offbeat towns in Massachusetts, Vermont and New Hampshire. Sometimes all three of us would hit the road toward Stockbridge, camera equipment in the trunk and Elton John's "Rocket Man" or "Benny and the Jets" on the radio. On those outings, I felt like I was part of something. More shards were coalescing.

I didn't know then but I do know now: The idea of Bob sat as a beacon on the periphery of my volatile life. Channeling my frayed emotions in his direction was like a life preserver that kept me afloat.

In my sophomore year at college, I had taken a modern dance class as an elective. It was an introduction to the Martha Graham technique, and it filled the same need that cheerleading had. Since returning to New Jersey, I yearned for those classes. I did a little research and found that Graham's actual school was located on the Upper East Side of Manhattan, which was only an hour away from Maplewood. As soon as I could, I caught the bus a few blocks from our house and set off for Port Authority.

The school was housed in a small but stately building. I stepped across the marbled portico and paused to take in the bedazzling scene. Girls in crisp leotards and tights, their hair pulled back in neat, tight buns, scurried down the corridor. My feet began moving forward on their own. I had to be a part of it, but the clothes that I had brought were old and shabby. I wavered for a second, but I refused to let it stop me. I took my first class.

Martha Graham classes always opened with floor work. From my position in the back of the studio, I saw that what I had learned in Bridgeport was a fraction of this comprehensive and technical method. But those fundamentals served me well, and I was confident that my body would quickly integrate the more advanced contraction and release actions. The spirals inherent in her choreography challenged me to move with more fluidity. I was inspired by the physicality and vigor of the other girls. I left with a schedule and a plan to return—but not until I updated my outfit. Capezio Dancewear was just a few blocks away, and there I bought my first real dancer's attire. From then on I went to the beginners' class once a week.

The city continued to be a place of discovery for me. Through the friends I met at Martha Graham's, I heard about the School of Visual Arts. One day I took the subway to 23rd Street and entered the six-story building. As the scent of linseed oil and turpentine enveloped me, I was transported back to my painting days at UB. It felt like a homecoming.

In the lobby, I took in the hustle and bustle of students and teachers crisscrossing in front of me. I caught sight of a wide, curved staircase, which I ascended in search of the admissions office. There, I picked up a catalogue and hugged it to my chest. It held so much promise. At home I combed through it and learned that I didn't have to matriculate; I could sign up for individual classes, and some of them were offered in the evening. Wow! I could go after work or after my dance class.

I didn't know then but I do know now: I did have a bond with myself, but it was so tenuous that a minor puff from my father's lips could blow it away. Still, the tiniest sliver remained intact, and glimmers of different paths appeared. I've likened these premonitions to the twinkle of Tinker-bell, and I marvel at my own inclination to follow her.

When I left UB and came home, my father assumed it was to work with him. As of yet, he wasn't sure what our "business" would be, but he was crystal clear that I was going to "help" him.

I was pretty certain that my enrolling in a class was not part of my father's plan, but my excitement pressed me to broach the subject anyway. During a lull at dinner that night, I started by telling him about the school. I was sure to emphasize that it was a non-traditional institution, unlike any other university. I explained that the teachers were professional designers, illustrators and photographers. I told him that their work appeared in magazines and advertisements and on movie and Broadway posters. Then I told him I'd like to take a class.

I was sure he'd disapprove, but instead he lit up. "It might not be a bad idea," he said.

Agape and shocked at my good luck, I collected myself, and as soon as dinner was over, I flew up the stairs. Sitting on my bed, I threw open the catalogue and searched for the right class. When I saw that Milton Glaser, the most famous graphic designer in the world, was offering an evening course, I planned to sign up.

The first class was held in a packed lecture hall. Glaser had a towering presence and delivered an inspirational presentation of his achievements. He showed slides of his acclaimed campaigns and those he was currently working on. But it was the description of his creative process, which he credited to his fine arts background, that caught me by surprise. I'd bought into my father's theory that design and fine arts were incompatible. Hearing the opposite from such an iconic figure made me consider that I might not have to compromise my love of classical art in order to have a graphic design career.

My bedroom would need to be rearranged to accommodate a desk where I could do my homework. The nicest part of the room was the casement window at the far end. It let in the most glorious light, and it overlooked a small stream. I estimated that the desk would fit under that window. My bed, which was across from the doorway, didn't need to be moved, but my dresser did. I pushed it as close to the door as I could.

Periodically, Bob visited me in Maplewood. On one such occasion, I solicited his help. In Bridgeport, I'd watched him put together a workspace with four wooden crates and a sheet of plywood. We found similar crates at the grocery store, and my father supplied the wood. We stacked two of the crates under the right side of the window and the other two on the left. The plywood made for a superb desktop.

Ready to tackle my first assignment, I sat with my hands planted far apart and my fingers spread on top of my work area. The task before me was to create a graphic image that illustrated a poem about a shadow. At UB the interplay of light on objects had touched something deep within me, and my confidence returned. My lungs filled with air, and my imagination began to stretch—I knew I was going to nail this project.

As my mind was combusting, the bright sun was streaming in through the window, casting a long shadow behind me. I turned around and looked down at the floor, knowing inspiration was moments away. As I sat musing, my father appeared in the doorway. He was holding something in his arms, and with a big smile he said, "I bought you a present!"

My father had never given me a gift. His gesture was so jarring that I didn't know what to make of it. Had something changed? Was it possible that he approved of what I was doing? Did he value me? Did *he* want to "help" *me*? Was it all going to be all right?

He handed me the box, which I eagerly opened. Inside was a shiny pen-like instrument with a little cone-shaped cup and a long cloth-covered tube. It was beautiful. "What is this?" I asked.

"It's an airbrush." The quizzical look still on my face signaled for him to continue. "It's a tool you can use for your homework." He explained that it was a more sophisticated way to get the same effect as his infamous spray cans.

"What are you working on?" he asked.

When I said I was trying to decide how to do my first assignment, he convinced me that the airbrush would create a dynamic image. "I guarantee," he said, "you'll be the only one who does the project with an airbrush." Then, "You'll stand out!" That's what I wanted: to stand out. Ever since the art classes I'd taken at UB, I yearned to present a project that impressed everyone. Perhaps my father was right, and this would be my time to shine.

He said I'd need a compressor to be the source of pressure that would run the airbrush. He just so happened to have one in his truck. He brought it upstairs, hooked up the tube from the brush and turned the machine on. It shook the floor and nearly broke my eardrums.

A little bit of paint went into the tiny cup below the nozzle. The instrument had a sensitive valve that controlled the paint stream; depending on the angle and velocity, I could get a dramatic effect. A spritz from the nozzle appeared opaque at one end and transparent at the other. After my father gave me a basic demonstration, I suggested he leave and assured him I'd figure it out.

Now I knew what I wanted to do for my project: an amorphous figure with a light source coming from the top left corner of the poster board and an elongated shadow ending in the bottom right corner. It was going to be a simple black and white illustration. Considering the love I had for the interplay of light and dark, or chiaroscuro, this would be right up my alley.

I got an 11"x14" piece of black poster board. The lone figure was easy, but the shadow would take some ingenuity. In actual life, when a shadow is cast, its proportions grow distorted and diffused the further it is from the light source. Mine had to be just right, otherwise it wouldn't look real. After many trials, I ended up with a simple, stark piece that I thought was striking. I slipped it into an envelope just big enough to protect it for my 90-minute trek to class. I removed it and placed it on the presentation ledge along with everyone else's. It was, in fact, the only airbrushed poster, but it did not get the overwhelming praise my father had led me to expect. It was hardly noticed.

I skulked to the front of the room to retrieve my failed project and was flooded with misgivings about the airbrush. At home, my father wanted to know how the presentation had gone. When I told him, he suggested helping me with the next one. Disheartened from my failure and dubious about my dad's offer, I vacillated between resistance and surrender. But I was weakened, and the latter won.

The next assignment was to redesign Milton's famous red poppy poster. Dad pulled up a chair and sat right next to me. He had already reimagined the graphic that we would be creating. As he barked out instructions, the shoulder closest to him raised rigidly toward my ear, and my eyes, nose and mouth squeezed together as though smelling the most awful odor. I was tumbling backwards. I leaned away from him. While my attention flitted between him and my project, between wanting him to leave me alone and feeling incompetent without him, he was saying, "I have a brilliant idea."

As though under water, I heard more words: "We are going to start a mural painting business. No one is doing what we will do. Those other morons are painting their artwork directly onto the sides of buildings. We will print our outrageous graphics onto paper, just like they do with wallpaper or billboards."

"One image printed limitless times will make us rich."

Then, loud and clear, I heard, "I will come up with the designs, and you will paint them. That's why you need to learn how to use the airbrush."

Could he have had an ulterior motive for his "gift?" Had his interest in my artistic expression been disingenuous all along? Was this all about him? Oh my God, yes!

CRASH—The truth slammed into me like a wrecking ball. I was shattered into a million tiny pieces.

I didn't know then but I do know now: Every reminder that my father did not love me triggered a sense of nothingness that was so impregnable it drove me back into his clutches.

Yet I continued to work with him on my project. It took longer than the first one, and I almost missed the deadline. I wasn't happy with the end result: The edges didn't match up, and it looked sloppy. At school, I half-heartedly placed it in front of the class and crept back to my seat. My piece did not even get a glance.

I swore I'd never use the airbrush again. I attended the remaining classes, but now I sat and watched as other students got the acknowledgement I so badly craved—more proof that I had no talent. I abandoned my SVA dreams and did not sign up for another course.

Once more, I gave up on myself and had no trajectory. All that lay ahead of me was driving my cab and taking my dance classes. Now my father swooped in like a raptor on its prey and dug his talons into me. It was full steam ahead with his book, his ongoing projects and "our" mural enterprise. As "partners," we were going to "breathe life into a dead industry."

He needed me to rewrite his latest theory, "Order from disorder." It was "the secret he'd been searching for." Albert Einstein, Max Planck and Erwin Schrödinger were stumped by it, unable to explain it. But he, Marcel Bau, was able to do "what the greatest scientific minds could not!"

He demanded that I accompany him to his "meetings" in the city. He now had a used white van with rust patches and balding tires. The back was cluttered with supplies, loose papers and discarded projects. I had to clear away food wrappers and empty cups before I could take the passenger's seat.

On the road, the banging and clanking of the van made it hard to hear anything, which might've been a blessing because my father never stopped talking. His incessant babble was of how everyone thought he was a genius, the "smartest man in the world," soon to be "recognized." As I'd been doing since I was six, I drifted off to a distant place beyond the car's window.

I hated working with my father, and the harder he wedged me into a corner, the more fiercely I searched for an alternative. I knew that driving a cab was not a viable long-term vocation, and my dream of becoming an independent artist or even a designer was still simmering. But how was I going to get a job without a college degree?

Tinkerbell fluttered in, and somehow I discovered that the School of Visual Arts had an in-house employment agency. Anyone who had taken classes there could use it. This could be my answer, so I made an appointment.

I didn't know then but I do know now: Compartmentalizing and dissociating had become my superpowers. Even though they took me out of my life, somehow they allowed me to reclaim what my father was trying to steal from me. Incredibly, at those dire moments when I should've vaporized and disappeared, a fuse that connected to a stick of dynamite was lit, and the explosion woke up my courage.

The office was in a building on the south side of 23rd Street, a small room painted a soft aqua. The counselor sat behind a desk that was almost as wide as the room, leaving him just enough space on either side to slip into and out of his chair. I sat facing him and a big window that overlooked several water towers on the rooftops beyond. He was asking me about my history, so I shared my UB experience and the class I'd just taken with Milton Glaser. He handed me a sheet of paper with a list of the jobs I'd be qualified for.

One stood out: National Lampoon was looking for a paste-ups and mechanicals artist. I was familiar with the magazine in name only; I knew it was similar to Mad Magazine. I had no idea what a paste-ups and mechanical artist was, but I didn't care. All that mattered to me was it had the word artist in it. The counselor made the call on the spot, and I left with an interview scheduled for the following week.

Now that I knew what a portfolio was, I spent time gathering and fixing up my recent artwork. I purchased a brand new 23"x31" black portfolio and filled it with the work I had from both schools.

My interview took place on a beautiful day in 1972. I'd learned that the magazine had launched in 1970; it was a satirical publication whose content was irreverent, controversial and funny. My outfit for the interview had to be hip and reflect the National Lampoon culture.

I still wore no makeup, and I had self-styled my hair into a shoulder-length shag ala Jane Fonda. I wore a long-sleeve black cotton turtleneck under a white peasant blouse with delicate embroidery around the neckline and the edges of the short sleeves. Both were tucked into my best-fitting bell-bottoms. I'd just bought a pair of high-heeled, round-toed, platform shoes. They were two different shades of brown, which matched my tan fringe jacket perfectly. A last check in the mirror confirmed that I'd chosen the right garments and looked exactly as I had intended.

National Lampoon was located on the corner of 59th Street and Madison Avenue. I stepped into the elevator and ascended to the third floor. I went through the glass double doors in front of me and stepped up to the receptionist, who sat behind a large desk under the magazine's huge logo.

"I have an appointment with Michael Gross," I told her.

While I sat waiting, I took in the professional surroundings and listened to all the activity beyond the waiting room walls. Even if I didn't get this job, I knew I wanted to work in an office in Manhattan.

A petite, dark-haired woman appeared around the corner, introduced herself as Ellen, Michael's assistant, and explained that he was the magazine's creative director. I followed her as she ushered me into his office.

Michael's long blond hair and beard gave him a Nordic look. His casual dress and friendly manner put me at ease. As we both sat down, I placed my portfolio in front of my shins. Strangely, allowing it to rest against my legs provided an extra layer of comfort. He told me a little about the magazine and what my job would be. Then he asked to see my work.

I hoped he didn't notice my quivering hands as I grabbed the handles of my book, unzipped the sides, and placed it on the desk in front of him. I'd filled the portfolio with a mix of the paintings from my class at UB, drawings from Mr. Novack's class, a zodiac sign graphic and both airbrushed illustrations from Milton Glaser's class. While he flipped from piece to piece, I flashed back to that dreaded snub I'd gotten by U. of Hartford. I shook it off and told him as much as I could about my two and half years at college and my latest experience at SVA. I more than expected him to thank me and say he'd get back to me.

But he didn't. "I really like your work," he said. "You're a talented artist." And he offered me the job, right then and there.

He asked if I wanted it. "YES!" I said.

"Do you have time to meet the rest of the staff?" Of course I did.

The creative department was small; I'd be working with Ellen in one of the two cubicles on one side of the space. He told me she'd be training me to do paste-ups and mechanicals. I liked her instantly; she was a happy, bubbly person who instantly took me under her wing.

Michael and the writers had their own offices on the other side. He introduced me to Henry Beard, Doug Kenney and Michael O'Donoghue. I couldn't wait to start working with this scruffy, intellectual and rambunctious crew.

"When can you start?" Michael asked.

"Today?" I said facetiously.

I didn't know then but I do know now: Behind the dizzying and abusive see-saw of my home life was a powerful force that drove me forward —no matter what. It's a source of great sorrow to understand that my father's intention was to kill it. But it's equally a sign of great triumph to know that he never could have.

CABBIE LASSIE. . .21-year-old Celia Gale Bau of 89 VanNess Court is Maplewood's first and only woman cab driver. "The idea of driving a cab appealed to me more than the alternative of working in an office," she explained. "But I'm not a women's libber." Driving daytime for the Loop Cab Company, Miss Bau attends art school in New York City nights.

A local newspaper piece featuring me as the "Cabbie Lassie"

24

BROOKLYN HEIGHTS

1972 proved to be a year that altered the arc of my life. Along with starting my exciting job at National Lampoon, my relationship with Bob was hitting a milestone. He'd graduated from UB with a degree in Industrial Design but decided he wanted to be an architect. He'd submitted his applications and was accepted to Pratt Institute, in Brooklyn. I'd been at the magazine for a month, and commuting from N.J. was untenable. So Bob and I decided to follow the latest trend and live together without being married. We'd been dating for three years and had no intention of breaking up, and we agreed to look for an apartment. I'd heard that Brooklyn Heights was a great neighborhood. We went there to explore, and I was bowled over by its charm. I knew that was where I wanted to live, and Bob concurred.

It didn't take us long to find the perfect place. It was on the second floor of a brownstone that had once been a rooming house. From the old and musty foyer, you could see the door to our tiny new home right at the top of the landing. The ascent up the wooden staircase was a creaky affair. Inside, the small room had an efficiency kitchen—more like a closet—that had been fitted with a stove and a mini-refrigerator. We had to use the bathroom sink to wash our dishes. But the rent was low, the ceiling was high, and the enormous windows let in the most glorious light. Through their panes we viewed a lush backyard with a magnificent tree that made me think of the book "A Tree Grows in Brooklyn." All of these amenities cancelled out any of the apartment's deficiencies.

With all the aerial space, Bob was inspired to build a loft-like structure out of two-by-fours and plywood, giving us a bedroom area on top and two workstations below. As a kid I'd always thought that bunkbeds looked like fun, so climbing the ladder that Bob built satisfied my childish longings. Waking up to the ceiling feet away from my nose and looking out through the tops of the windows was oddly cozy. Our double desks, thoughtfully arranged underneath, symbolized our shared love of creativity.

Our little haven was about five brownstones up from Atlantic Avenue, which was an oasis of diverse businesses: head shops, air conditioning and heating services, appliance stores, auto parts, electronics repairs, bicycle shops and office buildings. I found unique, international food products in the nearest bodega. Further along the block was a Middle Eastern spice store that knocked me over with its dizzying fragrances.

Sprinkled up and down Atlantic Avenue were antique stores, where I made periodic visits just to see what had come in. The smells of aging wood, furniture polish and rusting metal blasted my nostrils as I stepped inside. There was so much inventory crowded into tight spaces and the aisles were so narrow that I'd have to sidestep in order not to break anything. The lighting was always dim enough that I had to press my face right up to an item to see it. Upon leaving I always felt I must have missed something.

Small clothing boutiques with cutting-edge garments and assorted other gems were continually popping up. Perusing their wares frequently resulted in a purchase of something that no one else had.

Three blocks in the opposite direction was Montague Street, the heart of the neighborhood. Ornate brownstones lined the sidewalks. A canopy of low, leafy trees hugged the array of shops above and below street level. Colorful signs and awnings protruding from the buildings shouted everything from coffee to housewares, groceries, flowers, locksmiths and nail salons.

Bob and I settled into our new domestic life. We'd get up together and make our coffee, then he'd drive to Pratt and I'd take the N or R train to National Lampoon. The routine, sharing my life with someone and being part of a couple provided me with a new sense of balance.

I didn't know then but I do know now: As my emotional needs shifted to Bob, I was able to put a healthy distance between me and my father.

As for my job, my little cubicle on the corner of Madison and 59th was my entree to a previously unknown world. Ellen's and my role came at the tail end of a huge operation. The creative department couldn't have been any larger than 800 square feet. It had a communal feel, and I became intimate with every part of putting the magazine together. It started with the creative team's brainstorming meetings, where the theme of the issue was determined. After painstaking content decisions were made, Michael and James found freelance writers and illustrators, if needed. After that, the editing and proofreading process began.

As Ellen's paste-ups and mechanicals assistant, I had my own drafting table where I became proficient with T-squares, triangles, rubber cement, Exacto knives and tweezers. Our job started as soon as the first proofs arrived from the printer. The black, sometimes still-wet type was on a tan, transparent and crinkly-sounding paper called glassine. We'd lay it down in order to see how long the articles were and how much needed to be cut. The cutting of the copy was done by the editors with the writers' permission. Then we received the galley proof, which was the sheet that we'd cut, paste and lay out as it would be appearing in the actual magazine. I was surprised to discover that I found this precise and technical work strangely fulfilling. The nerve-wracking pace and pressure, repeated month after month, was exhilarating. I was acquiring skills that I would use throughout my career.

Plus I was coming into contact with some of the most accomplished and innovative illustrators, cartoonists and photographers of the time, among them Richard Hess, Jim McMullen, Milton Glaser, Rick Meyerowitz and Sam Gross. It was an honor to be handling their artwork.

National Lampoon was notorious for its "Foto Funnies," which were similar to a comic strip, but each frame was photographed rather than drawn. The shoots happened right outside my cubicle, and I was often asked to assist. I think they had a script of sorts, but for the most part it was improvised. It was disorganized, chaotic mayhem. The sessions that starred a nude woman with gigantic breasts gave the guys an excuse to be particularly lewd but hilarious.

I didn't know then but I do know now: I had no idea how iconic the magazine and the staff would become. I was an eyewitness to history.

The location of National Lampoon was right smack in the middle of everything. One block to the west was Central Park, where I'd sometimes seek out a bench to have my lunch or people-watch. The skating rink and the zoo, just steps away, was great for passing the time. Madison Avenue had the best shoe stores, and a few blocks east was Bloomingdale's, where I spent too much money. But when I discovered that the Alvin Ailey dance school was a couple blocks east of Bloomie's, my life felt complete. The school was housed in a three-story brick building twice the width of the surrounding structures, with arched windows that gave it a factory feel. Inside, the brick walls reverberated with the tinkling sound of piano melodies and the rhythmic beat of drums. Where Martha Graham dancers looked formal and polished, these dancers wore flowing, textured and colorful attire. The place was oozing with life.

The first class I took was with one of Alvin Ailey's principal dancers, who had the most beautiful body and moved in an otherworldly way. I worked my way up to the front of the class to guzzle rather than sip her instruction. I used my reflection in the huge, floor-to-ceiling mirrors to gauge my progress. I wanted to be there all the time, and some evenings I'd take more than one class. Dance smoothed my jagged edges, filled my vacant spaces and made me feel whole and in control.

I don't remember how I met Mimi in Brooklyn Heights, but we soon became best friends. She had come to NYC from Philadelphia to be a professional dancer. She and her boyfriend, also Bob, lived in a building a few doors from us. They were an odd couple who didn't look like they belonged together. Bob, who was slight, with a muscular physique, wore his long blond hair in a ponytail. Mimi towered over him, lithe and thin, with very short brown hair. It turned out that Bob was renovating the apartment they were living in because that was his business. Mimi and I suspected that our Bobs would hit it off, and they did.

Being friends with Mimi took my obsession with dance to a higher level. Her days were filled with classes all over the city, and that seemed like a dream-life to me. One day I accompanied her to a ballet class in Greenwich Village. I would never have gone on my own; ballet seemed like a reach for me, but soon I was doing pliés, battements, jetes and pirouettes. Ballet attire was the antithesis of the Ailey look: black leotards only and pastel or nude tights, soft pink ballet slippers, ankle warmers and hair pulled back in a tight bun. Exclusive to this studio, a woman came, took measurements of all the girls and custom-knit full body suits. They were so cool that I ended up owning several.

I threw myself into these classes as though I were also going to be a dancer. I learned all the intricate barre warm-ups and contorted myself for the floor work. I even overrode the booing audience inside my head to dance solo across the floor for the improvisational portion. I actually toyed with the idea of quitting my job to dance full-time.

But through Mimi I witnessed the competitiveness, the pressure and the narcissism required to succeed in the dance world. She worried about her weight, which was ludicrous because she had the ultimate dancer's body. Her long arms and legs formed an elegant silhouette, and she floated across the floor with the grace of a gazelle. Yet she lacked confidence and tolerated abusive treatment from her teachers. I had to ask myself if that was the world I wanted to be in, and the answer was no.

I didn't know then but I do know now: I could identify abuse when it wasn't happening to me.

Bob and Mimi eventually left Brooklyn Heights and bought a house in Pomona, N.Y. It was a "fixer upper," in a constant state of construction. The Bobs spent a lot of time working on it, which led to them speculating about starting a business together. The idea of us incorporating with our best friends seemed idyllic to me. And with it came fanciful notions of success, wealth and happiness.

I didn't know then but I do know now: This was the first of many entrepreneurial fantasies that Bob indulged in. Because I was still oblivious to my dad's delusional thinking and unrealized predictions, I was unaware of the same tendencies in Bob.

Our rooming house did not have a laundry facility, so I spent a lot of time at the laundromat on Montague Street. There I watched the young woman who ran it masterfully fold fitted sheets, a task I struggled with. After I befriended her, I beseeched her to teach me her enviable craft, which she did. I learned how to turn two of the corners inside out and tuck them into the other corners. Next I lined up the elasticized edges so that the sheet had four straight sides, which could be neatly folded in halves, ending up with a tidy 18-square-inch bundle.

It was during one of our practice sessions that I mentioned that Bob and I were growing out of our petite abode. She pointed to the bulletin board hung inside the entry door of the laundromat. It was covered with notices of all types. Among them, I spotted one for a floor-through garden apartment on Remsen Street. I called the phone number, reached a young man and made an appointment for the following day.

As I approached the building, my heart started to leap. It was an enchanting five-story brownstone, and inside, the apartment was huge. I could see our future there. I practically ran home and could not sit down until Bob came through the door. I described my find and took him back to see it the next day. The young man, who was the son of the owners, showed us around. Bob had the same reaction as I did, and we said we'd take it. A month later we moved in.

From the sidewalk we'd step through a gate onto a little cement courtyard. To the left, below the main staircase, was our own gated entryway, which opened into a vestibule and our front door. Once inside, the hallway was dark and long. To the right, a door led to the one large bedroom, with windows looking up to the sidewalk. An entire wall had built-in drawers and closet space. At the end of the hallway, toward the back of the apartment, was a full kitchen, which had a door that led to a utility room and out to our very own backyard. To the right of the kitchen, the large living room had a wall with windows looking out onto the garden area, another with a built-in shelving unit and the other with a working fireplace. And on top of all that, we were around the corner from Montague Street and two blocks from the Promenade.

Unlike our previous apartment, this one had room to spread out. The huge living room provided ample space for Bob to have a drafting table and me to have an easel. He was still in school, and I was fooling around with drawing, photography and macrame. Canal Street was practically in our backyard so, at a moment's notice, we could hop into the VW and make our way to Pearl Paint for art supplies. Across from the art store were shops for wood, plastic and hardware, all of which Bob needed to complete his assignments.

Bob claimed the utility room, where he set up his tools for building things and refinishing furniture. One day he brought home a set of four dining room chairs that were painted the ugliest chartreuse. I was appalled, but Bob had plans. "When I get through with these," he assured me, "they'll look like new."

He got to work. He applied paint remover, which made the old, thick paint bubble and liquify so he could wipe it off. It was tedious work; over the next week he reapplied the stripper and wiped the chairs clean until the original wood was exposed. Then we picked out the stain that would match our round butcher block table. The chairs did, indeed, look like new!

The kitchen, old but fully equipped, was my territory. I was all-in on the health food craze and using natural, unprocessed foods. Now I could practice cooking, experimenting with recipes and making meals from scratch. I discovered that I was a good cook. Soon, bottles and jars of herbs for flavoring, beans for soaking, spices for seasoning and all sorts of condiments filled the shelves that Bob had built on the wall. It was in that kitchen that my lifetime commitment to health and well-being began.

In a home goods store around the corner, I discovered Le Creuset cookware, and I bought a Champion juicer. For the fresh produce I'd need for my homemade juices, I found a food coop further down Henry Street. I'd arrive with my empty, folded shopping cart and wheel back bulk amounts of carrots, apples and greens.

This apartment was my first real home, and it was the catalyst for me to discover things about myself that I didn't know. For one thing, I enjoyed entertaining. We regularly invited friends for dinner or just to hang out. Our house became the hub of family gatherings, and my parents, along with Phyllis and my grandmother, often came for visits on the weekends. I relished showing off my new homemaking skills and welcomed the accolades that followed.

On one occasion, we introduced Bob's parents to mine. It couldn't have been a more unlikely pairing: They were vastly different. Beforehand I prayed for it to go well, and it did. In a show of unusual restraint, my father kept his contentious impulses at bay. That didn't mean he didn't dominate the conversation, but Bob's parents seemed interested in what he had to say. For all I knew, it could have been a display of good manners, but it was also an indication to me that my life was moving in the right direction.

Weather permitting, almost every get-together was capped off by a stroll on the Promenade. It was the crown jewel of the Heights. That first step onto the walkway began a magical one-mile journey. To the right were magnificent brownstones with their lovingly tended European-style gardens. To the left, the open sky and expansive East River lapped up against the Manhattan skyline and the Statue of Liberty. Along the way were benches inviting pedestrians to linger, take in the view, bask in the sun, read, draw or simply relax.

My parents were enamored with the neighborhood; they said it reminded them of Poland. It was uncanny how it did match the old photos from their homeland. It felt like another sign that I'd chosen well.

I didn't know then but I do know now: Moving into this apartment underscored what I'd been striving for: a serious relationship, a welcoming home and a sense of family. As it was coming together, I mistakenly thought I was leaving all my troubles behind.

In the warm weather, Bob and I took full advantage of the Promenade. We'd walk north from Remsen Street, then loop our way back to Montague where we'd pick up an ice cream cone at Haagen Dazs and find a wide stoop to sit on while we ate. Another pastime was riding our bicycles, which were stored in our long hallway. I still had my brown Raleigh 10-speed. Often we'd leave the apartment and head over the Brooklyn Bridge into Manhattan and cruise through the Lower East Side, the South Street Seaport or Battery Park. Sometimes we'd have no plan at all, riding aimlessly into Brooklyn, where we discovered Carroll Gardens, Cobble Hill and Boerum Hill. A couple of times we made it as far as Red Hook and Park Slope.

It might've been on one of our walks that we found an all-white, full-grown stray cat. He became the first member of our own, new family. We named him Quido, something to do with Bob's partial Italian heritage and his fascination with the mafia.

We wanted Quido to have the freedom to come and go as he pleased, so Bob built a cat door. He cut a 10-inch-high piece of plywood that fit snuggly in one of the windows facing the garden. Then he cut a hole big enough for the cat to fit through and constructed a flexible rubber flap inside the hole. The opening had to sit between two of the thick black bars outside the window so Quido could get in and out easily. Bob took great pride in solving these problems, and I admired his expertise.

Everything was going smoothly until late one night, when we were awakened by a thumping and scurrying sound. What on earth was it?

Turns out Quido had gone hunting, probably in the garbage cans of the Key Food behind our garden wall. At the foot of our bed, he presented us with a gift: a mouse—or maybe a rat—still alive. We hoped it was a fluke, but it happened again and again. We had no choice but to cover the hole with a wooden door and a latch to keep him in at night.

One of Bob and my favorite date nights was a Chinese restaurant on the corner of Henry and Montague, steps away from our house. It was up a flight of stairs, and we had a preferred table that overlooked the street. There was something about sitting above all that pedestrian traffic that made me feel like I was part of something special.

I didn't know then but I do know now: These first few years, immersed in my life with Bob, living in this delightful neighborhood and working at a great job in Manhattan, were as close to a dream-come-true as I'd ever been.

Me standing in for a
photo shoot at
National Lampoon

Just another day at the *National Lampoon* office
with Doug Kenney

A family gathering in our Remsen Street living room. Standing from left to right: Bob's dad, his mom, Bob, me, my dad and Phyllis, seated from left to right: Grandma, cousin Clila and my mom

Quido at Bob's window door creation

25

GURDJIEFF

And yet…while on the surface it appeared that the edges of my life had smoothed and the waters had calmed, below, dissatisfaction was brewing.

Sexually, I found Bob to be robotic and unaffectionate, which at first I ignored. I naively expected it to change once we began living together, but it did not. I began longing for passionate kisses, soft caresses, whispers of love and that lingering afterglow I'd heard so much about. In other words, lovemaking. Instead, each time, I was subjected to a sterile, quick and impersonal act; I could've been anyone.

"Stop hassling me," was Bob's terse reply when I finally found the courage to express my discontent. The exchange ended right there. I recoiled as quickly as a sea anemone retracts into its body cavity. Inside, I chastened myself for upsetting him; I wondered what was wrong with me. Eventually I landed on this: Whatever I wanted from him I did not deserve. So I dropped it.

I didn't know then but I do know now: I had not grown beyond the sexual trauma of my teenage years, and the scars that were left made me feel like a failure. The circuits that would've validated my own grievances were switched off. Shutting down was the only way I knew how to deal with adversity.

During this time, my father was worming his way back into my personal life, and inquiries into my sex life were commonplace. He saw himself as my sexual guru, and he was on a mission: "A woman's job is to maximize a man's potency." "The worst thing a woman can do is deny the man sex." "Women manipulate men with sex in order to get what they want."

The woman my father portrayed was an evil and unsavory creature out to steal a man's treasure, and his words felt accusatory. I could not be that woman. From what my father was saying, the woman's role was to please the man, and here I was complaining to Bob that I wasn't getting what I wanted. I was too needy, and I attributed Bob's lack of affection to the unattractive way I was behaving. I couldn't bear the thought of him not loving me, so I dared not withhold sex from him.

Tensions between us were growing in other areas, too. Bob was frustrated by my poor housekeeping skills. He was neat and organized, and I was not. He'd stomp around the apartment, pointing to my piled-up clothes or a sink full of dishes or the dirt ring around the bathtub, and call me a "slob." I wished I were cleaner; I cringed from his unpleasant reproaches, but I tenaciously clung to my messy ways, and the friction between us mounted.

I didn't know then but I do know now: My messiness was an unconscious response to his dismissal of my emotional and sexual needs.

My father already had a history with Bob. Years earlier, when Bob would visit me in Maplewood, my dad would bait him into a discussion any chance he got. In his usual pompous manner, he'd slouch in his chair with one arm slung over the back, projecting an apathetic air and posturing superiority. "So, what are you learning at that stupid school?" he'd ask. As Bob began to speak, my father would interrupt him, steering the conversation toward his own theories and accomplishments. When Bob grew silent, I feared that my dad would drive him away.

To my surprise, Bob was unfazed by my father's antics and manipulations. He actually agreed with a lot of Dad's "ideas." They shared a frustration with the way things were and a lofty belief that they were the agents of change. They had all the answers. One day my father turned to me and said, "I like your boyfriend. He thinks like me!"

I was relieved and supported their burgeoning relationship. I couldn't believe my good fortune.

I didn't know then but I do know now: My father's disrespect for boundaries was still wreaking havoc in my life, but I was clueless. It didn't occur to me that I should keep a distance between him and my relationship with Bob. On the contrary, I sought out my dad's blessing. The better their relationship was, the more positively it reflected on me.

Once we'd moved to Remsen Street, my father thought nothing of stopping by after his dealings in the city, usually without my mother. When he'd arrive at our door, I'd give him a peck on the cheek. No matter how well dressed he was, I picked up the scent of old food and mildew. He'd walk right in, and I'd fall in step behind him. He had a swagger, a loose and detached way of walking. But his nonchalance belied a ferociously spinning cyclone whose vortex I could not avoid.

I didn't know then but I do know now: The threat of danger hung around any interactions with my father. From the second he appeared, everything within me neutralized. Yet in spite of that, I was able to welcome him as any daughter would welcome her dad. I was still desperate for a normal relationship with him.

During one of his visits, I was in the kitchen kneading the bread

I was making. This was when Bob was finishing up his last semester at Pratt. He was sitting at his desk in the living room, putting the final touches on a building complex project, complete with people and trees to scale. As my father stepped up to the edge of Bob's desk, I overheard his usual cynical tone. "What's the point of this model?" he wanted to know.

Recently, Bob had expressed disenchantment about working a 9-to-5 job. He'd also begun questioning his decision to be an architect. I was caught off guard: This was not the life I'd envisioned, and worry began buzzing. I don't remember what our financial arrangement was, but at that point I was the only one bringing in a regular paycheck. Would his waffling put a strain on our finances?

From the kitchen I heard my dad's provocations, and I feared it would motivate Bob to move in the reckless direction I was beginning to sense he leaned toward.

Bob led my father away from his work area to our dinner table, which was right outside the kitchen. I was in the process of punching down my risen dough and kneading it for the second time. Earlier in the day Bob had put together a miniature model of a geodesic dome. Buckminster Fuller was Bob's hero, and I knew he was excited to introduce my father to his work. "The sphere uses the 'less is more' principle," I heard him explain, adding that it enclosed the largest volume of interior space with the least amount of surface area. As he handed my dad the dome, he continued, "It's both material- and cost-effective."

My father held it, turned it around and examined it with what appeared to be serious interest. But never one to be undone by someone else's fame or "brilliance," he gave it back to Bob and said, "This is a good idea, but how many people want to live inside a dome?" Then he said, "You're wasting your time. You should work with me. I'm on the verge of becoming very successful!"

Given Bob's recent flip-flopping and my sudden insecurity regarding our future, I thought perhaps this might be the solution. I had no way of gauging my father's accomplishments, so I thought, once again, "What if my father's right?"

And with that came a new daydream: My cool, visionary dad and my gorgeous, ingenious boyfriend standing in front of a huge, gleaming skyscraper. Two proud, impeccably dressed millionaires posing under their company name, which was engraved above massive revolving doors.

I didn't know then but I do know now: I had no mental safeguards, no anchors to keep me grounded in reality. Because I mistrusted my own ability to think coherently, I allowed my father's misguided projections to take over my operating system the way a virus infects a computer. And once that happened, the fantasies I was prone to generating seduced me away from reason.

Meanwhile, at work, a proofreader whom I'd befriended told me she'd joined an ashram a few blocks from the office. She convinced me to attend some yoga and meditation classes with her. There was too much chanting and reference to devotion for my taste. But it did spark my curiosity about the alternative cultures that were springing up in the city. Through the same friend I learned about George Gurdjieff, a Russian philosopher, mystic and spiritual teacher. She described a group that met once a week to study Gurdjieff's teachings. I was intrigued and accompanied her to the next meeting.

We arrived at a grand apartment building on the corner of Fifth Avenue and 11th Street. It was a classic limestone-and-brick masterpiece, with an imposing entrance flanked by two-story-high columns. We were greeted by the doorman and shown to the elevator, which took us to the second floor. We stepped into a spacious and well-lit parlor with two corner windows that overlooked the street below.

Inside, I stayed close to my friend. She introduced me to the apartment's owner, a warm, elegantly dressed, older woman. When all 12 members had arrived, the meeting started. I listened as the woman made a formal presentation of Gurdjieff's signature principle, "The Work." Words like "unified consciousness," "awaken to a higher state," "full human potential" and "waking sleep" caught my attention.

They echoed my father's grandiose spouting, but here, in this group, they exploded with meaning and possibility. The idea of learning under the guidance of what seemed to be a structured organization suggested achieving a new and different state of mind. Working on myself was a novel concept, which implied transformation and finding some sort of truth.

After the meeting, I rushed to get on the R train. In the brightly lit car, I sat on the edge of my seat, reviewing every detail of the evening. I felt privileged to have been included in what seemed to be an exclusive club. I practically ran all the way home. I burst into our apartment and found Bob in the living room watching television. As I repeated the new phrases I'd heard, he shut the TV off. Apparently they spoke to him as well. I went on to articulate that Gurdjieff had devised a method of study, which was what comprised the weekly meetings. Bob was eager to attend the next one, and we went the following week.

Gurdjieff's teachings became a big part of our lives. I devoured his book "Meetings with Remarkable Men." Through the group I was introduced to P.D. Ouspensky, Gurdjieff's pupil and disciple. I was equally inspired by Ouspensky's celebrated book, "In Search of the Miraculous."

The introspection that Gurdjieff's practices required marked the first time I'd turned my attention inward. Distinguishing between what was conscious and what was unconscious promised to be an invaluable tool. Any challenges were offset by the new control I was beginning to sense in my life. I saw the potential for evolution, and I believed I was heading toward a better understanding of myself. I belonged in this pack of "seekers."

This was a life-changing moment for me, and my enthusiasm spilled into my conversations with my father. I wanted him to embark on this journey with Bob and me. I believed that the teachings would improve everything. And I wanted him to be impressed that *I* might've found "the meaning of life."

I didn't know then but I do know now: Many of my irrational choices were driven by a persistent hunger for my father's approval—the deep need of a heartbroken, deprived and neglected little girl.

My dad began attending the meetings with us. I was ecstatic when he appeared to be as zealous as Bob and I. I couldn't believe that I had facilitated such an important addition in our lives. I felt equal, included and powerful. The highlight of my week was joining them before our sessions and discussing what we were learning.

But then…a couple of months into our membership, Bob and I met my father for dinner at our favorite diner. As we slid into our booth, I could tell that my father was disturbed. "Gurdjieff might've been a genius back in his day," he said, "but his teachings are already irrelevant and antiquated."

He sat back on the banquet with his eyes half closed and stroked his hair. "This woman isn't even the originator of this knowledge. We're getting it secondhand from an underling."

"Besides," he went on, "life is disorderly and can't be explained with rigid methodology. I'm writing *the* book that will explain the meaning of life. Soon people will be coming to *me* for *my* teachings."

I barely ate my dinner. As we walked toward the meeting, I slowed my gait to follow a few paces behind Bob and my father. I dragged myself into the room and braced for what was sure to come. About 20 minutes in, it started. My father began provoking the leader, implying that the teachings were out of sync with the times. He challenged her to explain how such austere principles applied to contemporary life, which was ever-changing and chaotic.

I was seated by one of the windows. As if in slow motion, I turned my head toward it, caught sight of all the movement outside and allowed myself to be whisked from the room into the stream of people passing by.

In the meetings that followed, my father arrived with the same arrogant and defiant posture. He continued posing his hostile questions. When he was asked to leave the group, Bob and I also left.

I didn't know then but I do know now: I didn't see that I had nothing to do with my father's actions and that there was no reason for me to stop attending the meetings. Without a second thought, I gave up something that meant so much to me.

26

THE VOICES

At the magazine, *The National Lampoon Radio Hour* was in the works. It required an expansion of the creative department, and the company rented some space adjacent to our offices. They broke through the wall behind me and constructed a doorway to the new wing. There I sat as people flowed by my tiny cubicle. Little did I know that I was witnessing a parade of future celebrities: John Belushi, Chevy Chase, Gilda Radner, Christopher Guest and Bill Murray streamed through to get to their temporary digs.

Everyone was abuzz with the news that a raw space on a higher floor had been taken for the show. It needed a soundproof room for broadcasting, and they were looking for someone to design the interior. I thought of Bob.

It had been months since he had graduated. He'd been taking odd jobs and was still unsure of what he wanted to do. I asked him if he was interested in the Lampoon gig, and he was. After I proposed my idea to the president of the company, they hired him.

To my mind, this new development would help Bob with his indecision, and if all went well, it could lead to more work for him. I was proud of myself for orchestrating his employment, and I hoped it would put me in good stead with the people who ran the company.

The project was time-sensitive, with strict deadlines. Bob was a chronic procrastinator, and he kept missing them. Things were not going as I had planned. Frustrated and embarrassed, I wanted to express my concerns to Bob, but based on how poorly that had gone in the past, I dared not confront him. I kept it all to myself.

One late morning, I sat cross-legged in the middle of our bed. The sun, which was pouring in through the windows behind and above me, warmed the back of my head and tops of my shoulders. With my sketchbook on my lap, opened to a blank spread, I encountered the same hesitation as I always did when faced with an empty page. As I fidgeted and changed my position, I caught sight of my bare feet, now outstretched in front of me. I studied the line from the tip of my big toe, over the ball, across the arch and around to my heel. I wondered if I'd be able to render the grace of my crossed ankles and pointed toes. I began to draw. After a few minutes, there before me sat a sketch that captured the elegant lines I'd observed.

I turned to the next white page. I scanned the room for something to pique my interest, but none surfaced. I thought about closing the book and doing something else, but I was rooted to my spot. I leaned back into the pillows that were stacked against the wall behind me and took a deep breath.

As I stared up into the corner, I felt agitated—something was bothering me, and it had nothing to do with the blank page that sat before me. All I could think of was the argument Bob and I had finally had the prior evening. He'd missed yet another deadline and was now holding up the project. It was becoming a big problem, and the president was expressing his annoyance to me. I tried to explain it to Bob in those terms and hoped he'd understand it from my perspective. "I feel responsible," I said.

His response: "Don't hassle me!"

Then, as he always did, he walked away, leaving me in a jumbled and contorted mess.

While the altercation was replaying in my head, I sprang up, grabbed my drawing pencil, which had slipped out of my hand, raised it toward my book and started to write. Instead of drawing, I began telling my sketchbook what had happened with Bob.

From that day forward, my book became a trusted friend with whom I could share anything: my conflicts with Bob, my irritation with my father and my frustrations with my colleagues and friends. I only wrote when I was alone in the apartment, and I hid my book inside my closet.

As I continued to chronicle and my writing became more fluent, my book represented a safe place for me to divulge intimacies and confidences. But simply recording was not enough. I wanted to know why I felt the way I felt, why certain things kept happening to me and what my role was in these events. I wanted—no, needed—a deeper understanding of myself.

I didn't know then but I do know now: My short association with the Gurdjieff group was my introduction to self-study. The hope and optimism it inspired never left me, and I recruited those skills to help me find the clarity I was searching for. Writing in my sketchbook and in the journals that followed became the means by which that end was possible.

My quest was to prove more convoluted than I anticipated. Turning inward touched a nerve: A deep edginess, a disquieting and restless energy that I didn't have words for. Whenever I put pen to paper, it grated at me like a pebble in my shoe. Each emotional entry came with the same discomfort. It was always there; I couldn't turn it off. It felt like I was standing in the middle of a multitude of high-powered amplifiers shooting the loudest, densest noise at me. Whenever I wrote, the ferocious frequency was there.

At some point, words emerged through the racket, and I transcribed what was being said. The messages were harsh yet familiar. All the unpleasant things that were happening to me were my fault. When it came to Bob, I wrote that I was "unlovable," "undesirable" and "unattractive," which was consistent with how I felt. Any problems I was having at work were because I was "amateurish," "inadequate," "derelict." My friends were all "smarter," "better," "luckier" than I. And the constant condemnation coming from my father was deserved. I experienced the words as "voices" and began referring to them as such.

Whenever I recorded something difficult, the "voices" made an appearance, and despite their cutting nature, I started to rely on their commentary. I waited for them to chime in because they always seemed to have an answer. They were like a sonar wave that I could send out in search of a solid object. Even though the echo that returned reeked of cruel judgments, it gave shape to what had previously been amorphous.

I believed the "voices" were telling me the truth.

I didn't know then but I do know now: A pre-verbal energy born out of my parents' hostility and critical words lived inside me. I gave that energy a voice. Capturing its words on the pages of my books was better than being ambushed by an invisible adversary. It was better to have the monster out in the open than hiding in the shadows.

For a time, journaling and the "voices" gave me some relief. I had context for the mysterious reflexes that would render me inoperative. But before long, the weight of my life would get the better of me, and

I'd sink into a murky pool of sludge. I'd tell myself I was tired or not feeling well. It gave me an excuse to stay in my pajamas and robe, with my heavy socks pulled up to my knees and my hand-knitted blanket wrapped around my shoulders. There I'd sit with an aching wish for someone, anyone, to notice and to care.

I didn't know then but I do know now: I have photos of myself during this period, and in them I see a young woman in crisis—severely depressed and haunted by dark forces. I recognize a frightening state of mind that is devoid of life. I've since discovered that in the mental health field, the major factors that contribute to the appearance of voices are stress, anxiety, depression and trauma.

Me in the grips of depression in Brooklyn Heights

27

WOODSTOCK

Earlier in our relationship, years before I began keeping journals, Bob and I cultivated a mutual love for the outdoors. Soon after I left UB and while I was living in Maplewood, Bob proposed a camping trip. Although that wasn't an activity I would have suggested, it did conjure up romantic scenes of sitting around the campfire and sleeping under the stars. I agreed to go, but I had no gear. Bob volunteered to pull together everything that we needed. I put my trust in him.

I packed the personal items I assumed I'd need: some warm clothes and my old, worn-out hiking boots. Bob pulled up to my parents' house and loaded my stuff into the trunk of the Beetle. We headed out for the five-hour drive to Mount Marcy, the highest peak in New York State.

The drive was beautiful; the farther north we went, the higher the mountains became. We stopped at several overlooks to take in the stunning views. We drove on narrow roads with sheer cliffs on one side and deep gorges on the other. The roar of the water racing over the rocks could be heard above the hum of our little engine. Eventually we pulled into a designated parking area for the trailhead.

The equipment Bob had gathered came from his garage and what he borrowed from Donnie. I had a small backpack that fit my few items, and Bob flung his bigger pack onto his back. We stood before the rustic map that showed the various trails leading to the peak. Bob had studied the map beforehand and knew the route he wanted to take. I followed close behind him, clueless as to what lay ahead.

The fresh, clean air, the cool breeze below the trees and the sound of the wind rustling the leaves above my head was as scrumptious as the best thing I'd ever eaten. At the base, closest to the entrance, the hard ground under my feet was flat, so our pace was brisk. Approaching the steeper parts required that we slow down and decisively navigate the roots and rocks as though they were steps—a new strategic ability. Our path paralleled a clear mountain stream. When it was time for a rest or lunch, we found a rock on the water's edge and imbibed the serenity.

Halfway up the trail, we came upon a small, level clearing. The ashy coals of a recent campfire sat in the center; a river for washing and drinking was steps away. We dropped our stuff on top of the picnic table and began collecting wood for our fire. Bob seemed to know what he was doing. I watched as he unpacked a dented aluminum mess kit that looked like a flying saucer. He unscrewed a wing nut and loosened a bar that held the kit together. He swiveled and turned the bar upside down, and it became the handle for the frying pan. Inside was a plate, a cup and utensils. He set up a pup tent, which stood no higher than four feet and just fit our sleeping bags. It looked cozy enough.

Once he got the fire going, we boiled some water and opened the cans of food that we had brought for our dinner. We pulled over some large logs that we could lean against while lounging beside the crackling flames. It was overcast, so when night fell there were no stars to gaze upon. We crawled into our tiny tent, which was open at both ends.

I couldn't fall asleep; it was cold, and the ground was unforgiving. I was sure I heard bears and other sinister creatures. Finally, the sound of the river lulled me into a light sleep.

It wasn't long before I was awakened by the tapping of raindrops. I listened. The tapping became a hammering, which quickly grew to a pounding. In no time we were overtaken by a deluge. Rain poured into the pup tent from above, and suddenly a stream was flowing through it from the back to the front. There was nothing we could do and nowhere we could go. We waited until daybreak and aborted the second half of the climb. Everything was soaked, our packs filled with wet gear. Somehow we made our way back to the car. If it were up to me, I'd never go camping again.

But Bob was determined to complete the mission. By the time we decided to return to Mount Marcy, we were living together in Brooklyn. We made so many trips to Paragon Sports that I knew the store inside and out. We bought a bigger tent with a floor and a door and a thin pad that was supposed to serve as a mattress. We each got down-filled sleeping bags, which were suitable for below-zero temperatures. We purchased state-of-the-art backpacks and upgraded the mess kit. The new hiking boots I chose reminded me of the ski boots I wore as a kid.

I mistakenly expected that the right gear would improve our excursions, but it did not. In spite of my distaste for camping, it became a regular recreational activity. I never minded the hiking, the views and the campfires, but the fake food turned my stomach, washing in cold water was agonizing, and I never got used to sleeping on the ground. Still, I didn't want to be viewed as a whiner or a wimp, so I kept it all to myself.

I didn't know then but I do know now: The same destructive pattern that existed with my father was appearing in my life with Bob. I was afraid to express my aversion to camping because I didn't want Bob to assassinate my character as my father had always done.

The best part of the many trips we took was the descent, when my backpack was lighter and we were heading back to civilization. In the Adirondacks, reentry into the world included a stop in Woodstock. I knew the town from my childhood. Whenever we skied at Belleayre Mountain, my parents would pay a visit. That was before the music festival in 1969. Woodstock was now famous.

The place oozed creativity: Artists and craftspeople crowded the sidewalks. Street musicians played in the center of town, and it wasn't unusual to spot a rock star at a restaurant. Prominent writers and movie stars were rumored to have houses in the vicinity. The eclectic shops were more authentically counterculture than those in the city. Bob hunted down vintage hardware, intricately carved old doors, unusual windows and rusted gates. I browsed the clothing stores in search of anything with interesting colors, unusual prints or fringes. The town was my source for handmade leather belts, bags, wallets and shoes. We became obsessed with this mystical place and returned frequently.

It was then that we began flirting with the idea of moving to Woodstock, which opened a new phase in our relationship. We became a team with a mutual aspiration, and it brought us closer. We had long discussions about feasibility, logistics and how we'd finance our new lifestyle. I liked the "we" of it; I liked functioning as a couple. It had a stabilizing effect on my emotions.

I didn't know then but I do know now: Being in a relationship with Bob and living with him in Woodstock were the two things I wanted more than anything. I was willing to overlook and minimize any of the problems we'd had—and were still having.

Bob and I had been together for five years and I was thinking about marriage. I'd always wanted to be married. Being a child of the '50s, I had idealistic visions of the man getting down on one knee and pulling out a little box from his back pocket. With fumbling fingers he'd flip the top back to reveal a sparkling diamond ring. Then, with a quivering voice, he'd pop the question. I believed in "Till death do us part."

I couldn't imagine Bob doing any of that, but I did wonder if he was thinking about it. It was the mid-'70s; everything had changed, and in many ways, so had I. The idea of breaking out of traditional gender roles was appealing, and I saw nothing wrong with initiating a conversation.

So on one of our trips home from Woodstock, when the conversation was bright and upbeat, I asked, "What do you think about getting married?"

"Aren't we fine living together?" Bob said.

"Marriage would be a commitment to our love," I said.

"Does it mean I don't love you if I don't want to get married?"

That was not the answer I was hoping for, and I glommed onto the words "…don't want to get married." Deflated, I melted into the back of the passenger seat, turned my head toward the window and closed my eyes.

I hadn't written in my journal since I needed to bitch about camping because I was floating on air about our new Woodstock plan. But the next time I was alone in the apartment, I retrieved my book from its hiding place. I had to record what I perceived to be the marriage debacle. The "voices" scolded me for being insecure and reminded me not to be a pest.

I didn't know then but I do know now: The voices convinced me that I was the toxic element in the relationship and it was incumbent upon me, not Bob, to change. It was always me who had to do better.

Things were getting serious: We made the bold decision to start looking for a house in Woodstock. We'd taken to checking the real estate section of the *New York Times* and the local Ulster County papers.

One Sunday morning, with the newspapers spread out in front of us, my courage kicked in. "If we're going to buy a house together, shouldn't we get married?" I asked.

I resisted the impulse to cower at the rejection I was sure would come. Instead, I sat there obediently, waiting for Bob's answer.

"I'm afraid that getting married would change our relationship," he said.

Well that was promising! He must have been thinking about it. "If we get married, nothing will change," I said. "In fact, things will only get better."

Apparently that was all the assurance he needed, and we began making plans. I was ecstatic. I was getting married to the most gorgeous guy I'd ever seen. We were going to live in the coolest town on the planet. I was back on solid ground, and my daydreaming had no bounds: We were going to be a power couple—he, a famous architect and I, a world-renowned designer.

We agreed not to have a conventional wedding. In Woodstock, we found unmatched turquoise and onyx rings. The announcement, which we designed, featured a funny drawing that Bob had done of our two bare feet, one his and the other mine. On each ankle sat a bracelet bearing our names. His big toe was affectionately hugging my smaller big toe. Inside we collaborated on a poem that spoke of independence, respect and forever.

On April 30, 1975, we made our way over the Brooklyn Bridge to City Hall. Granted, it was a gray, institutional space with hard wooden seats, but we were riding the hippie wave—bucking the system, blazing a new trail. As mavericks we stood before the magistrate and took our vows, with a couple of friends to witness. After the ceremony, we all went to the nearest diner and had some lunch. Neither of our parents were there; we planned to celebrate with them at our apartment the following weekend.

That summer we found our dream house: a sculptor's studio on the side of a mountain at the end of a dead-end road. It was a tiny wooden structure with 12-foot ceilings. A boulder at the foot of the entry door served as a stoop. Inside was a big, barren unfinished room with no insulation, heat or AC. On the left was a floor-to-ceiling window facing north toward the top of the mountain. In the middle of the room was a rusted wood-burning stove. A few steps to the right was another room with just a toilet. Adjacent and in the back was a space with a kitchen sink and nothing else. It was perfect. Bob's parents agreed to give us the down payment on the $16,000 purchase. I pinched myself every chance I got. I was the happiest I'd ever been.

The two-hour trip to Woodstock took us on the NYS Thruway to the Kingston exit, where we'd follow the roundabout to Route 28. Making the turn onto Route 375 meant we were minutes from Lewis Hollow Road. It was a steep uphill drive, past mature trees and rustic homes. At the top, a righthand turn led onto a bucolic little bridge over a babbling brook. The unpaved driveway was shared by three houses, all part of what had been the Osterman estate. As soon as I got out of the car and stepped onto our property, the smell of fresh air, the crunch of twigs and leaves, the sight of majestic trees and the water gurgling over the rocks transported me back to the best of those bungalow colony days.

Immediately behind the studio was a forest that began climbing up the mountain. Its thick tree growth and ground cover beckoned me in. From the narrow patch of grass that stood between the house and the woods, I'd search for an open space where I could start my ascent. I kept a vigilant lookout for clearings, which mapped my way up. And the boulders that were scattered everywhere served as resting places where I could gaze over our rooftop and beyond to the valley below.

The studio was a blank canvas for Bob. His first goal was making it suitable so we could stay there on the weekends. In the room that had only a toilet, Bob built a wall and installed a simple shower. Visits to local junkyards turned up a quirky old pedestal sink. We found a natural wood toilet seat and an antique mahogany medicine chest. The rest of the room became our bedroom.

No heat? Bob researched the best wood-burning stove and found the Defiant. We travelled to Vermont, bought one and installed it. It was a beautifully designed and crafted cast iron piece of furniture—totally different from the junky stove that was there upon purchase. Fashioned after a fireplace, it had doors with glass panels, so the flames could be seen at all times and the doors could be flung open allowing the glorious heat to escape into the room. It had a big flat surface that functioned as a cooktop.

In a way, camping had prepared me for this bare-bones, no frills endeavor. The discomforts or inconveniences associated with each improvement were all part of the adventure.

Soon we began discussing the renovations and additions we'd need in order to convert the studio from a weekend retreat into a home. Back in Brooklyn, Bob could be found at his drafting table whenever he had free time. One day I walked up behind him, looked over his shoulder and asked, "What part of the studio are you working on now?"

"I'm designing the kitchen," he said.

How exciting—the kitchen was my territory! He was sketching on yellow tracing paper that was taped over the floor plan. It was easy to read the layout, and I started visualizing where counters and appliances could go. Pointing to an exterior wall, I suggested, "Wouldn't it be great to put a big window on this wall with the sink right below it?" I imagined myself standing there, looking out over the front yard while I washed the dishes.

Bob stopped drawing, stiffened and spun around on his chair to face me. "This is my project," he shouted. "Stay out of it!"

His anger confused me. Hadn't we bought the studio together? Wasn't I an equal partner who deserved to have an opinion? Was I not going to be allowed to contribute toward the creation of our home? But the words that would've expressed my consternation were stuck in my throat.

I didn't know then but I do know now: The concept of abuse had not yet been introduced to me—not one fiber of my body recognized that Bob's callousness, disrespect and mean behavior amounted to abuse. I was conditioned to take a subservient and inferior position rather than stand up for myself. And breaking up with Bob was inconceivable: I couldn't bear the vast nothingness that life without him would portend.

During the week Bob's full attention was on the house and planning for the next weekend's project. When we were in Woodstock, he did a lot of the work himself, or he'd solicit friends to help—regardless, it started first thing in the morning and didn't stop until sunset. My unofficial job was to provide food and beer. At first I accepted my role, but I was acutely aware that all the time he spent on the studio was time he wasn't spending with me, and resentment began to creep in.

"Can you sometimes take a break from work so we can be together?" I asked.

His reply: "Get off my back."

I didn't know then but I do know now: Each time Bob lashed out, it was a reenactment of all the hits I'd already taken. It set in motion an internal response that started with a flashing warning: GO NO FUR-THER. What lay beyond posed a threat from which I thought I'd never recover. My retreat was impulsive.

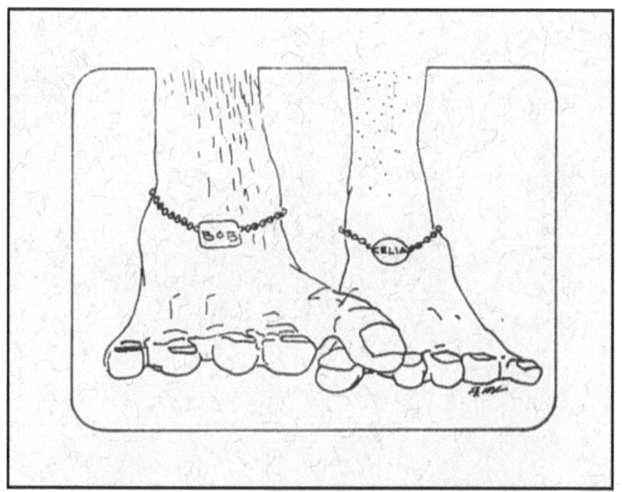

The cover of the wedding announcement,
designed and illustrated by Bob and me

Me doing Pilates in our still unfinished kitchen
in the artist studio on Lewishollow Road in
Woodstock, N.Y.

28

VW BEETLE

Soon after we'd taken possession of the studio, we began to hear the rumble of an engine barreling up our little dirt road toward the main house. It sped by so fast that all we saw was the dust cloud left in its wake. When we finally got a glimpse of it, it was an odd Jeep-like vehicle, driven by a cool-looking guy who often had two large black dogs in the back. Since it was springtime, we were outdoors a lot and always waved when he passed by.

One day he swung into our driveway, let his dogs out and walked over to introduce himself. Bruce owned the big white colonial at the top of the hill. He was a little older than we were, tan and fit, with thinning hair and the broadest smile I'd ever seen. We were soon to find out that he was a dentist on the Upper East Side, and this was his weekend house.

He had all the background information on our studio. It was built in the 1920s by Reginald Marsh, a famous painter known for his depictions of life in New York City. The previous owner, Mr. Osterman, a businessman and sculptor, had used the studio for the creation of his own art. I was already in love with the vibe of our house, but this new history gave it more panache.

Bruce had been coming to Woodstock for several years and had a circle of local friends, plus a coterie of the hippest, chicest and most beautiful people he brought up from the city. We had an open invitation, and soon our weekend agenda included a hike up to "the big house."

The door was always open. The huge kitchen counter was covered with a cornucopia of potluck contributions. Characters were mulling around everywhere.

Bruce had a charismatic personality, so it was no surprise when we learned that he had been a performer. In 1966, he was a member of Every Mother's Son, a sunshine pop band. He made sure that everyone knew his passion was music, not dentistry.

Many parties wrapped up with Bruce singing at his grand piano, which sat in front of a wall of windows in the living room. The tinkling of the keys drew people from all corners of the house, in various altered states. Pills, pot and any form of hallucinogens were abundant. I never acquired a taste for them; I preferred alcohol but hated those times when the room started to spin and I'd find myself vomiting into the toilet. It was a different story with Bob. He'd started to use drugs again, and I worried that he was becoming the "Bob" I'd heard about in college. I never knew if I'd be coming home alone because he was too "fucked up" to leave. Sometimes he was, sometimes he wasn't. When he didn't come home, I'd wake up regularly to check if he was next to me. The following day I'd complain, "What happened to you?" or "What were you doing?" or "You're doing too many drugs!"

"Stop nagging me!" he'd snap.

Oh my God, I was becoming a "nagging" wife.

I didn't know then but I do know now: I had the right to question him and worry about his wellbeing.

Despite these flare-ups, we began discussing our permanent relocation to Woodstock. Renovations were well underway. We set our move-in date for the summer of 1977.

After the completion of the *National Lampoon Radio Hour* project, Bob had taken a full-time job as an architect at a firm off Madison Avenue. He hated it and anything that distracted him from the design and building of our house. For several months, he'd been vacillating between quitting, finding a job as an architect in the Woodstock area, and starting his own firm. His hedging was reminiscent of earlier years, which had always made me nervous. On top of that, he was not including me in his decision-making.

My own professional life was going well. I had left *National Lampoon* and was now working as a freelance paste-ups and mechanicals artist for *Harper's Magazine*, the *Sunday New York Times Magazine* and *Psychology Today*. I was able to set my own hours, so my plan was to split my time between Brooklyn and Woodstock until we made the final move.

In the meantime, Bob was working on the blueprints for building a second story onto the studio. It would add a bright and spacious bedroom, a large luxurious bathroom with a clawfoot soaking tub and actual closets. We were going to have a porch instead of the boulder that sat at the foot of our entry door. Heating, cooling and plumbing systems would transform the place into a legitimate home. As I visualized all the creature-comfort improvements, I also hoped that things might get better with Bob.

Each weekend we needed to transport bigger items up to Woodstock, and our little VW was no longer practical. Toyota had just introduced the first mini pick-up truck, and Bob purchased a red one. That was going to be his car, and I'd be inheriting the Beetle. There was only one problem: I didn't know how to drive a stick shift. In the seven years we had been together, he had never let me drive his precious car.

We agreed that the next weekend he'd teach me. I got behind the wheel with Bob in the passenger's seat. He gave me a theoretical lesson on how to use the clutch, the brake and the accelerator. I kept my left foot on the clutch in order to practice shifting through the gears with my right hand. He repeated sternly, "When the car isn't in motion, the gear needs to stay in neutral, otherwise the car will stall out."

How hard could it be? As I turned the engine on, I released the emergency brake, and the car rolled forward ever so slightly. I caught it by stepping on the brake with my right foot. Bob told me to step on the clutch with my left foot, which I did. Now I had to put the car in first gear and move my right foot to the accelerator but not press down on it. A delicate dance!

I released the clutch too soon and took too long to give the car gas, and the engine sputtered. I glanced over at Bob, whose head was shaking in disapproval. I tried again from the beginning, but I was nervous, and my timing was off. Apparently I didn't have the clutch down enough as I shifted into first gear. I felt an uncomfortable vibration through my foot and heard a chilling, grinding noise coming from the engine. "You're stripping my gears," Bob shouted. "I'll have to get a new transmission." As he stormed out of the car, he said, "I can't do this!"

I followed him back to the house. "How am I going to learn if you don't teach me?"

"I don't know, and I don't care!" he said as he disappeared into the kitchen.

To my left and through the gigantic windows, I caught sight of the path that would take me to my refuge. I grabbed my journal and headed up the hill. There, with tears streaming down my face, I recorded what had happened.

The next day, I approached Bob. "Can we please try again?" I asked. "I promise I won't strip the gears."

He begrudgingly followed me to the car.

As I slid behind the wheel, I silently prayed to do a better job. Bob sat rigidly beside me. If the tension had been a vapor, in addition to being asphyxiated, we would not have been able to see through the windshield. I turned the ignition on and went through all the steps. I held my breath as my left foot released the clutch and my right stepped on the accelerator, but the car stalled. I looked over at him, apologized and said, "Let me try again."

I gritted my teeth and put my hand on the stick shift and my feet on the pedals. But my coordination failed me once more, and I heard the screech of metal. The passenger door slammed, and Bob was gone.

The walls of the car closed in on me. I wished they'd squeeze me out of existence. Comatose, I sat there staring at the dirt road in front of me. Then I felt my feet finding the pedals and my hand landing on the stick shift. They knew what they were doing, and soon the car was in first gear and I was moving down the driveway. I stepped on the clutch and the brake, took the car out of gear and stopped. I leaned back against the seat as my lungs filled with air once again.

Suddenly the car felt enormous, and I was alive. I got the car in gear, turned left onto the road we shared with Bruce and slowly headed over the brook and onto Lewis Hollow Road. I slipped into second gear, then third, and made my way into town without stalling.

The Beetle was now my car.

I didn't know then but I do know now: Left to my own devices, I was capable of teaching myself anything. I'd done it up till then, and I would do it for the rest of my life.

29
INFIDELITY

Six months before we were to move into our house, Bob announced that he had applied for the job of Building Inspector in Woodstock. It wasn't exactly what he wanted, but he rationalized that it was only for a year, and the pay was decent. Despite being surprised, I warmed up to the idea, and we both waited to find out if he got it. When he did, he told me it started in three months. Three months?

I hadn't yet discussed a part-time arrangement with my freelance clients. I didn't want to jeopardize my professional connections, and there was no way I could wrap things up within that time frame. Plus there was the matter of breaking our lease and losing our security deposit. And the Woodstock house was not ready for me to move into.

When I expressed my dismay to Bob, he brushed me off. Then he informed me that he'd decided to move as soon as possible, several months ahead of me. Once again, I was not part of his calculations, and once again, I was shut out. But I didn't want to be a "nag." I didn't utter a sound.

Bob and I had befriended Kathy, a single woman who lived a few doors down from us, on the top floor of a brownstone that she shared with her mother. After Bob left, I began spending more time at her place.

Kathy was plump, a little taller than I, with mousy hair and small brown eyes. Post work I'd walk over, ring her bell and wait for her to let me in. Her thumping footsteps could be heard as she descended the three flights of stairs. Dickweed, her white German shepherd, barked as he lumbered down behind her. He'd always greet me with a wagging tail and sloppy kisses.

Before I placed a foot inside the foyer, Kathy started in with all the latest gossip from the soap opera, *Days of Our Lives*. She was the manager of the popular show's wardrobe department and fraternized with the principal actors daily. I had no interest in the program, but I listened as she spoke of its cast as though they were her best friends.

She'd talk and talk all the way up to the third floor and into her living room, most of which was taken up by a huge table where Kathy did her work. It was always covered with fabrics and patterns. Kathy usually sat on a high chair at the table, while I ended up on the only other available seat—a settee between a big window and the fireplace.

Kathy and I became quite friendly. During an early evening visit, she noticed that I was preoccupied and asked if there was anything wrong. Close to tears, I confided to her that Bob was never home when I called him. "I'm afraid he might be cheating on me," I said.

I wasn't intending to share this embarrassing suspicion. I blindly assumed that, like me, Bob was faithful. After all, when guys at the magazine hit on me, I rebuffed their advances—marriage meant loyalty, and I never wavered from that principle. To me, infidelity was dishonest, and lying would decimate my ability to trust. But as of late, doubt had been percolating. What if I was wrong? What if I was being naïve and choosing not to see? The idea was bubbling at the surface that evening.

The air in the room condensed to an awkward silence. My gaze stayed fixed on Kathy, who was staring into the cup of tea she was holding. I waited for her to reply.

Finally, she did. "Bob and I had sex."

"What?" I needed her to repeat it—perhaps I hadn't heard her properly.

As she said those incomprehensible words again, there was only one more question I had to ask, "When?"

I heard a cascade of words flying across the table: "…the time he came over to fix my chair…" just happened…" and "… only happened once…."

This was my worst nightmare!

Minutes before, I'd been sitting with a confidante and a woman who did not threaten me. Now, before me sat a frumpy, beady-eyed, fat woman who was chronically unsuccessful with men. A woman I'd pitied. What had Bob possibly seen in her, and what did that say about me?

Without a word, I picked myself up, ran down the stairs and out of the brownstone. Somehow I made it to my gate and through the front door. It didn't occur to me to turn on the lights. I went right into the bedroom and threw myself across my bed, where I sobbed and sobbed.

When I finally had no more cry in me, I fixed my puffy eyes on the phone, which was a few yards away. I peeled myself up, put one foot in front of the other, took a moment and finally dialed Bob in Woodstock. This time he answered. "Kathy just told me you had sex with her."

A chill came through the receiver; he did not deny it, nor was he apologetic. He concurred that it was only one time and insisted that it didn't mean anything. For some reason that was worse. I wanted to ask him, "Then why did you do it?" But he was saying, "You're overreacting; it was no big deal." We hung up with no resolution. That night I didn't sleep, and the next day I didn't eat. The life that I'd been living was slipping away, and the vacuum it left threatened to suck me into a hole too vast for me to fathom. Exhausted, confused and in disbelief, I convinced myself that Bob was right: I was overreacting. His and Kathy's story matched; it had been a quick, impetuous and meaningless fling. I needed to get over it.

I didn't know then but I do know now: I had such an undermined relationship with reality that any inference of "overreaction" dropped a vault-like barricade between me and the truth.

With that "problem" solved, I was certain that he'd be calling—not just to apologize but to plead for my forgiveness and to promise it would never happen again. But the phone never rang. So I called him. When he didn't answer, I stayed glued to my seat with my fingers pressing his number over and over again. When he finally picked up, I was in a desperate state. I cried through most of the conversation, and Bob remained hostile until we hung up.

I called him back. He answered in a voice that was coarse and cavalier. "I'm not happy in this marriage, and I might not want you to move to Woodstock," he said.

CRASH—An unmerciful torrent of words came flying at me: He hated me, couldn't stand the sight of me. Ugly, stupid, unlovable, undesirable, pathetic, nag.

I didn't know then but I do know now: These were the "voices," my ever-present internal judges.

He'd hung up. With the receiver still in my hand, I looked around my beloved apartment. It now felt empty, cold and unwelcoming. Everything around me echoed with a hollowness that terrified me.

In the days that followed if I wasn't occupied or distracted, I had the last few years on a continuous loop in my head. I reran everything, searching for clues and pinpointing all the things I'd done wrong. I even flashed to all those guys whose sexual advances I'd spurned at work and thought, "Stupid me!" I didn't recognize my life; I was flailing, and if I wasn't in constant motion I felt like I'd wither away. I needed something to anchor me.

I'd been hearing about Scientology and thought that might be my answer. I found my way to the Upper East Side church and began attending meetings. The facilitator, a man I found mildly attractive, began showing some interest in me. My confidence with men had been pummeled, and I ached to be desired. When he asked me out for coffee, I said, "Yes."

Then he invited me to dinner, and afterwards he asked if he could escort me home. That seemed innocent enough. Scientology encourages openness, and I found conversation with him to be easy. Then, at the gate, he kissed me. It felt good, so I invited him in.

Even though it was surreal having a strange man in the home I'd shared with Bob, I was angry and determined to stop being stupid. It had been more than eight years since I'd been kissed with passion, and this guy was a good kisser. When he suggested we go into the bedroom, I agreed. It wasn't long before he divulged he was working out some sexual neuroses. He began acting creepy, and I asked him to leave. I never saw him or Scientology again.

What had I been thinking? I wanted my life back. I wanted to stay married to Bob.

The next day I called him and begged him to come back to Brooklyn so we could talk. He agreed to drive down the following weekend.

I had lost a lot of weight and knew I looked good. Leading up to his visit, I tried on several outfits and finally chose a new white eyelet dress that flattered my smaller frame. I wanted Bob to walk in and be reminded of what he was giving up.

The day he arrived was beautiful. The apartment was as bright as it could be. As I opened the front door, he stood there for a moment, giving me time to take him in. With the daylight behind him, he looked gorgeous. It was as though I were seeing him for the first time. The love I felt for him made all the misery of the past few months disappear. I flipped onto the tippy toes of my Dr. Scholl's wooden sandals and gave him a kiss. I ignored his flinch.

I followed him into the living room, and as he turned to face me, I gushed, "I love you, and I want to be with you."

There was no turning back. "I'm sorry for being a nag. It's just that I could feel us drifting apart. Let's take some time to work on our relationship and not make any rash decisions."

Silence. Bob was fidgeting and looking around. "I'm not happy in this marriage," he said again. "I haven't been for a long time."

There had to be something I could do to stop this from happening. I'll make him jealous, I thought. I told him about the Scientology guy, but rather than jealousy, he responded with disgust.

"I'm going back to Woodstock," he said, "and I don't want you to come with me."

He began collecting the few things he'd apparently come for. I followed behind him crying and begging him to stay. He stormed through the hallway, put his hand on the doorknob, but something stopped him from turning it. For a fleeting second I thought he might be reconsidering his actions. I waited with anticipation. But when he swiveled around, he was glaring down at me, "I'm having an affair with Lisa, and I'm in love with her!" he said.

CRASH—It was the end of the world. The void swallowed me up. From far, far away, I heard the front door open. I heard him step out into the vestibule, close the door behind him and leave through the gate.

What was left of me found the bed, climbed onto the mattress and curled up in a ball.

Lisa was the real deal—a legitimate supermodel who appeared in high profile TV commercials pitching the trendiest products of the time. She was being featured in all the magazines and had appeared on the cover of *Vogue*. She and Bruce had been in a relationship before Bob and I met them, and she was part of the entourage we'd been hanging out with. Her beautiful home in Woodstock was a venue for many dinners and parties. Oscar de la Renta had taken her under his wing and wanted her to star in a film he was producing. She was everything I perceived myself not to be: gorgeous, gracious, famous, rich. But Bob's last sentence—"…and I'm in love with her"—smacked me the hardest. I couldn't remember a time he'd directed that sentiment to me. I imagined him doting on her, taking in her beauty with adoring eyes. Grabbing her by the shoulders, drawing her in with his strong arms and placing a long, passionate kiss on her lips. If only he'd kissed me that way.

The pain was excruciating.

I didn't know then but I do know now: My understanding of love had not evolved. In my mind, only beautiful, charming women were deserving of it. And fame and wealth were the only measures of self-worth. My husband was leaving me for the illusion of perfection.

30

THE WHEEL OF MISFORTUNE

Like the "Wheel of Misfortune," my life was spinning round and round.

Space 1: Bob chose tall, blond, blue-eyed Lisa because he found short, brown-haired, hazel-eyed me repulsive

Space 2: Bob had been miserable with me, and now he was happy

Space 3: I was losing all my cool friends in Woodstock

Space 4: My beautiful garden apartment was now a dungeon

Space 5: I was stuck in the city while Bob was in paradise

Space 6: I was going nowhere in life

Space 7: No one was ever going to love me

Space 8: I'd be alone forever

After Bob's catastrophic visit and the limbo state it had left me in, our conversations were strained and unproductive. We were still married, our lives intertwined, but he was in Woodstock, and I was in Brooklyn. From day to day, I wobbled: One part of me could envision a new, single life in NYC, but my heart was in Woodstock. The battle raged on, and any way I looked at it, I was on the losing end. The wheel kept spinning. I needed it to stop.

Since Bob first hinted that I might not be welcome in Woodstock, a quiet drum had started to beat: Why couldn't I move into the house in spite of Bob's wishes? I dared not pay it any mind—it was too radical, and I couldn't imagine myself being that bold. Besides, how could it ever really come to that? But here I was, and my worst-case scenario had come true. The faint beat came back: Why does Bob get the last word? Why don't I have a choice in the matter? As the volume of the thumping increased, the turning of the wheel slowed down.

Space 9: It's my house, and I deserve to live in it

The wheel stopped spinning. Nothing was going to stand in my way. I was moving into *my* house.

I didn't know then but I do know now: The prospect of losing Woodstock and my house was unacceptable to me and set off a misguided emotional stew. It was a mix of belligerence, an insistence that I belonged there and the erroneous belief that I could keep my marriage from disintegrating. In spite of the consequences I knew I'd face, my resolve would not budge.

I had to tell Bob. I wrote my speech out and had it sitting in front of me as I called him. "I want to move to Woodstock," I said. "It's my house as much as it is yours, and I deserve to live there."

Silence. Then, "But our marriage is over."

A sting and a minor setback. My eyes darted to my notes, and I tried not to sound like I was reading them. "I've been planning this move for as many years as you have. I've gone to great lengths to arrange a part-time gig at *Psychology Today*. They've agreed to me working there one week per month, which means I'll only be in Woodstock for three weeks at a time. Why should I have to give up my dream?"

"I'm not going to stop seeing Lisa," he said. "If you can live with that, it's okay with me."

I had no idea if I could or couldn't live with it. All I knew was that I was moving, and I began to plan. I notified my landlord that I would not be renewing my lease. My new setup with *Psychology Today* was perfect, except I needed a place to stay for the one week a month I'd be working there.

My problem was solved at a lunch date with Sheila, the magazine's assistant art director. When I shared my dilemma, she offered me her one-bedroom apartment, in the heart of Soho. Turns out she was having an affair with Milton Glaser, and she was confident he would put her up in a hotel for the weeks when I was in Manhattan. (This was so juicy! Milton Glaser! My former teacher! The most famous graphic designer in the world! She also told me that he had a second home in Woodstock on none other than Lewis Hollow Road!)

Leaving the city presented another quandary. My obsession with dance had been replaced by Pilates. For the past year or so I'd been going to a studio that used the technique to rehabilitate dancers. My friend Mimi had introduced me to the owner, Robert Fitzgerald, who accepted me into the exclusive program. I was so wowed by this brand new form of physical fitness that I went every week. I discovered that I had a natural curiosity about the mechanics of movement and an interest in how the body worked. I couldn't imagine my life without it.

As I was stressing over this problem an idea popped into my head: What if I taught a Pilates class in Woodstock? Could I do that without training? I asked Robert what he thought, and he suggested I go down the block to the original Pilates studio. I did, and soon I was one of several people being trained by Romana, who ran the business. From her I learned the basics of teaching a mat class.

But where was I going to do this? I'd have to find a place. And then I remembered a gift shop on Rock City Road that I'd passed a million times. It had giant windows on the second floor. I'd often wondered what it was used for and, now, if it was available to rent. One weekend before my move, I swung into the parking lot and walked into the shop. The owner greeted me, and I asked if the upstairs space could be leased. He said yes.

I followed him up the steps into a huge open room with a high vaulted ceiling and those big windows overlooking the street. It was exactly what I had envisioned, and I agreed to rent it one day per week. I'd teach Pilates the three weeks I was in Woodstock and freelance at *Psychology Today* the other week. I was set.

I didn't know then but I do know now: Once again, Tinkerbell made an appearance, and I had the good sense to follow her sparkling light.

When my Brooklyn departure day arrived, Bob drove down to help me pack up, and our two cars headed north on the Thruway. As Brooklyn Heights faded in my rearview mirror, I reflected on what I was leaving behind and the precariousness of my future.

True to his word, Bob did not stop seeing Lisa. It took all my strength to shake off the indignity and to remind myself that I'd chosen the arrangement. I was to find out that a lot of the mutual friends Bob and I had made did not approve of what he was doing. Bruce, in particular, was happy to share his opinions with me. "Knowing Lisa as I do, this fling with Bob won't last very long."

It helped to have some allies, and it fueled the hope that Bob would wake up to realize that he truly loved me and our marriage would be saved.

But what really kept me from disintegrating was the arrangement I'd made with *Psychology Today*. When my weeklong hiatus in the city came around, I'd hop into my Beetle and leave the Woodstock scene behind. The reverse two-hour commute was like a cleanse, purging the stress from the crazy predicament I'd put myself in.

Sheila's apartment was on Spring Street, down the block from my favorite health food restaurant, the Spring Street Natural. It was the mid-'70s, and SoHo was *the* neighborhood—the most happening, hippest, funkiest in town. I'd wake up early each morning with plenty of time before I went to the magazine on 33rd and Park. The Cupping Room was on the corner of West Broadway and Broome Street. The early day sun streaming in through the windows, the brick walls and the rich wood interior cradled me. As I stood in line waiting to place my order, the aromas of brewing coffee, pastries baking and food cooking embraced me. Once nestled into my booth, with my cappuccino and homemade scone, I wrote in my journal or sketched in my pad until it was time to make my way uptown.

I didn't know then but I do know now: The time I spent in the city was my first taste of autonomy. I'd gone straight from my parents' home to living with Bob. The fear of being alone was the reason I chose to follow Bob to Woodstock.

At first, the three weeks up north were difficult. Bob slept upstairs, and I slept in the original bedroom downstairs. We were more like roommates, living separate lives and staying out of each other's way. Eventually I got into a rhythm. To teach my Pilates class, I'd have to prepare, which took a substantial amount of time. Unbeknownst to me, all those years of dance classes had amassed a body of knowledge I didn't even know I had. It turned out that teaching enriched and rejuvenated me. I looked forward to it, and it didn't matter that I started with one student.

I had met Anna soon after Bob and I began our weekend visits to Woodstock. She and Lester had made a wrong turn, and their two-toned Chevy Suburban ended up in our driveway one day when Bob and I were outside working on the house. Woodstock being a friendly place, we invited them to join us. Lester was an older man, tall and striking, with a shaved head and close-cropped white facial hair. He wore rugged clothes that seemed tailored to show off his impressive build. Anna, also tall, had a blond pixie cut. Underneath a fur-lined embroidered vest, she wore a flowing viscose shirt with long balloon sleeves. A thick leather belt with a handcrafted brass buckle hugged her narrow hips. Her jeans fell perfectly over her cowboy boots.

It turned out they were looking for a house, so they, too, were in Woodstock intermittently. From the moment we met, Anna and I struck up a friendship and would get together whenever we were both in town. It didn't take long for us to learn that we shared a passion for physical fitness. It became the foundation of our relationship. While I was speculating about teaching Pilates in Woodstock, she promised she'd be my first student. And she was.

Anna and Lester eventually rented a log cabin outside of Kingston, a few miles from Woodstock. I remember the first time I visited. I drove my little car up a steep dirt road in the middle of nowhere. Anna met me at the door, which opened into a spacious, bright room with a prominent stone fireplace to the left. She invited me in and showed me around. She had an ethereal quality, as if she were floating. She led me to one of two big leather club chairs set in front of a raging fire. As I curled into one, she offered me some tea, and while she was in the kitchen I looked around, noting the artful decor. Anna returned with two steaming cups balanced on an ornate tray, with a delicate pitcher of cream and matching dishes filled with sugar and honey. Dainty spoons sat on top of cloth napkins.

Sliding into the other chair, gracefully folding her feet underneath her, Anna told me how happy she was to see me. I was soon to find out that Lester was in the city, supposedly breaking up with his wife, a wealthy woman who lived in Florida and had an apartment in Manhattan. I was all ears, and Anna wasted no time telling me her whole story.

Anna was from Florida, where she had been a model. That's where she met Lester, who relentlessly pursued her. It was impossible to keep their torrid affair from his wife, and the situation grew so tempestuous that Lester whisked Anna and her two-year old daughter Kelly to Costa Rica for a year.

I'd never heard of Costa Rica and listened intently to Anna's exotic details. Lester set them up in a large open-air hut on stilts. It sat on the beach at the edge of the jungle, where howler monkeys and parrots of all colors lived. It was hot, so she and Kelly wore scant, light clothing, walking everywhere barefoot. The ocean, calm and balmy, was steps away. The beach took them to the market for fresh produce and other provisions. When the sun set, the house was lit by candlelight. Gentle ocean breezes blew the white gossamer curtains, and the clear evening sky stretched to eternity.

Then she divulged the more troublesome side of the story. Lester would only travel to Costa Rica periodically; he came and went arbitrarily. When he was there, he was everything she wanted him to be, and she couldn't resist him. But when he wasn't there, she knew he was with his wife. Anna was lonely, and her resentment grew until she finally gave him an ultimatum.

As I sat in the living room of the log cabin, she explained that as soon as Lester divorced his wife, he would come to Ulster County to be with Anna exclusively. Anna was excited to share the plans she had for their wedding.

I didn't know then but I do know now: It was serendipitous that Anna and I found each other. My friendship with her was a big part of what got me through a difficult time.

31

CALIFORNIA

Lisa did, indeed, dump Bob. But then rumors were flying that he was seeing someone else. I had grown disenchanted and doubtful that reconciliation was ever going to happen. The foul smell of divorce hung in the air.

In the midst of our messy situation, my cousin Elaine paid a visit. She'd travelled to Israel and was heading back to her home in California. Instead of flying straight to the West Coast, she proposed landing in New York so she could stopover and see me in Woodstock.

Elaine and I had been close since childhood. We were the same age, and her parents were also Polish refugees and Holocaust survivors. When we were little, our favorite pastime was to lie on either end of the couch, our legs in the air and the soles of our feet together. We'd repeat all the Polish curse words we knew, and we'd giggle our asses off.

We spent a couple of fun days together in Woodstock, and before heading to the airport, Elaine extended me an open invitation to come to Oakland. I promised her I'd think about it.

During one of our catch-up phone conversations, when I confided that things with Bob were increasingly uncomfortable, she insisted I come to California right then and there. I saw no reason not to go for a week; I wouldn't be missing work, and I could easily cancel my class. I purchased my tickets. Bob agreed the break would be good for both of us; he even drove me to the airport.

The only other time I'd been on a plane was when Bob and I took a camping trip to Colorado and the Grand Canyon in Arizona. I couldn't help noting that it had been during happier days. But we were pulling up to the departure entrance, and there was no time to wallow in melancholy—the cars behind us were already blowing their horns. I hastened to collect my stuff, step out of the truck and scurry into the terminal, which swept me into its tumult.

Once in my seat, I burrowed in and waited to take off. I recalled how my body responded the first time I experienced the speed that the plane had to reach before the nose went up and the wheels retracted. I wondered if I'd feel that same flutter in my stomach this time. I did. Once we reached cruising altitude I allowed my mind to drift. It was no surprise that I began to reflect on the past nine years with Bob— the good and the bad. Over the five-hour flight, which was taking me thousands of miles away, I was able to shed some of the weight. By the time I landed in Oakland, I felt lighter. Perhaps there might be more in front of me than behind.

Landing made me clutch the arms of my seat, squeeze my eyelids and pray. After all, I'd rarely heard about a crash take-off, but how many times had I heard of a crash landing? My breath didn't come back to normal until the wheels hit the tarmac.

I was in California! When Elaine met me in baggage claim, we pinched each other to make sure it was real. The minute her car left the airport, I could see that I was no longer on the East Coast. It was flatter and more sprawling. It felt like there was a different sun in Oakland—it seemed to sparkle more brightly. And due to the proximity of the bay, I picked up that delicious saltwater scent. The bare trunks of palm trees with their elegant fronds fanning out only at the top reminded me of huge umbrellas. The way they filtered the light felt so different from the dense greenness of the trees back home. We passed block after block of pastel-colored bungalows with neat kitchen gardens and beach-like landscaping. Young people, my peers, walking barefoot or hanging out on porches were everywhere.

Elaine and her boyfriend Jonathan rented one of those sweet little houses. A corner in the living room had been cleared for me, with a twin mattress on the floor and a small bureau for my clothes. California was in the middle of a drought, so residents could not water lawns, and flushing the toilet was prohibited. "How does that work?" I asked Elaine.

She showed me a jar next to the toilet that already had a hefty amount of urine in it. I hid my revulsion and looked at her quizzically. "You just pee in the jar," she explained, "and we empty it out in the backyard."

Yup, California was going to be interesting.

One night Elaine took me to her local YWCA for my first sauna. In contrast to Elaine, I was modest, and I reluctantly got naked in front of the other women. I wrapped a towel around me and followed her as she strode boldly through the locker room sans towel. As we stepped into the close, dimly lit space, the heat and the pungent smell of cedar welcomed me.

We took our seats on the top tier. The warm air kissed the skin that was uncovered. Elaine motioned for me to remove my towel and lie down, which I did. Having the dry heat hover over my flesh was strange, and as it grew hotter I felt as though I'd burst into flames. It brought me to the brink of panic. Just as I was about to solicit Elaine's help, the moisture broke through my pores. I let the perspiration drip out and onto the towel. The little streams of sweat felt as if they were washing the damaged parts of me away, as though my whole being was finally weeping.

The original plan was for me to stay in Oakland for seven days, but I felt so restored that I couldn't imagine flying back to the toxicity I'd left behind. I didn't have to return for another couple weeks, so I asked Elaine if it would be all right for me to stay longer. "Of course, we'd love to have you," she said.

The next day I called Bob. I pressed the buttons on the phone with purpose. When he answered, I didn't strain to analyze his tone; I didn't even wait for him to start talking. I simply informed him of my new plans and hung up.

I took a deep breath and inhaled the new person I'd become. There was so much I wanted to do and see. While Elaine was at work, I set out to explore. Oakland was adjacent to Berkeley, and I meandered over to the bustling U.C. campus, where I imagined myself going back to school. Several times I took public transportation into San Francisco. I window-browsed, serpentining my way through the streets, and checked out the different neighborhoods. The city was an urban version of Woodstock, with similar people and culture. What if I actually relocated?

I became fully immersed in the Bay Area experience. On the weekends we wandered through the redwood forests, drove over the hilly terrain of Marin County, visited beaches and spent afternoons drinking our way through the vineyards of Napa Valley. One evening I accompanied Elaine and Jonathan to their international folk dancing group, where they introduced me to the owner and manager. I couldn't resist a good dancer, and we began dating. I spent a few nights with him at his loft space in an industrial part of the city, where he hosted wild parties. At the same time, I looked up an old boyfriend from high school. We met for dinner, and I ended up spending the night with him. I never thought of myself as promiscuous, and these two trysts were out-of-character. I overrode my uneasiness about them because everything I was doing was breaking a mold. The idea of not being married anymore was growing on me, and I gave myself permission to behave as though I were single.

I didn't know then but I do know now: Being with other men acceler-ated my split from Bob.

As the end of my stay was approaching, I had to decide what I was going to do. In the course of those three weeks, I'd discovered a free-spirited me who could be self-sufficient and independent. I was no longer afraid to be alone. Yet the pull to return home convinced me that I had unfinished business in Woodstock. I felt confident that I could pick up my pieces and move on.

Back east I knew two things: I wanted to get a divorce, and Wood-stock was where I wanted to live. Bob was on board, and the only thing that was left to do was find a lawyer. Neither of us had experience in this area, so we asked around and found someone who would repre-sent us both.

Before our appointment, we had a tough conversation about the house. By this time, I had more of an attachment to it than I did to Bob. But he argued that his parents had made the down payment, he had done the bulk of the work, and there was still a lot to do before the renovation was completed. What could I say to that? Nothing, so I agreed.

It was an uneasy drive down Glasco Turnpike to the attorney's house. He led us into his dining room, where we took our seats on op-posite sides of table. The lawyer had an affable manner, as if trying to make an unpleasant situation tolerable. It didn't work for me; I sat on a razor's edge.

When the subject of my financial compensation came up, Bob threw out a number, and the attorney asked me if it was acceptable. I didn't know. I hadn't thought about it. I just wanted the whole ordeal to be over. So I nodded my head in consensus.

I didn't know then but I do know now: As with so much in my life, I had no one to advise me. It never occurred to me that I should have had my own council. I'm pretty sure if I had, I would have been advised as to how much of a settlement I deserved. It definitely would've been more than the few thousand dollars I received. To this day I regret that.

32

BEARSVILLE

Officially single, I needed a place to live. I checked the local papers and the bulletin boards around town. In the post office, I spotted a flyer that read "Room for rent," called the number and made an appointment. Bearsville was eight miles outside of Woodstock—a tad disappointing because I wanted to be smack in the middle of the action.

I followed the directions the guy on the phone had given me and pulled up to a big house with several entrances. He'd instructed me to take the staircase to the right of the parking lot, which I did. It brought me to a door, and I knocked. My future roommate greeted me and invited me in. He was a tall, fit fellow, about my age. He explained that he was the tenant and I would be his sublet. If that arrangement was all right with me, he'd be happy to show me the room. We discussed the rent, which was within my budget. I reasoned that I hardly had any furniture, and I'd only be in Woodstock three weeks out of each month. "I'll take it," I said.

The room was a little larger than my childhood bedroom. My mattress went on the floor in one corner, across from two big windows.

A rocking chair from Brooklyn Heights fit into another corner by the closet. My small drafting table stayed folded up against a wall, as did my disassembled round butcher block table, with its heavy, black base. The rest of my possessions were packed into boxes, which I stacked under the windows. The setup mirrored the suspended status of my life.

It was different with my clothes. I unpacked them and hung them methodically in the closet. The clicking sound as I placed each hanger on the pole punctuated this new phase—my first real act of being on my own. My clothes represented consistency. I knew who I was by what I wore, and I knew what looked good on me. In that department my identity was intact. Dressing was also a way to express myself creatively; combining diverse colors, patterns, textures and shapes was satisfying and fun. And now that I was a divorced woman, with the prospect of a new relationship looming, a plunging neckline, a bare midriff and well-fitted jeans were my sexual currency.

Waking up that first morning was loaded with emotion. Despite the space being flooded with sunshine, I did not spring out of my bed to meet it. I stayed curled up inside the cocoon of my covers. There was no reason for me to be anywhere but inside that room. I hibernated for a few days, tasting my aloneness and brushing up against my freedom. When I emerged I was revived.

I learned that my roommate was a homeopathic doctor and the apartment was his office. I had to pass through his "treatment room" to get to the kitchen, which was filled with little bottles, sugar pellets, gels, creams and mixing paraphernalia. At first I was curious about this unusual natural science, and he was eager to oblige my interest. But before long, he was seeking me out in order to dump mountains of homeopathic information on me. I found his feverish energy oppressive, and I began doing everything I could to avoid him.

My long drive into town wove through thick forests and open fields. It provided a necessary interlude to prepare for what lay ahead— hanging out at a friend's organic fruit and vegetable stand or the crowd I was likely to run into at the coffee shop. The radio was always tuned to WKTU-FM. Any song played from Fleetwood Mac's *Rumours* album cheered me on. "Dreams," "Don't Stop," "Go Your own Way"—these songs were written for me.

On sadder days, "I Can't Tell You Why" by the Eagles or "If You Could Read My Mind" by Gordon Lightfoot would open the floodgates. Sometimes I'd have to pull over, and in the privacy of my Beetle, I'd break down.

I resumed teaching my Pilates class, which added much needed structure to the weeks I was in Woodstock. Anna was always there. Lester had never left his wife, and Anna had finally broken up with him. Our friendship was a soft cushion where both of us could land. We spent hours together, talking about everything.

One morning, I was standing at my windows, waiting for Anna to pick me up. As soon as I saw her turn into the driveway, I ran down the stairs. She was driving a brand new SUV; I had to hoist myself up into the passenger seat. I glanced over my left shoulder and greeted Kelly, whom I was always happy to see.

"Very cool car, Anna!" I said.

She smiled and rolled her eyes. "My parents gave me such a hard time about buying a truck instead of a car," she said. "They don't think it's a proper vehicle for me or for Kelly."

I knew Anna had a complicated relationship with her mother. And I knew she had a trust fund, which her stepfather managed. I had no idea what a trust fund was, and when I found out that there was a pile of money sitting in a bank somewhere just for her, I couldn't believe her luck. She didn't have to work; all she had to do was show up in

Florida periodically, which she complained about bitterly. Small price to pay, I thought. But to Anna I said, "That sucks. It's your money—you should be able to manage it yourself."

It was hard for me not to compare myself to her. She could have whatever she wanted. Case in point: She got a new truck instead of a car. She was able to rent a house as opposed to a room. She needed furniture, she got furniture. My parents didn't have money, and I'd have to be in dire straits for them to pitch in. I would have given anything to be rich.

I didn't know then but I do know now: I knew a lot of people who came from wealthy families, and I thought they were fortunate. I didn't recognize that the coping skills I was honing had any merit. I have since seen many affluent people crumble under the weight of life, whereas my self-sufficiency has fostered strength and resilience.

After we dropped Kelly off at school, we headed out toward Route 28. Anna continued to complain about her parents. They didn't think Kelly was getting a good education in Woodstock; they wanted her to send Kelly to Florida so she could go to school there. "They just want to control me," she said.

We made a right turn toward Phoenicia, a quaint town about 20 minutes west. This was one of my favorite drives. Barreling down the open road, we passed clusters of fishing and hunting supply shops, gas stations, convenience stores, diners and roadside stands. On Anna's side was the mighty Ashokan Reservoir, which stretched for three-quarters of our trip. It carved out an endless space of shimmering water below and vast blue sky above. On my side, the heavy tree line started at the road's edge and ascended over the low hills. There I sat, the finite to my right, the infinite to my left.

The weeks I spent in the city were filled with traversing busy streets, weaving through people, hustling for a seat on the subway. I didn't mind that the work was intense and stressful. The contrast was a balance to my life in Woodstock.

With Bob still living on Lewis Hollow Road, I was privy to what was going on in his life. He was openly dating the woman I'd heard rumors about before I left for California. She was another tall, thin blonde, which irked me. But what truly baffled me was that she had a young son. I had gotten pregnant twice during our marriage. Both times we agreed we weren't ready to have children, and both times I had an abortion. My own choice not to have a child was partially based on an intuition that having a baby with Bob would be a mistake. He never expressed a desire to be a father, yet here he was on the cusp of becoming a stepfather.

I'd catch sight of them in his red pickup or strolling through town hand-in-hand. That was fine, but learning that she'd be moving into "my" house brought back a pain I thought was gone, and it made me feel replaced and conspicuously alone.

I didn't know then but I do know now: It was not about the house. Bob had someone to love, and I didn't. Someone loved Bob, but no one loved me. I felt ostracized all over again. The "voices" were back, and they were emphatic: "Only losers are single."

I had to find a boyfriend. On one of my drives back to my little room in Bearsville, I picked up a hitchhiker. He was a young, scruffy hippie on his way to his house, down the road from mine. Mark was the saxophone player in a small local band. In the car we had a flirtatious conversation. When I dropped him off at his house, he invited me to one of his gigs that weekend. I ended up going.

Mark was a passionate musician and looked sexy playing his instrument. During the break, he came straight over to me. I'd never dated a musician, and I'd always wanted to be that girl in the audience who gets the wink from the cool dude on stage. "What the hell," I thought and began spending time with him.

Mark's brooding nature made him an interesting subject to sketch. But a short time into our fling, he started whining about the weeks I was away in the city. His moodiness was turning into neediness, so I stopped seeing him. I still have my drawings, which are all I care to remember about him.

I didn't know then but I do know now: I didn't know who I was around men or what I wanted from them.

33

BROADVIEW ROAD

In Woodstock, Anna and I immersed ourselves in each other's lives. We spent all our free time together and relied on each other for advice. We had no secrets. Our friendship was our safe haven.

While I was subletting my room in Bearsville, she rented a house on Broadview Road, right outside of town. That was where we hung out, sat by her fire, ate dinner and got stoned. I was itching to have my own place, too. I didn't have a lease with the homeopath, and I was sure the money coming in from *Psychology Today* could cover the rent for a house. Scanning the local paper, I caught sight of an ad for an artist's studio. An artist's studio! What were the odds that I'd end up with my dream after all? I called and made an appointment to see it.

I was already familiar with the property. It was a lush estate, across the street from Anna's house. The landlord was waiting for me at the end of the long driveway. He was an older chap with an indistinguishable accent. He pointed to a separate building that was attached to the main house by a quaint covered walkway. After stepping through the doorway and into an unremarkable foyer, the light from an oversized window lured me into a room with a two-story-high ceiling. It was huge, and I needed a moment to take the place in.

With my back to the window I saw a mysterious indoor porch-like structure jutting into the space. It was supported by posts, which we had to pass by in order to get to a doorway that led into a full kitchen. At the far end of the main room was a wood-burning stove, a sign that I was meant to live there. The landlord asked, "Can I show you one of the bedrooms?"

One of the bedrooms! He guided me up a dark, narrow staircase beyond the kitchen. When we reached the top, I stepped into a sweet little room with a doorway leading to the porch that I now realized was an indoor balcony. It overlooked the big room and the enchanting grounds outside the window. I was already sold, but he was asking, "Would you like to see the other bedroom?"

"Yes," I said.

We trekked downstairs, across the studio to another small stairway. What I saw as I stepped through the closed door took my breath away. The large room, which was a separate wing, was surrounded by windows that were perched above manicured lawns, gardens and a pond. Fairytale images of a princess on a palanquin danced through my head. It was beyond my wildest dreams.

As soon as I could, I engaged some friends to help move my few possessions over. I unpacked my boxes, unfolded my drafting table and assembled my butcher block table. I painted the wall outside the kitchen a rich shade of magenta and decorated the posts with my drying herbs. My bed went into the middle of the master bedroom. Now when I awoke in my light-drenched room, I languished under my down blanket, drifting and musing about what might lie in front of me. With all this space, I realized I could teach my Pilates classes in one corner of the main room, which I did. My new life was about to start.

Anna had found a young, swarthy Mexican carpenter to do odd jobs around her house. Now that I had my own abode, I tapped Manuel to help me, too. Sometimes he'd just show up, happy to fix whatever was broken, and we slowly became friends.

Manuel fancied himself a spiritual guide, a guru of sorts: world traveler, purveyor of life's lessons, solver of problems and pot provider. He introduced me to Mayan culture and taught me how to ripen an avocado by putting it in a brown paper bag. He knew all about herbs and teas, which I was beginning to dabble in. Whenever I heard the roar of a motorcycle coming down the driveway, I knew it was Manuel. Soon I found myself on the back of his bike, cruising along country roads. It was on one of those rides, through a mountainous area, on a very narrow street with a steep drop to my right, that I discovered my preference to remain on the earth. I shut my eyes, clenched my teeth, grabbed onto his waist and prayed to stay alive. I have not gotten on the back of a motorcycle since.

I enjoyed my friendship with Manuel until he began making sexual overtures. I had no interest in getting involved with him in that way. I dodged his advances so as not to insult him, but he didn't get the hint. I finally had to tell him that I just wanted to be friends. He did not take it well, and I never saw him again.

Enough time had passed that both Anna and I believed we were ready for a serious relationship. But this was complicated for me. I perceived that Anna handled men better than I did: She was poised and charming, her words flowed smoothly, and she knew how to say all the right things. In contrast, I felt stiff, inelegant and inadequate, especially in the presence of men I was attracted to. I was inarticulate; my brain functioned at a fraction of its capacity. And flirting? I didn't know how; besides, I was devoid of charm. Anna shined, while I believed I receded into her shadow.

I didn't know then but I do know now: I was confusing Anna with my mother, who for me was the embodiment of a femme fatale—a woman who cast a spell that men could not resist. I didn't know that such a mythical creature did not exist, and it was the metric by which I measured myself. I falsely pegged Anna as one of those larger-than-life women.

One evening, Anna and I were sitting at the bar of the legendary Bear Cafe, a rustic and warm place that was the most popular restaurant in Woodstock. We were engrossed in conversation when Gene came over and stood between us. We knew him; he was a local doctor, and he hit of all the hot spots. This wasn't the first time he'd joined us at a bar. Anna and I ended our conversation to include him, and within a few minutes, Gene made it clear he was interested in talking to me. Meanwhile, another guy appeared at Anna's side.

Before that evening, I hadn't paid much attention to Gene. Slight, older and balding, he was not my physical type. It was easy to engage with him because I didn't find him attractive. But that evening, to my surprise, he was engaging and entertaining. When he asked for my number, I gave it to him.

On the way home, Anna and I debriefed about our separate experiences. Anna did not like the guy she'd spent time with. I said I was dubious about going out with Gene because, in my opinion, he was not good-looking. Anna's criteria were different from mine, and she made a case for Gene being a doctor—smart, funny and rich. If she liked him, I should give him a chance, I thought. When he called, I agreed to have dinner with him the following weekend.

It was late November. I scurried around, trying on these pants, this top, with that skirt, or maybe a dress? I settled on a pair of jeans, a tight low-cut shirt, my suede fringed jacket and Frye boots. My clothes never failed me.

Gene arrived on time, stepped into my house and, as everyone before him had, said, "What a cool place." When I gave him the tour, he was knocked out by the balcony and suggested we have a glass of wine up there.

Outside, he escorted me to his BMW. I hadn't been in such a fancy car since driving around in Sharon's father's Lincoln Continental. Gene opened the door for me, and I took notice of his gentlemanly manners. He told me we were going to another trendy restaurant on the other side of Woodstock. He'd reserved a table alongside the French doors, which in warmer weather opened onto a wraparound porch. Sitting across from him, I got swept up by his skillful discourse and his command of many topics. He was growing more attractive by the minute. Somewhere between the appetizer and the entree I found myself thinking, "I like him."

And then everything changed. Where seconds before I was composed and self-assured, now I was restless and self-conscious. I'd been enjoying our back-and-forth, but now I choked and was tongue-tied. The sound of my words incited a litany of internal criticism: bland, tedious, vapid, boring. I felt exposed, all my flaws laid bare, magnified and exaggerated. For the remainder of the dinner, I plastered a smile on my face, as if to say, "Please like me! Please."

I didn't know then but I do know now: As soon as I started having feelings for a guy, he became my father, and it was as though I picked up where I'd left off at 17. The stakes became super high: My self-esteem and confidence disappeared, and I became unworthy of his affection. I turned on myself in order to circumvent the inevitable rejection.

We left the restaurant, and with his hand still on the car door handle, he turned to me and asked, "Would you like to come back to my place?"

Relieved, I told Gene that I'd love to and slid into the bucket seat. I was sure I'd already blown the evening and he'd had enough of me. His invitation echoed the days when I mistook Allan's sexual advances as a sign that he "liked me." For the moment, disaster had been averted. But the trepidation from earlier in the evening and the silence between us thrust me deep inside my head. Suddenly there seemed to be less oxygen in the car. I needed more breath. I was gulping air. I couldn't help it, and I hoped he didn't notice.

"Are you all right?" came from the driver's side.

"Yes, why?"

"You're taking very short, deep breaths," he said. "Are you anxious?"

Caught, trapped, frantic—unable to lie. "Yes, I am."

"What are you afraid of?"

I had no idea, so I said the first thing that came to my mind: "I don't know you that well. I'm not comfortable going back to your house."

He assured me he'd take me home whenever I wanted to go.

I didn't know then but I do know now: I was having a panic attack. At that time not much was known about anxiety and its manifestations. I was oblivious to a battle that was raging between the part of me that wanted to be loved and the part that knew I was not exercising good judgment. The lack of control made me feel unsafe.

Gene lived alone in a house at the end of a long, private driveway. Inside, it was softly lit and cozy. He motioned for me to take a seat on his plush sofa while he put a match to the rolled-up paper placed under the previously stacked logs. His premeditated action settled me a bit. After he offered me another glass of wine, he put a Keith Jarrett album on the stereo. I'd never heard of Keith Jarrett, and it wasn't my kind of music, but Gene was a huge fan. Then he pulled out a joint, which posed a quandary for me. I never knew when pot was going to make me paranoid, and that night I was already compromised. Still, I didn't want to blow the evening, so I took a toke and then another.

It definitely made me appreciate Keith Jarrett a lot more, but it wasn't long before my eyes started to dart around, my heart began to palpate, and the room started to close in on me. What am I doing here? Who is this guy? Gene took notice and asked, "Is it all right if I hold you?"

His kind and attentive gesture brought me back into the room. Perhaps I could trust him; perhaps he wasn't judging me. I fell into his arms, and I spent the night. When I woke up, everything seemed to be fine. He made me breakfast before we took a leisurely drive back to my house. When he dropped me off, he kissed me and said, "I'll call you soon!"

I floated to my front door and reran the evening through my head for the rest of the day. Gene seemed to be a compassionate guy, tuned in to my feelings. I couldn't wait for him to call. He did, but rather than asking me out on a date, he invited himself over.

He arrived with a bottle of wine and suggested we have our drinks up on the balcony, which was right outside the smaller bedroom. From there it was a natural transition to the bed and an evening of lovemaking. But he did not spend the night. In spite of my dejected feelings, I allowed it to happen a few more times before he stopped calling me.

I didn't know then but I do know now: I had no idea how men perceived me, which created a gigantic gap between who I thought I was in the world and my inner experience. The two remained split, one betraying the other, leaving me somewhere in between, disarmed and vulnerable.

Bernard was the owner of the Bear Cafe—a mayor-like figure, magnetic, with an irresistible French accent. Anna had a relationship with him through Lester, and each time we went to his restaurant, we got special treatment: free drinks at the bar and personal care at the table. He often joined us, contributing interesting conversation and innocent flirtations. I never thought much of it until one evening when he surprised me with an invitation to dinner. He was much older than I; he could have been my father. Anna persuaded me to ignore that "minor" detail, and I accepted.

He took me to the Depuy Canal House, in High Falls. The chef/owner, Jon Novi, was his friend. Jon Novi greeted us at the door and invited us into the bustling and aromatic kitchen. Then we were escorted upstairs to a VIP table, which gave us a bird's-eye view of the chefs preparing the meals. I'd never been attended to like this, and I liked it. As we ate, Bernard's knowledge took me on a tour around the world.

I accepted a few more dates with him, but eventually our time devolved into an unpleasant routine: I'd meet him at the Bear for a drink or dinner, then I'd go across the street to his apartment and wait for him while he closed up. I knew, once again, that I was being used, yet I was powerless to change it. He must've known, too, because in a kind way he suggested our relationship was not healthy for me. "I'm too old for you," he told me. "You should be with someone your own age." When he admitted he was a forever bachelor, I snapped out of my fog and agreed to an amicable parting. But still I wondered what I was doing that led these men to take advantage of me. Why weren't they falling madly in love with me the way my mother told me they had fallen in love with her?

I didn't know then but I do know now: The illusion that my mother had cultivated created a smokescreen. I couldn't get past it; it was the period at the end of the sentence. Compared to her, I was unlovable and only good for sex.

Besides the landlord, my only other neighbor on the estate was Chester. His home, halfway down the driveway, was an odd warehouse-type building, similar to a Quonset hut. He, too, was older, with a strong build, salt-and-pepper hair and a full beard; he was attractive in a rugged sort of way. From day one, we'd exchange waves as I passed his house. Then he started to flag me down, I'd stop, and we'd chat. I'd noted he wasn't always in Woodstock; he'd come and go for weeks at a time. Most often he was by himself, but sometimes he had a woman with him, who I assumed was his girlfriend.

So when he asked me out to dinner, I was taken aback but chalked it up to our burgeoning friendship. I was curious and wanted to get to know him, so I accepted.

Chester was a sculptor who worked on large pieces in metal and wood. At dinner I found out why he was so transient: His work was shown in galleries and museums all over the country. He had to travel to install his exhibitions and meet collectors. I learned a lot about the New York art scene and how difficult it was to get pieces accepted into such prestigious venues. According to him, he was a highly sought-after artist, which impressed me. I wished he didn't have a girlfriend, and then he disclosed that they'd recently broken up. Now I understood why he'd asked me out. I was excited by the prospect of dating him.

We chatted on the short drive home, chuckled about living on the same property. Something about that set me up for what happened next. Rather than continue down the driveway to my house, he pulled alongside his place, and when he invited me in, I didn't hesitate.

The industrial exterior belied a stunning interior space that he'd designed and built himself. It was moody, modern and masculine. Artwork hung on the walls, and sculptures of varying sizes were displayed on all sorts of surfaces. There was no overhead lighting; instead, everything had a soft spotlight assigned to it. It had the dramatic feel of a gallery.

He handed me a glass of brandy and walked me through a doorway that went into a massive garage where he created his large-scale pieces. Several were finished; others were in progress. I was so dazzled that when he asked me to stay, I couldn't refuse. In the morning, as I was leaving, he informed me he'd be going to the city and would call as soon as he returned.

Even though I had an inkling of concern, I convinced myself that perhaps this time would be different. For the next few months, he'd call when he was home, then disappear without notice, then reappear and call. And I would wait. Not until late one night when I saw him pull up with his girlfriend did I finally understand. I'd become entangled in another deceptive web where I was not the one who was chosen, not the one who was respected, worthy and adored.

CRASH—All the traumatic pain that lived on the periphery of my life squeezed in on me. A choir blasted: You are such a fucking idiot, despicable, disgusting, dirty, useless. You are the worst of the worst.

He never explained, and he never called me again.

I didn't know then but I do know now: Between the abuses of my father and the fanciful narratives of my mother, I didn't stand a chance. In the dating arena I was crippled. Sex and love swirled together like a marble cake. And because I couldn't distinguish one from the other, blaming my shortcomings had become a reflex that kicked in automatically.

Me standing at the foot of my driveway on
Broadview Road with the estate in the background

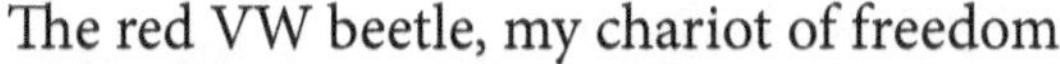

The red VW beetle, my chariot of freedom

34

THE HEALTH CLUB

While the choices I was making in my love life felt like a calamity, other parts were providing stability. The freelance situation was sustaining me financially, and the time I spent in the city helped to mitigate the Woodstock turbulence.

Thank God for my friendship with Anna. She, too, was finding her way through choppy relationship waters, and we spent endless hours talking about it. And Pilates, which had brought us together in the first place, was playing a huge role in shaping our views about fitness. Discussing "health" began to dominate our discourse almost as much as men.

With Anna and I living in such close proximity, we'd often have meals together. One evening we were curled up in her club chairs, feet tucked underneath us, with the logs blazing. Two glasses of wine sat on a small round table and "Just the Way You Are" by Billy Joel was playing in the background. Kelly, now four years old, was occupied in her room, and Anna's cockapoo, Pupper, was snuggled as close to the fire as she could be.

Earlier that day we'd been talking about what led us to our passion for exercise. Anna had cited her childhood dance classes, which she continued taking into her adult life. "It kept me in shape for my modeling assignments," she said.

Our conversation was so inspiring that I picked up on it now, in her living room. I explained to Anna that movement was intrinsic for me—as essential as breathing, smelling, tasting, hearing, seeing, touching and feeling. "It's a thirst I have to quench," I said.

I recounted to her how I single-mindedly learned to dance like the Black girls and became the captain of the cheerleaders in high school, and how in college I found my modern dance elective like a heat-seeking missile finds its target. As I got deeper into the subject of my dance obsession, I grew more introspective. Dancing took me out of my life and into a pure, untainted and peaceful state-of-mind. Anna knew exactly what I was talking about.

"Pilates bridges dance and exercise," I said. "It combines grace and fluidity with strength and power."

We picked up our wine glasses, clinked them together and said in unity, "I'll drink to that!"

Anna left the room to check on our dinner, and when she came back, she suggested I grab my glass and follow her.

Anna was a stained glass artist; her studio was set up on the all-weather porch. She was teaching me the art, and I had a work-in-progress on the table. I had no trouble drawing the pattern and choosing the colored glass, but cutting it, wrapping the edges with thin strips of copper foil and evenly soldering was not as easy as Anna made it look. I took a peek at my project, but Anna wanted me to see her latest piece, which was beautiful. It needed some final touches, and she asked if I minded if she did a little work on it. Of course I didn't.

My thoughts continued to race. As I grabbed another log to toss on the fire, I laughed to myself: My mind was ablaze just like the flames I was stoking. When Anna returned, I continued my stream of consciousness. I told her that Pilates was designed to enhance the body's natural way of moving, both laterally and circuitously. "The concept of strengthening from a center makes so much sense."

Anna reminded me that when she started doing Pilates with me, she had a hamstring injury. "Pilates healed me," she said.

The next day, after my class, Anna and I picked up coffees and headed out of Woodstock for another aimless drive. As she made the right turn onto West Hurley Road, my attention was drawn to the golf course on my left. I noted the vast, open space, the groomed landscape with its rolling hills and perfectly shaped sand traps. "I have literally no interest in golf," I said. "It seems so boring, and you don't have to be fit to play. Did you ever notice how out of shape these guys are?"

Unwittingly I'd sparked another conversation about fitness. It had occurred to me that most exercise venues were geared toward men. When I mentioned this to Anna, she concurred. We wondered: "Where do women go to exercise?" The YWCA, gymnasiums, body-building gyms? The Jack LaLanne show came to mind, and we both cracked up. We spent the next few minutes making fun of Jack's jumpsuit, funny soft shoes and bulging muscles. "Women don't want big muscles like that," I said. "We want to be long, lean and strong."

At that moment I noticed a building with a "For Rent" sign on it. Anna must've seen it, too, because we both blurted out, "Wouldn't it be cool if we could open a fitness place for women?"

That idea was the start of another nonstop discussion. We spent every waking hour evolving our vision. It would be a scaled-down gym where in addition to weights we would offer classes in Pilates, dance and other forms of exercise. Recently, Anna had gotten a juicer and was experimenting with different fruits and vegetables. "We could have a juice bar with health foods," she said.

"We could call it Body Works!" I said.

I didn't know then but I do know now: This was way before the advent of health clubs. We would have been ahead of our time if we'd gone through with it.

I designed a logo and wrote a mission statement: Body Works would be a place that promoted wellbeing and body awareness through fitness and nutrition.

But how were we going to do this? Between us we didn't have that kind of money. So Anna presented the idea to her stepfather, who said he'd consider funding our project, but first he needed to see a business plan. Neither of us had any experience with generating a document of that sort, and it felt like a daunting undertaking. For the next couple of weeks we continued tossing around ideas and dreaming. But the business plan became too big of an obstacle. And then Anna announced that she didn't want to be obligated to her stepfather in that way. Before long we forgot about it.

I didn't know then but I do know now: Expressing myself through my body remained undamaged throughout my life. It was a code by which I lived, a touchstone, a direct line to my soul—no matter what else was happening or how confused or hurt I was. And it still is.

35

CHARLES STREET

It was 1979, less than a year after my divorce, and my time in Woodstock was beginning to sour. Outside of my friendship with Anna, there was little keeping me there. Pilates was a treasured hobby, not a career path. Before Woodstock had come into my life, I had ambitions to become an art director or an illustrator. Now I felt like that could only happen in NYC. I was confident that with the connections I'd kept, and the new ones I'd made, it was possible to fulfill my aspirations. Everything pointed to moving back. But there was one problem: I still had a few months left on my lease.

I had an idea: What if I could find someone in Manhattan who wanted to swap their apartment for my house in Woodstock? I placed an ad in the *Village Voice*—one ad, one time. A couple who had an apartment on Charles Street in the West Village answered it. After my landlord gave his consent, I made the deal, sight unseen. My housing angels had come through again—or so I thought.

My new home was a one-bedroom on the top floor of a small building. My father helped move me in. My mattress went on the living room floor, along with the few pieces of furniture that I had accumulated. I piled my many boxes in the small bedroom off the kitchen and left them unpacked because I had an early dinner date with a friend. My father was heading to a meeting, so I said a quick good-bye and dashed down the block to Elephant & Castle.

When I came back several hours later, I turned on the lights to find the kitchen crawling with gigantic cockroaches. I'd never seen that many bugs; they were everywhere, including in the bedroom where they were swarming over my boxes. There were so many I couldn't help stepping on them, and the crunching sound made me want to barf. I ran out to the corner bodega, bought a can of Raid and sprayed everything. The apartment reeked, and I was sure I'd suffocate from the pesticide fumes. I pushed my mattress right under the window in the living room, opened it all the way and prayed I wouldn't die. As I lay there in the dark, I would have sworn the creepy critters were walking all over me. I hardly slept a wink that night.

I woke up to cockroach carcasses all over the apartment: The Raid had done its job. Clean-up was delayed by my gagging every other second. What a way to start a day. But I was not going to let a few bugs spoil this exciting moment. Here I was, back in the city!

That day I was starting my week at *Psychology Today*, and the following week I had an interview scheduled for a freelance gig at Milton Glaser's studio. I bounded out of the building, down the broad staircase and onto the village streets, practically skipping past all the iconic shops that gave the neighborhood its distinctive character.

The *Village Voice* was right around the corner, and I'd pass the Village Vanguard daily. Nearby was the American Bar, a restaurant that Bob and I had frequented. It had big barrels of peanuts throughout, and patrons were encouraged to discard the shells on the floor.

Getting to the tables or the bathroom was accompanied by a crackling symphony.

Speeding uptown on the subway mirrored my new sense of forward mobility. I was where I belonged; I had history and momentum on my side. My singleness no longer felt like a predicament, and that dark Woodstock cloud had drifted away. I was starting over.

I rekindled friendships I'd left behind two years prior. It was after a night out socializing that I came home to find that I couldn't get into my apartment. Someone had stuck toothpicks into the lock and broken them off so I couldn't get them out, nor could I get my key in the lock. It took me a second to realize it was deliberate.

The hair on the back of my neck stood up, and I swung around expecting to see someone sharing the hallway with me. No one was there, so I ran down to the basement, found the superintendent and told him what was happening. He grabbed his blowtorch and followed me upstairs. Clearly he'd dealt with this sort of thing before. The blowtorch burned the wood, and voila, I unlocked the door.

I turned the knob and slowly peered inside. My apartment had been ransacked. The still unopened boxes had been slashed, and my belongings were strewn all over the room. My stereo was gone, and a huge, scary boot print was on my mattress. The thief had climbed down the fire escape from the roof and entered through the window, which was wide open. He then must have taken a moment to put the toothpicks into my lock to deter me were I to interrupt him. Picturing this strange person going through my things spooked me and made me feel violated. I could not stay there for one more minute. I slammed the window shut, threw some clothes and toiletries into my car and drove to my parents' house. The next day I returned, packed up my stuff and moved back to Maplewood.

Now what?

I didn't know then but I do know now: Even though I'd been out of my parents' home for many years, my father still had the ability to undermine, unsettle and, at times, completely topple my world.

My interview at Milton Glaser's went well, and I started working there immediately. So I wasted no time getting down to the business of finding another apartment. I combed through the *New York Times* "For Rent" section, narrowing my search to between 23rd and 34th Streets. It took a few weeks, but I found a studio on 22nd Street close to 1st Avenue.

My spanking new apartment was on the third floor of an almost-finished, six-story brick box. The smell of sheetrock, spackle, paint and dust hung in the air. I was one of a handful of pioneers living amidst the noise and ruckus. Back in Woodstock, I'd furnished the artist's studio with found objects and mixed-and-matched pieces. Now I was moving in a professional direction, and I wanted my new home to reflect that. Pottery Barn was just a few blocks north, and it had everything I needed. Soon I had a sleeper sofa and director's chairs. I chose treatments for my south-facing, oversized window.

My 10-block walk to work took me through all sorts of aromas: coffee, spices, cigars; even newspaper had a smell. The sounds of brakes squeaking, horns honking, people speaking loudly and those iron gates rolling up to open a shop all reminded me that I was back on track.

An added bonus was that my building was right around the corner from the School of Visual Arts, where I registered for an illustration class with Jim McMullen. He was a watercolorist and one of the most popular illustrators of the time—another example of a successful fine artist. I admired his work, and I was ready to learn a new medium.

I didn't know then but I do know now: My spiffy studio apartment was like an incubator where I felt safe to process my 29 years of life. I stood at a crossroads, ready to take some bold steps forward in preparation for a different future.

36

THE JOURNALS

On a Saturday afternoon in the fall of 1980, I packed up my Pinto (which I'd bought when my Beetle died) with a change of clothing and all of my journals. I was on my way to a stranger's house in Sag Harbor. It belonged to a friend of the boyfriend of my new friend Kathy.

The house, a neat cottage with a white picket fence, was on a main street right outside of town. I parked in front, found the key and made my way to the door. Fiddling with the lock, I stepped inside. The house felt cold and dark—or was it I who felt that way?

My stack of over a dozen journals had followed me from Brooklyn Heights to Woodstock and on to Manhattan. In seven years I'd amassed a haphazard collection in all colors, shapes and sizes. They'd gotten me through my moves, my divorce and the never-ending storm that seemed to follow me.

But I was disturbed by what I had written in them. The pages were filled with my darkest thoughts, and I worried that the "voices" the journals contained were proof that I was truly crazy. I sometimes wondered if I might be schizophrenic or have multiple per-sonality disorder—a thought too deplorable to consider. I was deeply ashamed of the me depicted in those pages, and I wanted to erase any evidence of her. I no longer wanted to be tortured and self-loathing. I wanted my internal life to match my external profile: an independ-ent, single, professional woman with a purpose.

I had told Kathy I needed a weekend by myself, but that was not entirely true. I was not a good liar, and I was sure the guilt had shown on my face. Even though I had permission to stay in the house, I felt like an intruder.

The hallway in which I stood led directly into a living room with a low ceiling. A quick scan took in a lot of wood and chintz. But I was looking for something specific. When Kathy had told me about a weekend she'd spent at this house, she mentioned they'd sat around a quaint fireplace. A plan that required a fireplace had been percolating in my head. And here it was in the center of the wall opposite me. All the curtains were drawn; I walked over and parted them to see how close the neighbors were. I didn't want to be watched.

I carried the few things I had brought with me upstairs to a small bedroom and took a walk into town. It was late afternoon, and the weather was bleak, though I barely noticed my surroundings. Even as I sat at the edge of the dock overlooking the tranquil water, my reason for being in Sag Harbor was foremost in my mind.

I picked up dinner from a take-out restaurant and made my way back to the house. With my jacket still on, I sat at the kitchen table, took the plastic utensils and ate right out of the containers. I was intent on leaving no trace.

I'd decided that waiting until the neighbors were sleeping would call less attention to me. That gave me a few hours and an opportunity to take a last look at my journals. I was determined to do this thing, but it definitely seemed insane, similar to the way it had seemed when I was writing the many entries the books held.

At 10 P.M. I closed the last journal, and with my hand still on the back cover, I took a moment to reflect. Was I sure about this? Yes, I was. I gathered them up, with the biggest one on the bottom, and hugged them close to my chest. I headed down to the living room. I had left the curtains drawn, so it was pitch black, but instead of turning on some lights, I found my way to the fireplace using my lighter. There I saw a scanty supply of paper, kindling and logs, and for a moment I thought my plan would be thwarted.

Since I hadn't taken supplies into account, I worked with what I had and was able to make a small fire. Then I began feeding it with my journals—first the pages, then the covers, book by book. I poked and prodded the paper, keeping it burning until the last page disappeared into ashes. The flames had done what I needed them to do. As the fire's warmth and light bathed the front of my body, I had a sense that the darkness surrounding me was merging with the darkness that had spawned the journals. Together it was all passing up the chimney and out into the darkness of the night.

With just a few hours till sunrise, my tears kept me from sleeping. When morning came, I didn't have a plan; I just knew I had to leave.

I packed up my things, collected the garbage and cleaned out the fireplace. I didn't want to return to the city with any remnants of what I had done, so I found a dumpster behind some shops in town. Then I grabbed a coffee and a cheese danish and headed back to 22nd Street.

I didn't know then but I do know now: The "voices" were the verbalization of the trauma that began before I had words. They were a pure depiction of my childhood experience. Having them on paper did, in a way, save me, but they also revealed how warped my mind had become. I believed that destroying the books would free me from the anguish that had driven me to write them in the first place.

37

STAN

When I was still working at *Psychology Today* and shuttling between Woodstock and the city, I befriended Doug. He was the other paste-ups and mechanicals artist, and he, too, had artistic ambitions. He was my closest male friend; we spent a lot of time together outside of the office, and we knew a lot about each other.

When Doug told me he was seeing a therapist, I was curious. I'd never heard of therapy, but his description sounded like something I needed.

"I'm depressed a lot, and Stan is helping me," he said.

I had never referred to myself as "depressed." When I felt bad emotionally, I'd call it "feeling down" or in a "bad mood." From the way Doug described it, I thought I, too, must be suffering from bouts of depression. Was that why I felt snatched out of my life—withdrawn, shut down and despondent?

"What do you talk to Stan about?" I asked Doug.

"Anything that's bothering me," he said, and I was hooked.

"How does it work? How often do you go? How much does it cost?"

When Doug gave me Stan's number, I was still living in Woodstock, so I'd stashed it away. As soon as I knew I was moving back to the city, I found it and called to make an appointment.

It turned out that Stan's office was in a pre-war building a couple blocks west of Milton's studio, so I was able to walk over after work. It was a small, warmly lit room with a somber hue. The furniture was dark and comfortable. Stan looked to be in his mid-40s, with unkempt brown hair and a cropped beard. His slightly rumpled shirt was tucked into loose pants fastened over a bulging belly. He wore a button-down sweater with a shawl collar and well-worn, gum-soled shoes. Being in the presence of a sensitive man who was receptive to my thoughts was novel, and Stan's mild and patient manner engaged me. It seemed the decision to solicit his help was the right one, and I never missed an appointment.

When I'd enter his office, Stan was usually at his desk, located diagonally across from the door. After we exchanged greetings, he'd move to a wingback chair, and I sat on the sofa opposite him. My initial sessions were marked by uncertainty. I wasn't sure what to discuss, so I stuck to my social and love life.

One evening, I shared that I was struggling with a decision—I'd been offered a full-time job at Sudler and Hennessy, a pharmaceutical advertising agency uptown. I'd still be in the production department, which didn't concern me as much as other aspects. I'd only worked in publishing and design, and I saw my future there. I wasn't sure how my creative aspirations would fit into the advertising field. But I was most conflicted over moving from Milton's prestigious and high-profile studio to what I ascertained to be the dull and lack-luster pharmaceutical industry.

"Do you think I should take a job with a company that has no name recognition?" I asked Stan.

He asked in response what I saw as my career path, and I explained that I wanted to make my way out of production and into creative.

"Which company do you think would best get you there?" I tried to describe the competitive atmosphere at Milton's studio. The "talent bar" was set high, and Milton was an intimidating figure. "It's pretty obvious that I will not be given that opportunity there," I said.

It was unprecedented for me to have a pragmatic source like Stan. Our subsequent strategizing steered me to my answer, and I took the job at Sudler and Hennessy. It was a decision that would improve the arc of my professional life.

Stan's rational point-of-view was in such contrast to the chaos and delusion of my father's world that I began sharing more exchanges with him. I started with the pressure my father had imposed on me to become his partner in all his "business" endeavors.

"Your father has the right to express himself and make requests," Stan said, "but you have the right to oppose or decline those demands."

It took a while for me to grasp what Stan was saying. First, he was implying that I had a choice, and even more profound, he was saying I had a right.

I didn't know then but I do know now: Since I'd never had anyone to talk to about my father, I had no perspective. The notion that there was a "me" in the equation did not exist before Stan. He might've been the first adult who made me feel visible.

At first, I could only speak of my father in vague and superficial terms. I told Stan about his eccentricities, his unconventional ideas and his strong opinions. It felt good to have a person listen to me. With Stan's support I ventured further. In one session, I reported a phone conversation with Dad where he said, "What's the point of working for an advertising agency? What good is it doing in the world?" He called advertising "conventional, mediocre, meaningless and unimportant." Then, "You'll never go anywhere working for someone else."

"Is this how he always talks to you?"

I wondered why Stan was asking me that question. "Yes," I replied.

"How does that make you feel?"

"I don't like it," came out of nowhere.

Those simple words shook me. They were foreign, and after speaking them, I found myself waiting for some force to strike me dead. When that didn't happen, a tiny part of me began poking its head out of a hiding place. As I talked more to Stan, words like "caught," "suffocated" and "trapped" began showing up.

I didn't know then but I do know now: Stan was the first person to pierce the seal I'd placed on my true feelings. They were locked away so deep that I had no access to them.

Within the sheltered walls of Stan's office, I began to perceive my feelings with more acuity. One day I blurted out, "My father terrifies me!"

Stan reminded me of the original reason I'd sought him out and delicately suggested there might be a link between the depression I'd complained about and my father. I was stunned. I'd never made that connection. My "moods" had been a mystery; I viewed them as an affliction due entirely to my deficiencies. Considering that my father could be the source was an alien concept.

The bolder I became, the more I noticed something strange happening within me. As the words emerged from my subconscious, my conscious mind floated away. As I was speaking, it felt like there was a two-second delay, like a beat was skipping. Something was out of sync, but I couldn't tell what it was.

During one session, the split was so profound that I couldn't ignore it. I'd been whisked so far out of my body that I felt myself to be up in the far right-hand corner of the room. For the rest of the session I hovered up there, hearing myself and seeing myself, but from afar. I had to tell Stan. I stopped mid-sentence, pointed to the ceiling and said, "I'm up there!"

I didn't know then but I do know now: This was the clearest manifestation of my dissociation and the first time I sensed it consciously.

I expected shame to follow the huge leap I'd just taken. Stan had to be thinking that I was in fact crazy and needed to be institutionalized. But instead he was asking, "Where are you?"

I pointed up again and immediately looked back at him. I barely blinked, and my diaphragm stopped moving as I waited. Stan tilted his head. He appeared pensive. His eyes were sympathetic.

"Have you ever considered that your father is abusive?"

What was he saying? What did that mean? I stared at him from above.

He must have known, and he gave me a moment. My mouth began to move, and words passed through my lips. "Are you saying that my father intentionally hurts me?" From a very injured place I whispered, "Does that mean he doesn't love me?"

It didn't matter what Stan said after that. All the usual sensations associated with the crashes that had come with each of my father's assaults returned. I was unreachable. Before I left, he made sure I was all right. What could I possibly say other than I was fine. I didn't know how to tell him I wanted to be a ghost that no one could see.

I dragged myself through the dingy hallway and waited with unusual patience for the elevator, which thankfully was empty. I had no idea if I were alive or dead—everything around me stopped. The buildings liquified, the lights dimmed, the loudness that defined NYC life was silenced. It was me and only me passing through this unrecognizable world. Undetected, I walked into my lobby, rode up to my apartment, sat on my sleeper sofa and peered into nothing.

Subsequent meetings with Stan focused on this bombshell. For a time it was so hot I couldn't touch it. I was blindsided by the notion that my father's abuse was meant to hurt me. Like a movie with an unexpected ending, I had to rewind the film and watch it from the beginning in order to make sense of the unforeseen conclusion.

It took many sessions for Stan to guide me to a new state of mind. When he cited other patients who had also been victims of abuse, it helped: I wasn't alone. However, when he said, "In situations like yours, I usually encourage a confrontation with the perpetrator," it was a setback.

Such an encounter was unfathomable. The terror associated with expressing myself about these things to my father was insurmountable. To face him felt like stepping off a cliff with no parachute. The prospect shut everything down.

I explained this to Stan, adding that I wouldn't know what to say. He understood that there was work to do. Together, he and I played out all the angles until I began to feel empowered. Until I could envision myself making my case and my father hearing me. I planned a visit home.

I didn't know then but I do know now: I'd never found a way to stand up to my father, and I'd never fully advocated for myself. Anything I'd managed to accomplish I did by blindly charging forward—and away from him. I remember that with Stan's new tools and my broadened perspective, I was full of hope and optimism.

38

VAN NESS COURT II

"If you're honest with your feelings, they will be met with warmth and compassion." That was the one statement that Stan made that I clung to. It sat foremost in my mind as I drove to Maplewood. I made the left-hand turn that put me on Van Ness Court and parked my car. Before I opened the door, I sat back in my seat, closed my eyes and tried to collect myself.

I repeated my own pep talk: I have the right to express myself, and it can only amount to a better relationship with my father. "And whatever you do, don't cry!" I told myself.

After I grabbed my things from the backseat, I headed down the hill and continued my words of encouragement. When I reached my parents' garden apartment I rang the bell. My mother opened the door with her perfect smile, her beautiful teeth and her recently coiffed hair. She was wearing a plaid button-down shirt tucked neatly into her jeans to accentuate her tiny waist. As she always did, she checked me out from head to toe. Her opinion mattered to me. Her disapproval, which she did not hesitate to share, could bury me. Today, with her heavy

Polish accent, she said, "You look good."

I didn't know then but I do know now: I had yet to understand the giant and destructive role my mother played in my emotional life.

I followed her through the living room, which narrowed into the dining room. My father's papers were spread out on the dinner table. The air was stagnant and smelled of dust. Through a doorway to the right we stepped into the tight kitchen. While my mom tidied up, I took a seat at the minute table with my back to the refrigerator. Then she joined me, sitting in the chair opposite me, facing away from the door that led outside. With our knees practically touching, she asked, "So, how are you doing?"

She wanted to know about my new apartment and if I'd started my new job. Then came the "boyfriend" question, which annoyed me unless I had one. "Are you hungry?" she asked. I nodded my head yes. She got up and made me a turkey sandwich with cheese and mayo on a Kaiser roll. As I ate, it occurred to me that she had no idea why I had come home.

"Where's Daddy?" I asked. She said he'd be back for supper.

Eventually I made my way upstairs into what had once been my bedroom. All the furniture was where I'd left it, but the surfaces were cluttered with papers, cardboard, ink bottles, rags, rulers, a pencil sharpener, stapler, pens and paintbrushes. The airbrush, which was connected to the compressor on the floor, was still under my desk. The bed I was supposed to sleep in was disheveled. There was no sheet on the old blue mattress; my blanket was threadbare and rolled up haphazardly; the flat, stained pillow had no pillowcase. Large poster boards leaned against the furniture and any exposed wall. I recognized my father's distinctive lettering and drawing style, but I couldn't tell what he'd been doing. And I didn't want to know.

Dinner was tense, but dinner with my father was always tense. I had rehearsed what I would say many times, but now, in his presence, I couldn't retrieve a single word. The blankness turned into panic: Maybe I won't do it this time. Maybe I'll do it another time.

I went upstairs, closed my bedroom door and sat on the bed. My thoughts were ricocheting. It took some time to recover my resolve. Then I told myself: "It's now or never."

I planted my feet on the floor, straightened my knees, smoothed my clothes and walked toward my parents' bedroom, where they were watching television. The door to their room was open. I reminded myself again, "Whatever you do, don't cry!"

I didn't know then but I do know now: Stan was the only champion I'd had, the only person ever to acknowledge that my father's treatment of me was wrong. When I arrived that night at my parents' house, every ounce of my being believed that what I was doing would result in a better relationship with my father. I wanted that more than anything in the world.

39

AGAINST PROTOCAL

My dad's hideous cackling coupled with my mother's indifference sent me into a new stratosphere. I arrived at Stan's office utterly broken. Still in a dissociated state, I stammered through a recount of the dizzying episode in my parents' bedroom. Stan listened, and when I finished, I was desperate for his feedback.

"Your father is a severely abusive man who cares little for your wellbeing," he said. "I'm certain he will never take responsibility for his actions, and he'll continue to hurt you."

Then he looked deep into my eyes. "I'm going to tell you something I've never told another patient," he said. His tone was earnest, solemn and full of compassion. My interlocked fingers tightened as astonishing words left his lips: "I don't think you should ever go home again."

The proposal was so startling I almost floated away. But before me sat the only person on the planet who understood my life. The only human being who wanted to protect me from further harm. A man who believed what I was saying. I trusted him, and he was telling me that the situation with my father was bad enough that he, Stan, had to go against protocol. All I could do was take in the moment. I had no response.

The notion of never going home again was too much to abide. The dream of reconciliation with my father was still fresh. Even though I knew intellectually it would never happen, I couldn't abandon it. The part of Stan's message that registered was that my father was, in fact, a danger. The least I could imagine doing was putting a physical distance between him and me.

I didn't know then but I do know now: The nothingness implied by a full break with my father was a step I was unable to take.

INTERLUDE

Stan had opened the door—but only a crack.

I never confronted my father again. Our relationship remained flawed and broken. I did make some futile attempts at speaking to Mom about the abuse allegation. She didn't take me seriously, not the way I wanted her to. "Celia doesn't get along with her father," was the way she phrased it, and I went along with her. I did not yet have the will or the understanding to refute her. Denial continued to blanket everything.

By the age of 30 my ability to compartmentalize was well honed, and I set my sights on my professional ambitions. Over several years I worked my way up to assistant art director in the pharmaceutical advertising field before I began a freelance graphic design business. As for my love life, for about five years I went in and out of some complicated and interesting relationships. I was intent on improving my skills with men and not repeating the mistakes of the past. By the time I met my future husband, I had learned a lot and did not fall into any of those old traps. We were married in 1985. We had our first daughter in

1986 and our second in 1991. For me, marriage and parenthood were everything I had always wanted, and I expected the problems from my past to fade away.

My mom paid regular visits with Phyllis, my grandmother and other friends. Interactions with my dad were limited to big family events.

Over time, my father's mental and physical state deteriorated. He was struggling with heart disease and suffered a serious heart attack. His delusions multiplied, causing him to be more erratic, demanding and belligerent. My mother was more forthcoming about the difficulties she was having with him. She eventually moved out of their garden apartment and in with Phyllis, whose husband had died several years before. By 1992, my mother and father were legally divorced. I wish I could say that my mother left my father because of what he had done to me, but that was not the case.

My father died of a heart attack in 1994. When the news came, my family had just moved into a new house in Westchester County. Unpacked boxes were everywhere, and our neighbor was at the front door with a welcome basket. I let my husband greet her as I found my way up to our bedroom. I threw myself across our king-size bed and wept for what seemed like hours.

The next morning I awoke with the clearest, most visceral sense that the world had changed. As I stepped out of the house and down our flagstone walkway, the air brushing my arms felt like silk. The gravity that kept me pinned to the ground lifted just enough for my feet to glide above the pavement. My energy pulsed out to the edges of the universe.

It was grand, and I expected my father's death to erase all those punishing decades. The monster was gone, and with him would go all the torment, pain and fear that had hijacked my life. But that did not turn out to be true.

— 292 —

PART 3

40

PHYLLIS'S FUNERAL

"I can't imagine how my mother will be when they put Phyllis into the ground," I said to my husband on the way to pick up Mom before the funeral.

It was 2013, and Phyllis had died. She and my mother had been living together for the past two decades. Neither of them had remarried. They functioned as a couple, doing everything together. They had worked for the same company, they had shared friends, and they had been travel-mates.

There were about 30 people standing at the graveside. It was a typical Jewish ceremony, with the Rabbi saying the traditional prayers. They lowered the casket, and we each threw a shovelful of dirt into the grave. The sound was harsh and hollow as it hit the coffin.

Standing next to my mother, with my arm around her shoulders, I felt enormous. Mom had been barely five feet tall in her youth. Now she was even tinier.

On that chilly October day, she wore her warm khaki-green jacket with a matching fur collar. Before we left for the funeral, she had asked me to smooth out her thin, red hair so it lay flat in the back. Standing beside her, I couldn't see her eyes through her rose-colored glasses, but I could tell she was not crying. How could that be?

At the luncheon that followed, Mom was her usual charming self. She flitted around, talking to Phyllis's sons and their families. She checked in with all of her and Phyllis's friends. I watched in dismay. When she returned to our end of the table, I leaned over and asked, "Are you okay?"

"I'm okay!" she replied.

I asked her often in the days that followed: "How are you doing?"

Her answer was always the same: "I'm fine!"

Finally I asked, "Don't you miss Phyllis?"

"I miss watching TV at night and eating ice cream with her," she replied. "We had a good time and lots of laughs!"

This was her answer whenever I asked about Phyllis. I didn't understand. Since the day I was born, their lives had been intertwined. To me, it seemed as though Phyllis was the most important person in Mom's life. I expected her to be grief-stricken and inconsolable. I expected to hear a stream of fond memories. I thought there was more to their relationship than television and ice cream. My mother's passivity rocked something fundamental within me, and I couldn't shake the disturbance. What else didn't I know?

I had to face my own indifference, too. It was notable but not surprising. As far back as I could remember, I'd been guarded in Phyllis's presence; a deep resentment sat at my base like silt sits at the bottom of a pond. Whenever it got stirred up, I'd wait for it to settle down.

Mom's apathy was causing a new sediment cloud to billow, and it was not clearing. The particles were so opaque and choking I had to pay attention. I'd never examined their relationship or its impact on me. Their friendship was simply a part of my life that I'd blindly accepted. Sometimes it was easy, but more often it was not, and I was not inclined to ask why.

I recalled several exchanges with Mom years before Phyllis died. Mom and Phyllis regularly visited our family. Sometimes they came for the day and other times for the weekend, but they always came together. One day I felt compelled to ask my mother, "Can you please come without Phyllis sometimes?"

"I can't leave her alone," she'd say. "She'll feel bad, and she always takes me to visit her sons." It was final; there was no discussion. The need that burned in me had fallen on deaf ears, so I buried the wound it inflicted.

But now Phyllis was gone, and a soft, auspicious voice began to speak: Maybe now I will have my mother to myself. An unusual lightness took the place of a more common heaviness, and with it came an epiphany. This was something I'd always wanted, and now it felt possible.

At the time I lived in an old farmhouse with a wraparound porch that overlooked 15 magnificent acres. I visualized Mom and I spending hours together lounging and talking while taking in the view. She'd accompany me as I went about my life. We'd prepare chicken soup, chopped liver and other Eastern European delicacies, just the two of us. I was so overcome with joy that I expected the heavens to open up, sunbeams to stream through the thick clouds, and angels to sing.

I would have bet anything that was going to happen.

But it didn't. In the six years between Phyllis's and my mother's death, Mom and I did spend time alone together, but the moments I ached for never came to pass. Instead, my time with her remained troubled.

The voice that had spoken auspiciously as a whisper now began to shout: "There's something you're not seeing!"

I didn't know then but I do know now: HERE IS WHERE MY TRUE STORY BEGINS.

41

ABUSE

A week before Phyllis died, my husband and I visited her in the hospital. Howie, Phyllis's older son, was there by her bedside. He was his usual affable self, but outside her room he confided that he was leaving. "I was supposed to be staying for several more days," he told me, "but my mother is being so abusive that I'm going home today!"

I'd never heard Howie say the word "abusive." I was struck by how effortlessly it flowed out of his mouth, as though it weren't the first time he'd said it, and as though I wouldn't be surprised to hear it. But I was. My mother was the only person in my family who I'd spoken to about my father's abusive tendencies. I'd never had a conversation with Phyllis's sons about it and certainly never in the context of my feelings toward Phyllis. But here Howie was pointing out that his mother was treating him so badly that he had to leave. "Yeah, she can be pretty nasty," I said, too flustered to continue the conversation.

A few days later, my mother joined Phyllis in the hospital. She hadn't been feeling well, and when she went to see her doctor, he determined it was her heart. He directed her to a cardiologist, who sent her straight to the hospital where she was to be given a pacemaker. Mom was in relatively good health, and this new development alarmed me.

The following week, when my husband and I arrived for my mother's procedure, both of Phyllis's sons were already at the hospital. Before we went to Mom's room, we went upstairs to see Phyllis. She was in dire shape. She had been given morphine, but she was moaning in pain and gasping for air. I'd never seen a person in the throes of death, and I stood paralyzed in the doorway, horrified by what I was witnessing. I struggled with whether I should tell Mom. I decided she needed to know, and I braced myself for her reaction.

At first Mom seemed to hear me, but then her eyes glazed over. She just stared at me. I asked the nurses if Mom could see Phyllis for the last time. My request was denied because they had to monitor my mother's heart. When I explained this to Mom, I was sure she'd beg them to let her see Phyllis, but there was no reaction, none whatsoever. I hadn't yet encountered Mom's indifference in the face of losing Phyllis.

Monica, one of Phyllis's daughters-in-law, came down to Mom's room, and in the course of our conversation she said, "Phyllis has been very abusive to everyone, including your mother."

There was that word again. And this time from Henry's wife. And did she say Phyllis was abusive to my mom?

Abuse was an intricate and loaded subject for me. Thirty-three years had passed since Stan cited abuse as the agent of my problems with my father. When my mother thwarted all my attempts to petition her support, I relegated the whole "issue" to a secret place. The emotions associated with it were trapped in a labyrinth with no exit. They banged into walls and slammed into dead-ends. Yet here I was, amidst people who were freely throwing the word around—and in reference to my mother.

So when Monica said, "I don't understand why your mom takes it," I was ready to burst. Here was my chance to tell her about my father and even about Phyllis' abusive behavior toward me. But Monica excused herself to return to Phyllis' bedside, and I returned the whole matter to the maze.

Days after Phyllis's funeral, I had a conversation with Wanda, Mom's and Phyllis's friend. When I expressed my concerns regarding my mother's unemotional reaction to Phyllis's death, Wanda said, "The last exchange between your mother and Phyllis was bad. Phyllis implied that it was your mother who should be in the hospital bed instead of her. Your mother thought that Phyllis had given her the 'evil eye' and that was why *she* was in the hospital." Then Wanda added, "Your mother was so upset she was crying."

I had no idea such craziness went on between them. I'd never viewed their relationship in the context of abuse. But I was reminded of how menacing Phyllis had felt to me. It was conceivable that my mother had also been on the receiving end of her caustic nature. Suddenly I recalled past scenes of Phyllis's frustration and impatience with my mother. Had Mom also been a victim of abuse? This was a massive nugget—the one I'd been waiting for, the piece that held the key to Mom and me bonding. I envisioned us healing together and finally speaking about what had been unspoken.

42

THE REHAB CENTER

Before Phyllis died, had someone asked me to describe my mother, I would have gloated. "I have the best mother in the world," I'd tell them. "My mother is as gorgeous as a movie star. She's like an elegant Kewpie doll."

Then I'd go on. "Her beauty is matched by her charm. She's the nicest, most considerate person, and everyone loves her."

Whenever my friends complained about their moms, I felt lucky. "My mother doesn't bug me, and she's my best friend," I'd say. "I can talk to her about anything."

To me, my mother was perfect. My love had no conditions; I held her in the highest esteem, and she was my role model. There had never been another narrative in my head.

Due to her pacemaker, Mom had to go to a rehab center. It was a few miles from where she lived, so I already knew that, without traffic, it would take 90 minutes each way for me to visit. I planned on four hours in the car. Thank God for my music.

I was now a member of the "sandwich generation," and I'd listen intently to friends and clients who were caring for aging parents. Most of them shared the responsibility with a sibling or two. Mom's care was going to fall solely on my shoulders. But she was my mother, and I'd do anything for her.

As I drove up to the facility for the first time, I was delighted to see that it was pleasant. Inside, a friendly receptionist pointed me in the right direction. I walked through bright corridors until I reached Mom's room. She was in the bed by the window; lots of sun was streaming in. As she flashed me her beautiful smile, I was relieved to see that she was herself again.

I kissed her on the cheek. "You look great!" I said. Mom loved compliments.

I took my seat in the corner by the window, and we began to chat. She told me that our relatives, the ones who'd brought her to America, were donors to the rehab center. I'd be able to find their names engraved on one of the walls on my way out.

It felt so good to have gotten beyond Phyllis's passing and Mom's medical emergency. With the cheerful atmosphere and the effortless conversation, I thought, "Caring for her might not be so bad."

Then an administrator appeared at the door, explaining that my mother needed to fill out a disability form. She placed the papers in front of Mom, who stared at them blankly, and then, with a tinge of alarm in her voice, said, "Celia, can you please fill this out for me?"

I asked "Why can't you do it?

"Oy, these kinds of things confuse me," she said. "Please, can you do it for me?"

Really? Had she never filled out a form before?

I knew it was a simple request, yet I felt my jaw clench as I picked up the papers. She's just asking me to fill out some stupid forms, I thought.

Yet a palpable sense of defiance made me want to resist her.

This tug-of-war between what I should do and what I wanted to do was familiar. It was reminiscent of other times when her incompetent ways caused a tightness in me. Like when she'd come to my house and act like she'd never been there before. She'd stand in the middle of the kitchen with a fork, or a dish, or food that clearly belonged in the fridge, and act like she had no idea where any of those items should go. It irked me then, and it was irking me now. More than irking. I wanted to blast her. But within seconds, guilt made me turn my ire inward. It was me who was at fault, and I labelled myself impatient, intolerant and mean. This is what you do for the people you love, I told myself.

I commenced to put pen to paper and entered the answers. When I reached the part where I needed work details, social security and insurance policy numbers, I turned to my mother. She appeared undone. "Oy, oy, I don't know where to find them," she said, her tone tinged with panic.

The shift in her voice and her helpless demeanor intensified the tightness I'd felt moments before. And from within a spinning vortex, I stared at this confusing creature. This unhinged, child-like version of Mom raised my internal temperature to boiling, and I had no idea why.

I searched for her purse and fished out her wallet, which she fumbled through before handing me what I needed.

While I was delivering the finished forms to the administrator, my mother's roommate returned from lunch and took the visitor's seat by her own bed. She was nice and quite chatty. When Mom shuffled her way to the bathroom and closed the door, the woman leaned toward me and said, "Your mother is a star. Everyone loves her."

"Of course she is, and of course they do," I thought. I did what I'd always done: I thanked the woman and expected to forget about it. But that day the words had sharp edges. The roommate might as well have scratched her nails on a blackboard or hit a nerve while drilling one of my teeth. The tightness returned, and it wouldn't loosen.

I'd teetered on the fulcrum between disparate versions of my mother before. But until this day I was able to steady myself quickly and move on. Now I couldn't recover. There was something about the duality of my perfect mother and the sputtering, inept, fumbler that rattled me. But why did that matter? Why was I so critical and intolerant? Where was the compassion I should have had for my aging mom? The tightness wouldn't let go.

On the way home, I was so distracted that I didn't notice the traffic, which normally triggered me to spew obscenities. Instead I was consumed by what had been set off in that room. Whatever it was, it felt like a burden I'd been carrying most of my life. It felt almost primal.

My curiosity was aroused and for the first time I wondered about my mother—who she really was and the role she'd really played in my life.

I likened the tightness to a knotted tassel that would have to be untangled one strand at a time. This would be the first strand.

43

THE TRIANGLE

Instead of the peaceful time I'd anticipated with Mom, I stood at a most precarious crossroad, pondering the existential question of my reality. I wondered about my childhood. Had it been different from the one I thought I had? I was aware of the damage inflicted by my father, but what about my mother and Phyllis?

Before Phyllis died, had I been asked to describe them, I would have said, "I don't remember a time that Phyllis was not part of my life. She and my mom were best friends, and they were lucky to have each other."

Then I might go on to elaborate their differences. My mother was the pretty one, I'd explain, always a few steps ahead in hairstyles and fashion. Like Mom, Phyllis was petite, but her stooped posture and ample breasts gave her a heavier appearance. She wore clothes that hid her figure, which made her look matronly. Where my mother exuded grace and charm, Phyllis had a sour disposition and a sharp tongue. Where my mother was sunny, Phyllis was gloomy. Her light blue eyes and her long, thin hands were her most striking features. I was drawn to how her diamond ring sparkled on her slender finger.

If I'd been asked what Phyllis meant to me, without thinking I'd say, "She was like my second mother."

But I was thinking about everything now. I realized that the "second mother" role was the premise around which my relationship with Phyllis had been shaped. And it was my mother who had thrust it on me. I'd never been asked if I felt that way or if I liked Phyllis having that authority over me. Which she did. And I didn't like it.

I found myself reflecting on the mysterious and ubiquitous tension I'd always felt around Phyllis. During my teenage years there were times when her intrusive behavior, her grouchy disposition, her predilection for kvetching and her judgmental nature suffocated me. When the pressure would build up, I'd seek out my mother and ask her to intervene. But I never got the relief I was hoping for. Instead, "Phyllis is your second mother," she'd say. "She loves you like a daughter." That was that, a fait accompli, followed by my own whirling guilt tornado. Second-guessing would commence: Why should I have any grievances? And why didn't I appreciate everything Phyllis did for me? Blame and shame were imbedded in my relationship with Mom and Phyllis. That was the part I needed to explore: Where did I fit into that triangle?

Each attempt to look back came up cold. It was similar to the wall I'd recently slammed into when thinking about my mother. Now it seemed as though my perception of Mom and Phyllis's friendship was just as shallow and vague. There was no data.

Until, unexpectedly, cracks began appearing in what had previously seemed impervious. As if refusing to remain buried, old narratives and disjointed memories began seeping through the fissures.

My mother's account of how she and Phyllis met showed up first. They lived in the same apartment building on Hillside Avenue. "The building was full of refugees, and we were all friends," my mother would tell me. Gossip among the neighbors began to buzz about the new couple who had moved in down the hall. As a child the wife had lost her whole family in the Holocaust and had spent the war years alone, living in a barn with farm animals.

"It was a terrible story," my mom would say. Then she'd lean in close and tell me that during the war she'd heard rumors of such a girl hiding all by herself. And with great fanfare she'd add, "Can you believe I knew about Phyllis while Grandma and I were still in Poland?"

"Even though we were very different, we became the best of friends," she'd say. "I was a big city girl, and Phyllis was a peasant." She relished calling Phyllis a peasant.

From that point forward my mother and Phyllis were inseparable. From Newark, my parents and I moved three more times, and each time we either shared a house with or lived next door to Phyllis and her husband. The garden apartments in Maplewood would be the farthest apart my mother and Phyllis had ever lived: eight units between them. They both got their first jobs in the same liquor distribution company and worked for the same businesses thereafter.

Phyllis was a homemaker and, unlike my mom, a great cook. Our families observed holidays and celebrated special occasions together. Phyllis would often take care of me, and frequently I'd eat dinner at her house. She had two sons who were younger than I, and I was referred to as their big sister. Phyllis enjoyed making me sweaters, fixing my clothes and combing my hair. And she never missed a birthday.

Those were the facts, but I knew there was more digging to do. I had to look beyond my surface recollections and search for my own memories. Soon one led to another.

Memory: I'm ten years old, sitting in Phyllis' living room watching Leave it to Beaver. *She's sitting across from me knitting. Her fingers work the needles and yarn so nimbly that I watch her rather than the TV. I want to learn how to do that, so I ask her if she'll teach me. I nestle close to her on the couch and wait for her to hand me two long needles and a ball of bright red yarn. With her needles, she shows me how to cast on with the first stitch. She continues the same action until the needle is completely covered with yarn. It doesn't seem too hard.*

"Now you try," she says. I take my yarn and make the loop, just like she showed me. I stick the point of the needle through it and loop the yarn until my needle is fully wrapped. When I look up at her, she nods her approval.

Next, she slips the point of the other still-naked needle into the first cast-on stitch, masterfully flips the yarn across, catches that loop and slips both stitches off. She makes it look so easy and elegant.

I begin to follow her steps, but when I get to the point that I have to transfer the first stitch, I drop it. I try again, but it keeps happening. My frustration makes my hands feel clumsy. I can't knit one single stitch on the second row, and I'm losing my cast-on loops.

I can feel Phyllis's impatience. When I look up this time, I catch her frowning. "You can't knit because your fingers are fat," she tells me.

I look down at my enormous, chubby hands and say, "I'm not good at this. I hate knitting!"

Memory: Around the same age, I am standing in the bathtub washing myself when I see Phyllis and my mother, shoulder to shoulder, in the doorway. They're looking at me and speaking so softly in Polish that I can't make out what they're saying.

I continue to lather up my hands. As I make my way down my torso to my private parts, I glance in their direction. Tonight their presence embarrasses me, but there's nothing I can do about it. I begin to gently rub my soapy hand against my skin, and it produces a squeaking sound. They're still speaking Polish, but now they're pointing at me and laughing. It could've been the sound that they think is funny, but I know it's me they are laughing at. I'm familiar with their tone. They're making fun of me. I stand there, ashamed and confused.

Memory: I am a sensitive, self-conscious teenager, and I'm on my way out to meet my friends. My mother and Phyllis are sitting on the couch when I walk by them. "You walk like a duck," my mom says. She gets out of her seat and struts across the room with her toes turned out, her feet stomping widely and heavily. She looks hideous. "That's how you look," she sneers. Then Phyllis chimes in. "You look like a klutz." Phyllis joins the performance, and they both clomp around the living room. "Straighten out your feet, keep your knees closer together and take smaller steps," they say. "Learn to walk like a lady."

Memory: It's midday when I walk out of my bedroom. I can hear Mom and Phyllis jabbering away in Mom's bedroom. She's trying on a new outfit and asking Phyllis's opinion. I love to see my mother dressed up. When I enter, Phyllis abruptly turns to me and says, "What are you doing here, you miserable kid?" I slink back into my room.

Memory: An uncomfortable pressure is growing in me, and it feels like it's coming from Phyllis's insults and harassment. I need my mother to get involved. She's in the bathroom across from my bedroom, and I wait for the sound of the door to open. I step into the hallway and ask if I can speak to her for a second.

I know I have to choose the right words. "Phyllis is such a pest," I say. "Can you ask her to stop telling me what to do?"

"Phyllis does so much for you. She loves you like a daughter." Then she adds, "Don't be like that!"

Memory: I'm waiting for my breasts to grow so I can wear a real bra like all my friends. I'm standing in my room, in front of my mirror, and I'm naked from the waist up. My mother and Phyllis open my bedroom door and stand in the doorway. I freeze. They're scrutinizing me. Phyllis steps in, approaches me and cups her right hand under my breast. She gently bounces it up and down. With her hand still under my breast, she turns back to my mother. "Look how firm they are," she says. I cringe and stiffen even more. Her touch makes my skin crawl.

These memories had been orbiting in my mind as separate planets, one having nothing to do with the other. Now they were surfacing en masse, and I began to make connections:

Connection: When I was in high school, my typing teacher said, in front of the whole class, "You have spastic fingers!" I never understood why I was so decimated by her criticism and why I remained ashamed of my short, stubby hands.

Connection: My mother and Phyllis regularly repeated a phrase in my presence: "Ona jest gruba"—"she is fat," in Polish. I knew what it meant, and I believed it because that's what I saw in the mirror. It caused a morphed body image that I struggled with all my life.

Connection: When they imitated the way that I walked, their humiliating ambush was no different from the mean girls in Newark calling me "big foot." I added my clodhopper feet to the rest of my inadequacies.

Connection: Since the day I could understand language, I remember my mother and Phyllis calling me "paskudny dzieciak," which translates from Polish to English as "bad kid." Whenever it was lobbed at me, it reinforced my own suspicions that there was something wrong with me.

Connection: In addition to the many liberties that Phyllis took, she'd often call me names in front of my mother. "You're a slob," she'd say, or, "You're funny looking!" Sometimes she'd scold me: "Stop being so nasty to your mother." Never once do I remember my mother coming to my defense. In fact, she most often took Phyllis's side.

Connection: Inappropriate behavior and sexual violation had been normalized in my household. My father had been sexualizing me for years; no one acknowledged it, and it was rampant. I'd learned early to dissociate, and that's what I did in all these instances.

The mother in these fragments collided with the mother I believed I'd had for six decades: my best friend, my advocate, my champion. I never attributed any of the difficulties I'd had as a child to her. If anything, I held Phyllis responsible for the problems I couldn't attribute to my father. But that's not what the memories and connections were telling me. They were telling me that my mother and Phyllis were a team who constantly ganged up on me. It was both Phyllis *and* my mother who were belittling, denigrating and sexually inappropriate. The memories and connections revealed that I had been at the bottom of a totem pole, the third component of the triad. It was two against one—them against me.

A little girl in those circumstances would have felt under siege, judged, inadequate, clumsy. She would have felt like she didn't belong. The more I pictured her, the more my own body swelled with the rejection she had suffered. I felt excluded because I *was* excluded.

Suddenly I remembered times that I wished my mother would stop being friends with Phyllis. That my mother would love me more than her. It saddened me to think that my little brain was having thoughts like that, but it did.

I could no longer view Mom as a victim or an innocent bystander. She had actively participated with and enabled Phyllis to mistreat me.

I'd found another strand of the tassel.

44
THANKSGIVING

This new rendition of my childhood was unbearable. The damning memories and flashbacks were too raw for my psyche to absorb. Instead I clung to hope. I rationalized that within the time I had left with Mom, we could potentially undo the damage that had been done. She could still become my ally, and that would redeem any of her perceived transgressions.

Thanksgiving was my favorite holiday, and Mom always attended. But now, with Phyllis gone, she was hesitant to drive by herself, so my husband and I agreed to pick her up and take her home. The plan was, we'd go to get her on the Tuesday before Thanksgiving. In every conversation prior to her visit, she asked me to repeat the details. She'd then go to check her calendar to confirm that she had written it down. So early on Tuesday morning, my husband left for New Jersey.

When the phone rang that morning and Mom's number showed up in caller ID, I suspected she was calling again to ask when someone was going to be there. I prayed for patience.

"Celia?" Her voice was low and full of anguish. "I don't feel well. I don't think I can come."

"Ron's already halfway there! What's the matter?"

"I'm still in bed. I didn't sleep well. My back hurts. I don't think I can come."

I reminded her that her back always hurt her. I told her Ron would help her when he arrived. "No, no, I'm not packed. And he makes me nervous."

Then the truth: Howie had come to West Orange to tie up loose ends after his mother's death. He was staying at the townhouse with Mom. "Howie took me to do errands yesterday," she said. "We were up late last night eating pizza and ice cream." Her tone had abruptly switched from sullen to playful. Mom liked people to think she was naughty, and I could tell she had a devilish smirk on her face. I was not amused. She didn't get the gravity of the situation. But I had to compose myself.

"Ma, you don't have to do anything. You can even take a nap when you get here."

"But I don't feel well." The anguish was back in her voice.

I lost it. "I told you last month what the plan was. You had it in your calendar, and now you're telling me you wore yourself out so you're not coming?"

"Oy, don't be mad at me. I'm sorry. I'm all screwed up!"

Ron had to turn around and ended up in massive traffic. Before he got home, my mother called back several times. "Are you mad at me?" "I think I should come." "I don't know what to do."

"It's too late," I said and practically slammed the phone down.

I was standing by my night table, stiff as a stone statue. Remnants of my newly-discovered mother, the one who'd ganged up on me with Phyllis, flashed through my mind. With them came a hazy, noisy sensation. Similar to the "crashes" I'd experienced with my father, it obscured my ability to think. But one thought did manage to get through: My mother's actions did not feel innocent or ingenuous. They felt deliberate, irresponsible and inconsiderate.

The day after a wonderful Thanksgiving celebration with friends and family, Mom called. She was upset. "Don't be mad at me," she said again. "I'm all mixed up." When she hinted that she wanted to come for the weekend, I was speechless, incredulous at her audacity. Did she have any idea what it took for us to transport her back and forth? Did she consider for one moment how her actions affected me?

I had answered the phone in our family room, where everyone was relaxing. I kept the receiver to my ear, walked into the living room and dropped heavily onto one of our huge white sofas. Out of my scrambled mind, a bullhorn blared: "Ma chose not to come, and she doesn't care if it hurt me!"

There was no way I or anyone else was going to get into a car and drive the 90 minutes to N.J. An unusual clarity kicked in, and I knew I had to take care of myself. "I'm sorry, but no one can pick you up now," I said.

But when she called again the next day, this time begging me to come get her, my assertive surge from the day before clashed with decades of restraint, and my resolve weakened. Once again, I got sucked into a centrifuge of guilt—"Don't be so hard on her. It's only been a month since Phyllis died"—and I conceded to visit her later that day.

Several weeks passed, and on the Friday before Christmas, Mom called to tell me she was in the hospital.

"What happened?" I asked.

"I fell on my face."

My gut reaction was to go straight to the hospital, but I had obligations and couldn't just pick up and leave. In 1995 I'd started to do yoga for fitness. It went from a passion to a vocation. I taught in a studio until 2010, when I'd teamed up with a Pilates instructor to open our own business. I had a full schedule of private clients to teach, and I was managing several teachers and classes.

Plus my stepsons and their families were coming to stay with us for the holidays. I didn't have room for my mother. I decided to wait and see how serious it was. She said she needed a few stitches, and then she'd be discharged. Wanda would pick her up and take her home. I couldn't have gotten there in time anyway.

Still, I was overcome by worry, and I decided it would be best for her to come stay with us. Perhaps I could pick her up, and my stepson, who lived in New Jersey, could take her home on Wednesday. I asked him, and he agreed. Then I asked my older daughter if she minded bunking with her sister so Mom could stay in her room. She was fine with that arrangement. I called Mom with the good news and explained the plan. "Oy, I'm not feeling well," was her infuriating reply.

I now understood what those words meant: She didn't want to come. And with that, the sizzling returned. It felt like a vast, impenetrable white space. It was visceral, numbing and all-consuming. It came with a static so loud that I lost contact with my auditory functions. It was like the black and white snow that suddenly obliterates a TV screen, obscuring the clear picture that had been there just moments before.

On Sunday I decided to get into my car with an open-ended plan. I'd check her out and determine whether to leave her at her home or bring her back with me. Thankfully I had my iPod and blasted Pharrell, Ed Sheeran and Sam Smith. But Adele's "Turning Tables" moved a weary and beaten part of me. Waves of sorrow wracked my body as tears flowed down my cheeks. I needed to cry, so I kept hitting rewind.

The scene I encountered when I reached Mom's townhouse startled me. She was far more banged up than I'd imagined, but it was her disoriented mental state that alarmed me most. She couldn't remember what had happened, and she seemed to have no awareness of how severely injured she was. Maybe everything did boil down to her age? Maybe she had more than a mild case of dementia? How could I have been so heartless and impatient with her?

No matter what, I was bringing her home to Westchester. I assured her she'd be back by Wednesday. All of a sudden, her tiny, ravaged frame grew. She stood up straight, put her hand on her hip and with absolute coherence and clarity declared, "I can't be gone for that long. I have things to do."

As I witnessed this indignant and obstinate version of my mother, the buzzing I'd experienced the day before was back. It encased me in sheer whiteness, and the crackling sound deafened me. I had to get away from her; I swiftly turned and left the room. I stopped in the TV room, just outside her bedroom. My fists were clenched by my sides. I shifted to my right, and I punched the wall.

Everything stopped. The pain of my fist smashing the plaster was no match for my devastated spirit. Why did such a seemingly harmless occurrence cause me to disintegrate so completely? Such violence had never broken through my surface; I didn't recognize myself. Where on earth were these vehement and angry feelings coming from?

The scene and my bewilderment would haunt me for days. I had to let it settle and eventually it boiled down to a wound I knew had been there since infancy. The present choices that my mother was making cut into the festering gash. She was not prioritizing me. Not for one second had I ever thought that my mother would have harmed me. But here it was in full view: The rage I felt had nothing to do with my father or Phyllis. It was triggered by my mother.

As I picked at this strand of the tassel, I had to ask myself: What other painful choices had my mother made throughout my life?

45
SENSATIONS

The question of my mother's choices followed me day and night. It spun and spun until disembodied images and sensations began to bombard me. They were chilling, disturbing, and I wanted to dismiss them, but I could not put them out of my head.

Sensation: I am a tiny lone figure, a baby suspended, almost levitating, in a vast and barren white landscape. In the distance are two people barely visible in the mist. They're my parents, and they're ignoring me. The air around me feels cold and unwelcoming. My tummy is tight, and I'm aching for someone to see me.

The vision reappeared whenever I thought about my mother. The solitude and sadness surrounding the "tiny lone figure" felt familiar. It was an eerie and heartrending perception arising from within me. The baby's anguish had seeped into my bones—it was *my* anguish, *my* pain, *my* loneliness, *my* longing. Identifying with the lone figure allowed me to feel what was missing: The warmth of my mother's skin, the smell of her hair and the comfort of her embrace. I felt the ache for Mom's soft whispers of assurance and sweet kisses of affection. Then it hit me—even now, I did not feel my mother's presence.

This was a portal, a new entry point, and like an archeologist spotting a tiny protrusion, I began gently brushing each grain of sand away.

Sensation: I am in our apartment in Newark, standing in my crib, looking around the bedroom. It is dark, and I am alone. My little hands grasp the railing. A window is behind me, and the shades are drawn. My parents' big bed sits a million miles away, between me and the door to the living room. The door is closed, and I wait for it to open. I wait for someone to come get me. I hear the muffled sound of voices in the next room, but none approach the door.

Where was my mother?

As I wove the child I was channeling into my life, I began to notice that memories were emerging in the shape of stories I'd heard since the day I understood language.

My mother's story: "One summer, when Celia was a baby, we were staying at Kessler's Hotel. We were having dinner in the dining room with a group of friends when our waiter showed up at the table. We thought he was going to take our order, but instead he asked, 'Are any of you in room seven?' 'Yes, that's our room,' I told him. 'Is there something wrong?' 'There's a motor running in your room, Mrs. Bau.' I looked up at him and laughed. 'Oh, that's just our baby, banging in her crib!'"

My mother told this tale over and over again. She performed it to perfection. Before she delivered the punchline, she'd pause and take a coy scan of her audience. Then, with a practiced curl of her lips, she'd smile and bring the story to a mirthful close. As a child, I hung on every word, laughed along with everyone else. I loved hearing her talk about me.

But now I wanted to know why she left me alone in a hotel room? Why was I banging? And why did my mother think that was funny?

It horrified me to understand that as early as infancy, I had already learned to provide comfort for myself. There was no other way to interpret what the story revealed—it wreaked of neglect. My mother was more interested in entertaining her friends than attending to her young daughter.

As the gravity of this discovery sunk in, a new vivid memory was spawned.

Memory: I am rocking. I'm in my spot on the couch in the living room, and in full view of my parents and anyone else, I rock. Each time my back hits the sofa and I am gently bounced forward, I slip further inward to a secret place behind my eyes. With my peripheral vision fading, I don't have to see anything I don't want to see. The soft thuds of my movement muffle anything I do not want to hear. The rhythm transports me to a safe, peaceful place where no one can reach me.

As an adult I knew that I'd rocked until I was eight years old. Secretly, I wondered if it meant that I was mentally challenged. As a girl, I'd watch newsreels of infants and children rocking in orphanages and mental hospitals. I'd stare at these poor, broken kids in their deplorable confines, and I'd say to myself, "I'm not an orphan, and I'm not 'retarded,' yet I rock." It was more proof that there was something wrong with me.

But now I saw that the banging in my crib had evolved into the rocking, and my mother had remained oblivious. Why did it not worry her? Why was she not paying attention? And worse, why did she not care? Why didn't she slip alongside me, put her arm around me and ask, "Sweetie, are you okay?"

My mother's story: "Your father is sitting on a bench with his friend Max. They're facing each other, engrossed in one of their intellectual conversations. Daddy is gesturing wildly with one hand while the other is holding a rope. Behind them is a small pond. The rope your father is holding is tied to a rowboat, which is floating in the pond, about 12 feet away. The boat is empty, and I start screaming, 'Where's the baby? Where's the baby?' It turns out, Daddy thought it was a good idea to place you in a boat. He'd forgotten about you, and you'd fallen out and were under the water, drowning."

As frightening as the story was, recalling the unapologetic way that Mom told it sent a shiver down my spine. To her it was another tale meant to get a laugh. There was no mention of the poor judgment that put my life at risk. Nor had she ever shown an ounce of remorse or contrition.

Phyllis's story: "Your mother had an abortion several years after you were born. But don't tell your mother that I'm telling you."

For whatever reason, Phyllis repeated this many times when I was growing up. As a little girl, I knew abortion was a bad thing, and it scared me. When I got older, I understood it to be taboo, and I was surprised that my mother had done it. Later, I sympathized with how difficult that decision must've been for her. But I never thought about what it implied. Why hadn't she wanted another child? Why didn't she want a sibling for me?

The timeline of my birth had not been of interest to me until I began thinking about these tales. As I did the calculation, it gave me pause: My parents got married in June of 1949, and I was born exactly nine months after their honeymoon, in March of 1950. My mother was 23, my father 26. They were Holocaust survivors who had just immigrated to America, and I wondered: Was it too soon for her to have an infant. Did she have any idea of what it meant to care for a child? Was she ready to sacrifice herself for me?

Everything I was facing was the opposite of what I'd always believed about my mother. Reconciling the discrepancy was almost impossible. But what I couldn't overlook was that the implications began to fill the holes I hadn't even known were there.

And what about my father? I recalled something I'd put out of my mind.

My father's pronouncement: "I never wanted to be a father."

My dad made this confession during a heated exchange with me when I was in my late 30s. I'd buried it along with all the other cruel assertions he'd made. But now it completed a picture that was crystallizing: an unplanned pregnancy with a husband who had no interest in being a father. That left my mother as my sole caregiver. How did she balance his demands, her own desires and my needs? Was I in the way? Did they want me at all?

Phyllis's story: "When you were three years old, your father came home and announced that he no longer wanted to work for money. He was going to explain the meaning of life. Your mother had a nervous breakdown and left for a few weeks."

This single story, which Phyllis repeated more times than the others, encapsulated the bizarre circumstances of my young life. Anytime I asked my mom about it, all she'd say was, "Your father was driving me crazy with his crazy ideas." Perhaps that was true, but where had she gone? What about me? Who took care of me during the time she was away?

And what did it say that my father's behavior was already threatening her sanity? Had she had enough? Was she contemplating leaving him? If so, why didn't she? What happened when she came back? Had I been a factor in her decision at all?

I could only speculate. What I did know was that she had chosen him—a man who did not want to be a father and a man who had abused me. What concessions had she made then and throughout my childhood?

How different would my life have been had she chosen me?

No wonder these memories, stories and sensations had been spinning independent of each other. No wonder they'd escaped me. Now, as their revolutions drew closer, I saw what they had in common. My mother had been negligent and careless. It seemed that she did not plan for me and may not have wanted me. And once she became my mother, her choices would define the rest of my life.

Before I could tackle the enormity of my new reality I needed time. I needed to identify with the little girl whose childhood was scarred by neglect. I had to rewind to my earliest days and reconstruct what it must have been like to be her.

Without a doubt, this was a strand of the tassel, but the emotional stamina it would take for me to unknot it evaded me. The most I could accept was that my oversized reactions to all the seemingly benign interactions with Mom were coming from somewhere that might eventually make sense.

46

MOVING

I was in new territory—split between a radically different account of my childhood and the present-day care of my mother. I ping-ponged between anger and love, retribution and empathy, self-sabotage and self-care. My heart wanted to swing in Mom's favor, but I could not deny the impact of her actions on my wellbeing. Paying attention to what was happening on the surface was seminal to understanding what was hidden in my depths.

Henry, Phyllis's younger son, owned the townhouse where she and my mother had lived. They paid him rent, and it was an ideal arrangement for everyone. But after Phyllis's death, he wanted to sell it. He let my mother know. There was no rush, he said, no pressure, which gave her license to procrastinate.

Years prior, she'd pointed out an independent living facility run by the JCC and told me that when the time came for her to move, that's where she'd like to go. With her relocation looming, I suggested she put in an application for an apartment, but she resisted. "There's a long waiting list," she said. "I'll never get in."

Finally, I convinced her to apply, and I soon learned that Mom had gotten a call from the JCC-affiliated Jewish Federation Plaza informing her that she'd been accepted and a one-bedroom apartment was available for immediate occupancy. But it wasn't my mother who was sharing the good news with me; it was Monica. Mom didn't even tell me she'd gone to see it, and I wondered why.

After I hung up with Monica, I sat down at my kitchen table. Staring out over the porch and into the distance, I tussled with my mixed-up feelings. Any conversation I'd had with Mom regarding her move was contentious, leaving me feeling nervous and guilty. I was the one urging her to do something she didn't want to do.

When I finally spoke to her, her tone became hostile. "Why do I have to move?"

She insisted that Henry and Monica said she could stay in the townhouse as long as she wanted to. When I'd spoken to them, they'd assured me that they would never kick her out, but their intention was to put the place on the market as soon as she found a new home. I explained that to Mom and pointed out that if we didn't expedite the new apartment, she would lose it.

I could see it was all too much for her, and I knew I'd have to take over if she were to move in a month. When I went to the townhouse to assess what she'd be taking, she couldn't make up her mind. She walked behind me, muttering that I was the only one who thought she had to move. She was provoking me. With the recent wall-punching episode fresh in my head, I tried not to feel antagonized. I took a deep breath, calmed myself down. I told her I'd find a moving company to do the job; all she'd have to do was decide what to bring. Then I left.

It took me a week to compile a list of movers who could work within her timeframe and budget. When I called to discuss the options with Mom, she had another idea. She'd already arranged for Agata, her cleaning lady, to pack her up, and Agata's husband would do the moving. Mom could not be dissuaded from this plan.

A week before the move, I went to check on the progress. When I entered the townhouse, I saw a handful of boxes lined up by the sliding glass doors. "These boxes are barely filled!" I said. "I thought Agata was packing you up."

My mother just stood there, pale and drawn. She had not applied makeup, not even lipstick. The jeans she was wearing were too big, and her sweatshirt was stained. She still had on her pink slippers, and her hair needed tidying up. She bent her arms at the elbows with her palms facing the ceiling, as though the matter were out of her hands. "Agata only comes here on her day off," she said, "and besides, I couldn't tell her what to pack."

My foundation was crumbling. Burning magma threatened to bubble up but I collected myself enough to say, "I'm finding a mover who will do the packing and moving, no matter what it costs!"

When it was time to leave, I kissed Mom goodbye and headed for my car. As soon as I backed out of the parking spot and made the left turn to leave the complex, I started to sob. It was hard to know what I was crying about. My heart clung to the mother I'd once adored, and it broke for the old woman I'd just left. My mother was approaching the end of her life. Her light was fading. Time was running out.

With moving day pending and so much to do, I aspired to stay in a peaceful state. There was no shortage of challenges—not the least being Mom's incessant stressing—but for the most part I checked myself and circumvented any explosions.

Until the evening before the move, when I was in my kitchen, preparing dinner. The phone rang: Mom.

"Celia?" That voice.

"I have to speak to someone. I'm so unhappy about this move. I don't know why I agreed to it, especially because I don't have to."

I kept the phone glued to my ear as I stomped onto our back porch. I could hear my mother breathing on the other end, and then I heard her ask, "Celia, are you still there?"

"Yes," I said.

Words eluded me. I was standing outside overlooking 15 acres of beautiful open space, with hills, meadows and a spring-fed pool. At any other time it would have been my source of tranquility. But that day, the static returned, and it obstructed everything. It felt ancient. I knew it had followed me from my childhood into my adulthood. I'd begun calling it white noise, and I was in the throes of it.

I erupted. "Ma, you have to move!"

The next day, after the movers left, Agata came to Mom's new apartment, and the two of us managed to unpack and put away most of my mother's belongings. The only disruptions came from Mom, and she must've known my tolerance was waning.

"You have to be patient with me," she said. "I'm an old lady."

White noise hissed. It felt like it would penetrate my flesh. But instead of imploding, a ferocious energy vibrated my vocal cords, and out of my mouth came words I'd never imagined saying and with a force I'd never felt. "No, you need to appreciate me for what I'm doing," I told her. "Saying you're an old lady is an excuse, and it offends me!"

Before I left, after a 12-hour ordeal, Mom stood in the middle of her almost-set-up apartment and said, "Oy, what a mess!"

"What mess? There's no mess. You're in good shape because all the people around you made that happen."

My outbursts stunned me. They tousled me like bingo balls cranked up in a cage. As they tumbled and twirled, something else was brewing. At the tail end of what felt like an honest outpouring came a palpable sense of danger. I was learning not to turn away from these ephemeral sensations, but to embody them. This one felt as though my neck sat in a guillotine waiting for the blade to drop and chop off my head. Where had such a macabre image come from?

As I continued to interact with Mom, I noticed that each time she dismissed and negated me, it ignited the same internal chaos, and it was not isolated to the most recent episodes: It went all the way back to the days before I had words. What I was sensing in real time was the terror of a little girl who felt invisible—unseen and unheard and unsafe. Her only means of defense was to disappear and stay silent.

The voice that was finally escaping through my lips belonged to that forgotten and bruised child. The words she spoke were never supposed to be heard. She knew things that were supposed to remain secret. Along with my charged reactions came a peculiar sense of betrayal—as though I'd broken a trust by divulging my true feelings. The threatening blade of the guillotine was meant to keep me quiet.

And what about the white noise? It was part of this elaborate system, and I suspected it was a protective shield. Without a doubt I'd have to begin loosening this tightly knotted strand of the tassel.

47

BOND

With Mom finally moved in, things calmed down a bit. I checked in with her regularly.

"So, how do you like it?" I asked.

"It's different," was her tepid reply.

There were problems with the windows and the heat. She needed a shower curtain, and she hadn't unpacked the wardrobes with her endless articles of clothing. I took care of everything.

"Have you met any of the other people?" I asked.

"Oh, you know me. I like to keep to myself." That was interesting—I'd always thought she thrived on being a social butterfly. I noted the contradiction and moved on.

Months later, I asked, "Is it getting any better?"

"Yes," she said. "A neighbor who lives down the hall is a very nice Polish lady who checks up on me." Then, "There's also an Italian gentleman who lives right next door, and he likes me."

Hearing that she'd acquired a regular seat at a dinner table in the dining hall and listening to her gossip about her fellow diners comforted me. She'd resumed her Friday movie night with a group of Polish friends. Restarting those activities was a sign that she had settled in. I recognized my mom of days gone by. Returning to her part-time job, from which she'd taken a temporary leave, indicated that her life was getting back to normal, which meant that mine might, too.

Her sunnier tone touched a part of me that was not ready to give up on her. Maybe we had turned a corner. I even joked with her about how she'd recently driven me crazy with her anxious antics.

When she said, "I'm sorry," I said, "It's fine as long as you're happy."

And I meant it. I was desperate to have my quintessential mother back. It wasn't difficult for me to attribute all the disturbing events since Phyllis's death to an anomaly: a solitary isolated, unpleasant moment in time. I clung to the notion that the bond I'd always thought we had, the bond I had always longed for, was there.

But most of our phone calls were empty, and most of my visits were tense. As my optimism began to dwindle. I reverted to questioning whether the whole mess was my fault. Why couldn't I chalk it all up to the challenges one faces when dealing with an aging parent? But I was changing, and I hesitated before blaming myself for the way things were.

Then two seemingly innocuous conversations with Mom reminded me that there was more truth waiting to be unearthed.

If I didn't call my mother, weeks would go by without her calling me. "Did you forget that you have a daughter?" I'd ask.

She'd say she was so busy with work, errands, friends. This ran counter to the other mother, the one who'd made her many agonizing phone calls. The one who was so incompetent and feeble that she couldn't accomplish minor tasks without my help.

"But why don't you ever call me?"

"I guess it's because I called my mother every day, so I expect you to call me every day."

Where did this tit-for-tat rule come from? Did it mean she'd never call me if I didn't call her? This wasn't how the gracious mother I thought I had functioned.

And then, another day, in the car, on the way to a cardiologist appointment, my mother began talking about a friend who, for more than 20 years, had been taking care of Mom's money matters. As I was getting onto the freeway, my mother turned to me and hinted that she'd like me to take over. When I explained that I was already overloaded with managing my family and business finances, she did not seem to care. "When Grandma was as old as I am, she said to me, 'Irena, it's time for you to take over,' and I gladly did."

Was my mother playing me? Was she guilting me into doing what she wanted me to do? To me, manipulation felt dishonest and deceitful, and I had never before considered Mom to be manipulative. Now, it felt deceptive. How had I not recognized this before? The simple answer was: I was not ready to see it. I could not bring myself to relinquish my idealized mother. But this version of her felt too wicked for me to assimilate.

Well into 2015, more than two years after Phyllis had passed away, I was driving home from my studio when Mom called.

"Hi, Ma."

Her anguished voice came through the speaker. "I had an accident. I totaled my car."

She had back-ended another car, and when the police officer asked her if the other car had stopped short, she said no, which made the accident her fault.

I could understand the tizzy Mom was in, and I tried my best to be patient.

Her court date was set for a Tuesday in January 2016. She pleaded for me to go with her. I didn't think it was an unreasonable request, so I conceded. I cleared my teaching schedule and tried not to stress about the lost revenue. But over the next few days, she called repeatedly, relentlessly changing her mind. "Don't come." "Come." "It's not necessary for you to come." As I was getting ready for bed that Monday night, the phone rang at 9:30 P.M. I answered.

"Ugh, I changed my mind," Mom was saying. "Can you please come with me tomorrow?"

White noise. Blinding and deafening. My mother's maddening twists and turns were too much, and my newfound voice kicked in.

"Are you kidding? Do you have any idea what it takes for me to come to New Jersey? I already canceled my clients and rescheduled them because you told me not to come." Silence on the other end. "Do you ever consider the impact your actions have on me?"

I hung up and went right to sleep. But during the night, once again, my guilt gobbled up my clarity, and in the morning I called Mom to tell her I'd be there in time for her court appearance later that day.

I drove to West Orange in the snow. Turns out there was barely anything for me to do. All she needed was a ride. I might as well have stayed home.

The court determined that she had to retake her driver's test, including the written part. She failed the written test six times, and in 2017 she lost her license.

My high-voltage reactions were still unnerving until it struck me that I'd been appearing in my own court, where I was both judge and jury. I continually found myself guilty, and I escorted myself out of the courtroom in handcuffs. The final verdict: I was a terrible daughter. I'd been living with that stain all my life. From the day I was born, my mother had indicted me as "bad," and I made sure that I stayed incarcerated.

This was undoubtedly another knot in the tassel. As it loosened, it revealed a truth I could not unsee: The final years with Mom were not going to heal the wounds that had broken my heart. And the love I so urgently longed for would never come from her. The bond that I now knew was missing would remain so forever.

48

AN EXCITING LIFE

Some strands were untangling, while others remained knotted. Sometimes the white noise broke up, and other times it didn't. I found myself in a suspended state, but it was better than being deaf, dumb and blind. At least I was mindful of something I'd never been aware of before.

During another visit with my mother, we were watching the news as the anchor was reporting on the Winter Olympics. The Alpine skiing event was on the screen. "I loved to ski," Mom said. "I was a good skier."

My eyes rolled, and I gave her a sideways glance.

"We went to all the best ski resorts and always had a great time," she continued.

Rather than the stressful family ski trips I recalled, I realized she was speaking of the vacations she'd taken later in life, with my father and their friends. I let her talk. Suddenly she paused, leaned her elbow on the armrest, turned her head, looked straight into my eyes and said, "Your father was quite the flamboyant skier. You know how outrageous he could be!"

Her tone was mischievous, and the deference in her voice seemed to be inviting me to join in the glorification of my father. The woman staring at me was erasing part of the childhood I knew I'd had, replacing it with the one she preferred. Before white noise could steal me away, my newfound voice snapped, "Do you ever consider the chaos and insanity I was subjected to being his daughter?" I couldn't stop. "It was *not* fun for me!"

Although the words shooting out of my mouth rang with truth, within seconds a tempest swooped in. What was I talking about? It hadn't been so bad, and why couldn't I get over it?

While I was fending off the storm, my mother was lifting her gnarly hand to her heart, and with exaggerated sincerity she said, "I didn't know."

White noise! It was a furious blizzard—a whiteout.

There was nothing left of me. All I could do was check my watch. It was 3:00. I explained to Mom that I didn't want to hit traffic and said good-bye. I spent the 90 minutes it took for me to get home taking stock of myself. What was happening? What was this white noise? What unwanted sounds was the static drowning out? What was I not supposed to see?

One winter weekend, Mom paid us a rare visit. After breakfast, she and I were sitting together on the couch. With her elbows hugged tightly to her sides, she shivered. "Brrr, it's cold in here," she said. "Can you push up the heat?"

"I have a better idea," I said. "I'll make a fire."

"I'd like that," she said.

I removed the screen from the front of the fireplace and grabbed a couple of the brown paper bags that I'd saved. I had a foolproof method:

The bags got rolled up and shoved under the grate, then a large hand-ful of twigs went on top. I chose the smallest pieces of chopped wood because I knew they'd catch quickly and produce the embers that were needed for a hot fire. Within seconds we had a roaring blaze.

When I returned to the sofa, I took my seat next to Mom, who was wrapped in a blanket with a couple of pillows propped up behind her. "I love a fire," she said.

I savored the harmony of the moment.

"How are you doing?" Mom asked.

I would have loved to tell her about my new yoga studio and all the things I was planning. But the past had taught me that she was not interested. So instead I got up and went into my study to fetch my computer. I showed her my new website and the recent postings I'd created for social media.

"That's nice," she said.

I placed the computer on the ottoman in front of us, sat back, put my feet up and stared at the fire. Suddenly Mom started talking about Germany after the war and before she came to America.

"Grandma and I had to stay in Germany for a few years after the war, waiting for our papers," she said. "That's when I met your father. He was very handsome, a sharp dresser and extremely romantic."

He wined and dined her, brought her flowers, took her dancing; it was very exciting, she said. "He was madly in love with me and asked me to marry him."

But, she continued, she'd also met Bernard, a young American sol-dier who was equally as handsome. "He was also in love with me and wanted to marry me. They knew about each other, so they competed for my affection. Your father sent me love letters, and Bernard prom-ised me a wonderful life in America. I was torn. In the end, obviously I chose your father."

Another tale I'd heard a million times, but that Saturday she was telling me more about Bernard than she had before. The uncharacteristic lucidity in her voice compelled me to say, "I'm surprised Bernard still holds such a prominent place in your life."

"I almost married him instead of your father," she said. "I even went to America to meet his parents."

That was news to me! "I thought you were in Germany waiting for your papers?" I asked. "How could you have gone to America?"

Her answer made no sense. I let it go and asked her the same tired question I always had. "Are you sorry you didn't marry Bernard?"

And she answered as she always had. "If I'd married him, I wouldn't have you."

The sweetness of her words touched me, softened me and soothed me as it always had. But the trance was broken by more words from her—a different answer. "If I had married Bernard," she said, "I wouldn't have had such an exciting life!"

White noise! Another stratospheric explosion. There was no trace of me in her answer. All that mattered to her was that she had lived an exciting life. There was that feeling of invisibility again. Pure anger straightened my spine, dropped my feet to the floor, slid me to the edge of the couch and twisted my whole body to face her.

"How do you think that makes me feel?" I said, as heat flushed my cheeks. "*My* life with my father was anything but exciting. He inflicted so much pain on me. To this day I'm struggling to undo the damage he wreaked, and you so flippantly talk about how exciting he was!"

I was sure that the power of my words had finally reached my mother. She had to see me and hear me now.

But shock, dismay and disbelief flashed across her face, as it always had. I could no longer delude myself: It was fake, manufactured, manipulative. "I didn't know," she told me, once again. And this time

I blasted back, "YES YOU DID! I've told you so many times that he *abused* me!"

All those years ago, when I finally found the courage to tell my mother about my father's abusive treatment of me, her responses shut me down. "Oh, he didn't mean it." And, "You know how crazy your father can be." And, "Don't be so sensitive." As my mind scanned further back, I recalled the many times I'd needed her mediation and she'd dismissed me with the words, "Don't be like that." I had no idea what "that" was, or how I was "being" that was so offensive to Mom. The words always whacked into me. They became code—an evil side of me or "bad Celia" had escaped, and I'd better do whatever it took to return her to captivity. I had no voice back then and assumed that she was right and I was wrong.

As I slipped back into the present moment, I heard her preposterous reply. "I thought you and your father were the best of friends."

Silence.

Satisfied with her answer, Mom went back to gazing at the fire. The flames were not going to calm me down. I knew I was never going to get any more from her than I'd just gotten—than I'd ever gotten. I rose and found something to do in the kitchen.

When I returned to the living room, she had fallen asleep. The sight of her frail figure almost transformed my perturbed state into forgiveness. But the memories of Mom's deflections lingered. "I didn't know" was just another way for her to swivel and swerve in any direction but mine.

Now, in the safety of my home, with the warmth of the fire behind me, I courageously stood with my younger self. Her energy was my energy, and it was frantic, desperate and terrified. It was her anger that was alive in the subterranean network that I'd locked away behind the wall of static.

Finding and loosening the tassel's strands was freeing my vocal cords. It felt like a phantom limb was coming back to life. And with it, the blinders that had obstructed my vision began to fall away.

49

ANGER

The friction I was encountering with my mother was analogous to the battle that seemed to be raging within me. On one side was the daughter I thought I'd always been, the daughter I thought I should be—loyal, devoted and selfless. On the other was a different daughter who was hurt, disillusioned and angry.

The anger was complex—I did not know how to express it. It felt too harsh and scary. I'd let it agitate, bang and churn, but it rarely came out in its raw form. Had I been asked, I would have said that I was not allowed to be angry.

The rage that I was struggling to contain was an unknown entity, and I imagined that a dire consequence would follow its release. But I could no longer let it intimidate me nor stand in the way of resolving the issues with my mother. I couldn't bring myself to cut Mom out of my life as I'd done with my father. Instead I began asking myself, "How much do I owe my mother?"

This counterintuitive question punctuated all my interactions with Mom. It challenged the very essence of my romanticized relationship and unconditional allegiance to her. Although it was an unpleasant way of thinking, it did interrupt a cycle that I'd been stuck in forever. I used it as a vetting tool—a new, conscious, protective device. I began checking in with myself to make sure it was *my* choice to do the things I did and that they were in my best interest. I called Mom more sporadically. When too much time passed, I paid her visits, arriving around noon and departing by 3:00 to avoid traffic.

With the sliver of distance the question afforded me, I began wondering how much Mom had added to the chaos and turmoil that I had always blamed on my father?

One Sunday in the springtime I visited Mom. She had to let me into the building. She no longer got dressed for my visits, and she appeared more fragile. I watched her grasp the railing that had been installed there for that use. As I fell in step behind her and followed slowly down the hallway, I was gripped by an acute sense of melancholy.

Her apartment was oppressively hot, so I walked straight to the window and opened it. Passing the dusty coffee table, I pointed to the dead, dried up flowers in a waterless vase and asked if she'd like me to throw them out. She said no. The small table where we were going to eat needed to be cleared of piled-up mail. Over lunch we talked about the food.

After we ate, as usual, Mom complained about her back, so I told her I'd clean up. She protested, but I insisted. She shuffled into the living room and over to her recliner, where she arranged the heating pad and pillows that were set up to support her. When I finished in the kitchen, I flopped onto the couch to her right and put on the TV. Something must have reminded her of her life in Poland before the war. "I had an ideal childhood," she said.

White noise! It puzzled and disarmed me. Then I remembered that the static was a sign that something was bubbling up from the subterranean bunker below ground.

Mom had been characterizing her life in such idyllic terms from the time I was a little girl, and I'd hang on her every word.

Mom's story: My father adored me. I was the apple of his eye, and he spoiled me rotten. We were rich because he owned a hardware store and had many employees. Your grandpa was a tall and handsome man, charming and funny. He loved practical jokes and played them on me and my friends all the time. He was a pillar of the community, admired and loved by all. You would have loved him.

As a child, I'd picture my perfect mother bathed by rays of sunshine streaming through a double rainbow. She was a princess encircled by butterflies, hearts and doves. Now, as I recalled the impact her tale had on the child who worshipped her, I saw that it had lured me into a fantastical world that was the opposite of mine. I wanted to be my mother, the daughter of an adoring father. I couldn't imagine what that felt like. As for my grandfather, I would have given anything for him to be alive and a part of my life. Maybe he would have adored me, too. Instead, I was left with a big hole that could never be filled. I'd missed out on something special, something that would never happen to me.

I recognized the cocktail of envy and despondence. It was alive in my bone marrow. Now that I had the courage to let those emotions dance closer to the surface, rather than a first meeting, it felt like a reunion. I was on the cusp of an alliance with those turbulent feelings invoked by Mom's adorned stories. What else had I shielded myself from?

The answer lay in the other tales my mother had told.

Mom's story: I was a good student, the teacher's pet. I was also very popular and had a lot of friends. And all the boys liked me.

In school I adopted her vision as my benchmark. And as hard as I tried, I could not measure up to the standard she'd set.

Mom's story: Your grandpa had to leave Krakow with all the rest of the men. Grandma and I were alone. As the war was escalating, it became unsafe for us to stay. I knew a Christian boy, and he was in love with me. He convinced his relatives up north to take us in, and he orchestrated our move out of the city. He saved our lives.

A harrowing story, yes, but back then, all I pictured was a boy with stars in his eyes. So in love that he risked his own life, and the lives of others, to save my mother. Throughout my life, each and every time my mother mentioned a boy or a man, she'd say, "And he was in love with me!" As a young girl I was awestruck; I'd picture my magnificent mother entering a room and casting a spell. I wanted to be the star of that movie—bewitching and tantalizing men, causing them to swoon over me and pronounce their everlasting love. When that did not happen, I chalked it up to my inadequacies.

I'd never had a reason to doubt that what my mother was telling me was true. Whether she needed to embellish her life, or she needed me to idolize her, or she needed to keep herself from falling apart, I'd never know. What mattered to me now were the pieces I was in as a result of her magical thinking. The fanciful webs that she spun excluded and condemned me. I was not good enough to fit into her world. I was relegated to my own deluded world, where I was on the losing end—left behind. She was everything I wanted to be and everything I thought I was not. She was tiny, I was big. She was skinny, I was fat. She was elegant, I was coarse. She was smart, I was stupid. She was shiny, I was dull. She was lovable, I was not.

My mother needed to sparkle the brightest, even if it meant putting out my light and casting me into her shadow. It was a painful insight, but as pain often does, it gave rise to a new sensation.

Sensation: Sitting alone and at a distance, I watch as my gorgeous mother puts on her charm and allure. Though her back is to me, I know exactly what she's doing: flaunting her perfect smile, speaking with her Zsa Zsa-like accent and impressing everyone with her command. But a storm is brewing inside me, and I want her to stop. I'd shout if I could, but my vocal cords won't work. My throat is parched. "Don't fall for her act," I want to say. "She's not really like this!" I want to tell them that at home she yells at me and calls me "bad kid." I want them to see how she sneers at me and looks at me with disdain. If they did, she wouldn't get away with this.

There was a reason the gravity of this vision held me for days. It was in accordance with how I'd always felt in my mother's presence. It was a clear portrayal of the dichotomy that was my mother. Mom's priority was the way she presented herself to the world. I had no place on her stage. But I knew too well what she was like behind the scenes.

My identity had gotten completely entangled in the facade that my mother had crafted. In all matters of my life, it was my guiding light; my viewpoints and values were shaped by her mythical personae. It was the glue that kept me together.

But now I needed to know: Who was the little girl who'd watched from afar? She was intimate with the mother behind the curtain. I'd been estranged from her, yet she held the key to the mysterious source of my anger. She was the one who wanted to know what I owed the mother who had caused my anguish.

This knot was the most complicated of all; it would require a magnifying glass.

50

SILENCE

I'd reached a milestone in my quest for the truth. Curiosity was supplanting doubt. My faith in the tassel and my courage to untangle the strands were mounting. I was about to encounter the most monstrous knot of all.

Memory: I'm with my first-grade classmates at Bergen Street School, in Newark. We're sitting cross-legged on the rug in front of our teacher, who's seated on a small chair. It's cold outside, but the room is warm and cozy.

She's reading us a book, carefully enunciating the words as she holds it up to show us the colorful illustrations. I'm mesmerized by the pictures.

Suddenly a monitor enters the classroom and calls my name. I'm singled out. I shrink. I reluctantly uncross my legs to stand up. As I walk toward the door I can feel everyone's eyes following me, and I'm mortified. The monitor leads me down a chilly hallway, our footsteps echoing off the walls. We enter the speech classroom, and I'm the only kid there.

There's something wrong with my tongue. It gets in the way of me pronouncing my Ss. I have a lisp; they call it a speech impediment. They want me to keep my tongue from slipping through my teeth, but I can't do it.

I don't remember a time that my voice did not betray me. The words I chose and how I delivered them were under constant self-scrutiny and brutal judgment. They were as grating to me as someone singing off-key. No sooner were they out of my mouth, I'd want to suck them back in.

"It feels like I have marbles in my mouth," I told a friend decades later. That disclosure was like a flare illuminating a dark space. There in the center of the spotlight sat I, a bewildered three-year-old in a jumbled world of language.

Sensation: I'm surrounded by adults who are making sounds to one another but not to me. I want to be a part of it, but no one is paying attention to the noises coming through my lips. I stay quiet.

Now, as I witness my granddaughter learning to speak, I can't help but wonder: Did anyone try to communicate with me as I do with her? Did my grandmother pick up an object, hold it in front of me and patiently name it? Did she wait for me to make a comparable sound? Did my mother string words together to form sentences just for me to understand? Did she squeal with delight as I was able to ask for what I wanted? I knew the answers were no.

One could say, "Your parents were new to this country; they only spoke Polish." Then why didn't they teach me their native language?

If a lisp were all I sustained from the neglect, I could live with it. But my life had been marked by a different form of silence. A more nefarious type of silence. My father was an unchecked, unmoored and resolute force. He had free rein over me. His verbal abuse was an unmerciful assault, and he did it in full view of my mother. She looked on blankly, eyes cast downward, and waited for it to be over. Not a word was ever spoken. Life went on as though nothing had happened.

I now wondered, if my father had inflicted physical harm, if he had left me bruised and bloodied, would my mother have come to my defense? Would she have taken care of my wounds. Perhaps she would've hugged me close and softly whispered, "Sweetheart, I'm sorry that your father hurts you like that. Don't worry, I'll take care of it." Nowhere in my being could I find a scene like that.

Sensation: I'm trapped, running around in a frenzy, my arms flailing above my head. My mouth is wide open, my throat pulsating, but nothing is coming out. I'm desperate for someone to see me, to rescue me from something dreadful and frightening, but there's no one there.

That terror was my terror, and it had been my constant companion since my earliest days. How had I endured this scrambled, narrowed and alienated world? I knew the answer: I'd exiled the fear far, far away. Not only was it sequestered, it was silent.

For my mother's part, her silence gave everyone permission to mistreat me. Her silence made me a target. She was the only person who could've stopped it; only she could have validated my experience, but she never did. Her silence signaled to everyone, "There's nothing wrong here!" So not a soul, not a single human being, came to my aid.

The absolute isolation that the daughter of that mother had to suffer belonged to me. It was the air that I breathed. Had I witnessed this in another mother and child, I would have been furious. The time had come to face the anger that I felt toward the mother who was never there. The mother who turned her back when she was needed most. The mother who chose to deny the abuse that was happening right in front of her. The mother who was not my champion, my advocate or my protector. The mother who was my mother.

It was my mother who had expelled me into a chasm, a space so cold, barren and dense that it went on forever. I understood why white noise had to obliterate such an inhospitable and adversarial place. No wonder I'd always felt split, disconnected, dissociated and, yes, crazy. The crazy allegation had been haunting me ever since I correlated my rocking with those mentally challenged children. That was the seed from which my worries about insanity had been spawned. Then I remembered the journals I'd kept all those years ago. The reason I'd burned them was that I was embarrassed and confused about the "voices." I thought they were proof that I was unstable. I'd hoped—no, I'd prayed—that destroying the books would close that chapter of my life. But it hadn't.

Whenever I couldn't find a reason for things that were happening in my life, the insanity verdict waited in the wings. It stood at the end of the line, poised to demolish me with its final blow. I'd never linked it to my mother until now. As each crystal-clear memory of Mom's icy dismissals returned, so did my recollection of the doubt they had cast on my mental stability. Time and time again I'd ask myself if what I was reporting to Mom had really happened. Was I overreacting? Or was I making it up? Only an insane person did that!

Whether she knew it or not, Mom had been gaslighting me all my life. Her most recent claims that she "didn't know" served that end. She "didn't know" because she chose not to know. She "didn't know" so it didn't happen. She "didn't know" gave her a pass; she was oblivious, and therefore she could remain silent.

Now I understood that my mother's silence made her complicit and culpable. And yes, it made her a perpetrator. It was an agonizing punch in the gut. Like a catchy tune, this new truth stuck in my head, except it was a melody wracked by sadness and loss.

For the moment, these strands of the tassel had to remain knotted.

51

SEXUAL ABUSE

"Have you ever thought that your father sexually abused you?"

When I turned 39, in 1989, I started seeing a new psychotherapist, Arlene. It wasn't long before problems with my father began to take over my sessions again. During one of those emotionally charged meetings, Arlene posed her question.

Back then, sexual abuse was taboo; I thought it only referred to rape. Was Arlene inferring that my father had raped me? That my father had had sex with me, his daughter? That was incest! That couldn't have happened to me! That only happened to people in depraved, underprivileged conditions. Not in a normal and respectable family. Not in my family. Not to me.

My mind fought to divert the shameful and despicable images that arose. Had I really been violated? That made me dirty, different and deviant. And what did it say about my father? He was a perverted degenerate, an immoral and vile human being.

Arlene had dropped a massive bomb: The idea that my father could've done something so heinous broke me into a million pieces. I had *no* memory of a sexual assault; my mind was a blank. But when I asked myself if he was capable of doing such a thing, the answer was a clear and resounding YES!

At the time, I was conflicted about what or even whether to tell my mother. I still believed her to be an innocent bystander. I felt protective of her when it should have been the other way around. I chose to keep my secret to myself—perpetuating the family tradition of carrying on as though nothing had happened.

So when my mother proposed a visit with my father, I acquiesced. He had something he wanted to talk to my husband and me about. At the time, my husband and I were living with our four-year-old daughter on West End Avenue in Manhattan. Being married and a mother made me feel safe, and I thought, what could possibly go wrong.

On the appointed evening, before I opened our apartment door, I noted my shallow breath and sweaty palms. I turned the knob and swung the door open. There before me was my beautifully dressed and coifed mother. My father, who stood close to her, was similarly well-dressed. He reminded me of a messy little boy who'd been spruced up for a special occasion. As they stepped into the foyer, my daughter came flying down the hallway and ran to hug my mother. But she stopped short in front of my dad. She hadn't had much interaction with him, nor he with her. To break the awkward moment, he lowered himself to her level and said something akin to "koochie koochie koo."

My father hated formality. As soon as we got all the "phony" niceties out of the way, he pulled out a looseleaf notebook filled with writings and illustrations. He jumped right in. He'd invented a video conferencing system that used biofeedback technology to read and transmit the emotional reactions of the participants.

Words and sentences began flying out of his mouth: "I'm going to change the world." "My invention has global implications." "I will bring world peace." "People at the U.N. are backing me."

The familiar phrases, the velocity of his voice and his manic gestures yanked me back in time. I was no longer an adult sitting in my own living room in the city; I was back in Newark, a mangled, shrunken, dissociated mess. I'd underestimated the impact my father still had.

He kept talking. He wanted us to become his partners. He wanted us to invest. He rattled off a list of upcoming expenses that included the application fee for a patent, hiring a lawyer, building prototypes and future manufacturing. "As early investors you will make a lot of money," he declared.

Despite feeling like I'd been put through a meat grinder, I managed to thank him and tell him we'd think about it. I kissed my mom goodbye and shut the door. My back caught the nearest wall while inner forces clashed ferociously. I had to tame whatever had me in a death grip. I had to walk.

I went outside and headed south. Each brisk step smashed my heels into the pavement, and the buildings on either side of me whizzed by like a train speeding on its tracks. I knew this state: I could feel myself decomposing. But just as I was about to crumble, a voice within me boomed, "There's a reason I hate my father so much."

I abruptly stopped walking. It was the lifeline needed to halt the total shutdown that I was spiraling toward. I repeated the line several times, waiting for the usual assault on my sanity. But it did not come. It was the deepest knowing I'd ever experienced. From that day forward I severed my ties with my dad. I no longer saw him or spoke to him. We remained estranged until he died.

It wasn't long after my epiphany that my mother began considering her own separation from my father. When she took the audacious step of leaving him, it told me that she agreed with me: He was an impossible, evil and dangerous person. Even she couldn't tolerate him, and I had been right to "divorce" him myself.

Some time after my father's death, in 1994, I began planning to tell my mother about his sexual misdeeds. With my father out of her life, perhaps she was ready to hear what I was ready to tell her. In anticipation of her validation, a sense of peace enshrouded me. There would no longer be anything to fear or lose. It was the right time.

On a rare weekend when Mom came to visit without Phyllis, I asked her to join me in the family room. Sitting rigidly on the edge of my couch, knees pressed tightly together, my quivering hands in my lap and my eyes downcast, I began. "You know, I've been telling you for years that Daddy was abusive to me." She nodded. "That wasn't the only reason I cut him out of my life."

Her quizzical look encouraged me to go on. I gulped a bit more air and tried to keep my voice from shaking, but to no avail. "The real reason is that he sexually abused me," I said.

I'd just told my mother my ultimate secret. All at once the multitude of defenses I'd created throughout my life came flying in.

She sat motionless. Something was processing, and she said, "Are you sure?"

I shuddered. "Yes, Mom, I'm sure."

"When could this have happened?" she asked.

"I don't remember," was the truthful answer. But I could sense her skepticism, and it threatened to annihilate me.

In an effort to catch my fall, I asked her what I'd asked myself. "Do you think he was capable of it?"

She took a moment and said, "I suppose so. But your father said and did a lot of crazy things. If you don't remember, how do you know it happened?"

Before I tumbled into the pit, I salvaged whatever lucidness I had left. "Ma, it was so traumatic, I've blocked it out of my memory."

She sat there stone cold. Her disbelief had triggered my own, and I was in a panic. I wanted to—no, I needed—to get through to her, but all I had were those horrific incidents that had occurred when I was a teenager. I wasn't even sure they amounted to sexual abuse. I went down the list anyway. I started with the time I told my father I was not a virgin and he made the frightening suggestion that he should have been the first man to have sex with me. I told her about the atrocious kiss he planted on me in the basement. And about the afternoon on the hill in South Mountain Reservation when he propositioned Sharon and me to have a ménage à trois with him.

I was no longer in my body. Was I really making these most dire confessions to my mother? A tug-of-war ensued between all the dark forces that had kept those events hidden and the freedom their release promised. Breathless, I raised my eyes to my mother, and before me sat an expressionless woman.

Give her time, I thought.

Finally, she said, "I didn't know."

Of course she didn't know. I'd never told her. There was nothing more for me to say. Even though my body settled back into the sofa cushions, inside I was as pulverized as I'd ever been.

As the dense air began closing in on me, Mom sat deep in thought beside me. And then she said, "So Daddy wanted to have sex with Sharon?"

Was she really asking me that?

Then she said, "I always told you to watch out for her!"

Yes, she had planted that seed about my best friend, and it had poisoned aspects of my relationship with Sharon. But that day it wasn't the point. The point was: She'd leapt past everything I'd just told her. It hadn't reached her that I'd lived through hell, all by myself. She hadn't comprehended what it was like to be prey to a man she knew was capable of it. And she didn't appreciate what it took for me to keep it all inside. It was as if I hadn't said anything. Once again, it was perfectly all right for me to continue carrying the burden as long as she could stay in her narcissistic fantasy world.

At the time, I knew nothing of the mental defense systems I'd created. When the jaws of a vice began compressing my temples and metal started clanking, it was too much for me. I stuffed it all back down, and for the next 16 years it was easier for me to oblige my mother than to face the monsters and demons. On the rare occasions that the subject of sexual abuse came up, she stuck to her story.

So the issue lay dormant, and I continued to shoulder the weight of my father's actions. But now, all these years later, reviewing the wrenching moments when Mom abdicated her maternal responsibilities, I knew I was picking at a crucial knot in the tassel. Searching for the barriers between me and my mother was a flawed exploration. It was the barriers within myself that would lead me to the healing I coveted.

52

PHOTO ALBUMS

Mom died in May of 2020, at the height of the COVID pandemic. Fortunately, she died of natural causes in her apartment. Unfortunately, I was unable to see her before her death.

My feelings about all of it were mixed. I'd followed the clues from the tightness that had never gone away, to the burdens I continued to carry, to the white noise, to the tassel's tangled strands. They had led me directly to my mother, but I still needed proof.

So which mother was I mourning, and what loss was I grieving? Should I have confronted her? Should I have tried harder to speak up for myself? Should I have fought for the bond I so desperately wanted? Had I missed an opportunity for answers while she was alive?

Clearly my search was not over. What was it that I really wanted to know? I was still unsure of where I had fit into her life—then and now. The only evidence I had left was her photo collection. I had another deep sense of "knowing": I'd find the last knot of the tassel there.

Several years after Mom's move to the JCC's Federation Plaza, I started thinking about—no yearning for—a photo album I had loved as a kid. I hadn't seen it in years, nor had I noticed it among all the other albums she kept on the bottom shelf of her coffee table. Whenever I asked her where it might be, she didn't know. Rummaging through her stuff in order to find it was out of the question. I muffled the tiny voice that feared the photos might be gone. That was unthinkable.

Memory: I pull open the drawer of a side table in the living room where my mother keeps a dark brown, leather-bound photo album. With the book pressed to my chest, I walk over to the sofa. I put it down so I can climb onto the cushions. Taking my seat right next to it, I stretch my legs straight out in front of me without crossing my ankles. When I pick up the album, it feels enormous in my little hands. A shiver of excitement passes through me as I set it on my lap and get ready to open it. But before I do, my eyes catch sight of my scuffed black leather Mary Janes and my soiled ankle socks. The last time I'd looked at this album, my heels barely hit the end of the sofa seat. Now my calves hit, and my feet dangle with nothing but air beneath them. I have grown.

There's something printed in gold on the cover, but I can't read the words yet. I like the way the raised letters feel as I run my fingers across them. I stare at the first blank black page, which feels like the construction paper we use at school. With my right hand I lift the bottom corner. The weight of the many photos on the other side make it feel floppy.

The album is full of different sized black-and-white pictures, all arranged neatly and anchored with black corner tabs. I quickly leaf through the first few pages, past the photos of my parents as children before the war. I pause briefly to admire the post-war shots of my beautiful mother, arm in arm with my handsome father.

I rush through my parents' wedding in America in order to get to my birth soon after. There I am, a few months old, professionally photographed in a tiny light-colored dress. In one picture I'm sitting up next to a toy with a suction cup base, and in another I'm lying on my tummy propped up on my elbows. My dark hair is combed with one curl on the top of my head, and my big eyes stare into the distance.

I turn the page to another studio photo. Now I'm one, with a lot more hair and that same baloney curl on the top of my head. Me, in another dress with puffy sleeves holding a black-and-white stuffed animal. Is it a penguin? It's so well-worn it's unrecognizable. I'm smiling, almost laughing, with a bit of my tongue sticking out between my teeth. In other shots I'm very serious. As I view these baby pictures, it's hard to imagine I was ever that small.

I have my favorites, and I seek them out. Me wearing the same dress that I wore in the studio shot when I was one. Perhaps it was taken the same day. I'm standing on a park bench in white leather lace-up shoes. My feet are firmly planted at the same width as my shoulders. My pudgy arms are outstretched, resting on the back of the bench, and the look on my face conveys steadiness and certainty.

Another: My father pushing me in a big pram with the hood up, strutting in his shiny new shoes and his dapper suit, his head tilted to the left as he looks down at me. He appears relaxed, almost serene, as if he's cherishing the precious cargo in the carriage.

My birthday parties fill page after page. They're festive occasions, with lots of kids and parents. I always have on a new crisp dress, and my hair is neatly combed with big bows. All the kids sit on the couch with pointy birthday hats on their heads. The same shot is taken of the parents lined up on the sofa, but there are so many of them some have to sit on the floor. The photos that catch my attention are of me in the kitchen, blowing out the candles on my birthday cakes. I'm surrounded by my friends singing "Happy Birthday;" a huge smile is on my face. My mother always stands nearby in her apron, looking commanding and protective. I gaze up at her.

Newark has a big park where families gather. There are shots of us walking down the sidewalks, standing in front of monuments and playing in the playground. I'm drawn to the one of two-year-old me standing with a line-up of adults but several feet away from them. I'm wearing a plaid jacket with a miniature purse slung across my chest. My brimmed hat has flaps to keep my ears warm. I'm in long dark pants that look too big on me. I see a secure little girl, comfortable being by myself.

By this point the album has started to slip off my lap. I move it so that the spine rests between my legs, and the opened book sits perfectly balanced on my lap. Before me are all the photos from South Mountain Reservation. The page to the left is filled with Mom, Dad and me sleigh-riding on a snow-covered hill. It's a light, fun-filled day. I treasure the one of me sitting on my father's back while he makes believe he's going down the hill on his stomach.

On the opposite page is a series of photos at the reservation's Turtle Back Zoo. Me in my red, hand-knitted sweater with big white snowflakes across my chest. I have a matching hat with a long white tassel. My warm corduroy pants are tucked into my red rubber boots. With my hand stuck through a link in the fence, I'm feeding the deer on the other side. As I peer at this shot, I can feel the deer's gentle lips fluttering on my palm as he eats the snacks we brought.

Of all the pictures, the ones I most prize are from our summer vacations. When I reach them, my back burrows heavily into the sofa, time stops, and I'm transported to those carefree, warm days, under the trees, on lawns and in pools. I always linger on one of the first shots in this grouping: me, around two years old, standing between my parents, holding each of their hands. We're in front of our white Chevrolet and next to the Kessler Hotel sign. I'm so little, and I look adorable in my full-length nightgown with a tiny flower pattern. My mother is clutching a bottle of milk for me, which I will have as soon as I go to bed.

Right next to that photo is another from the same time: My father tenderly holding me in his arms, with one hand around my legs and the other across the front of my body. Me, safe in his embrace. My mother standing on the other side, leaning into me, her fingertips affectionately poised on my father's protective hand.

Perhaps it was the next day when someone snapped another shot of us in Kessler's gigantic pool: Mom in her bathing suit showing off her gorgeous figure, standing next to Dad in tight swim trunks, looking quite fit. They're posing in knee-high water, and I'm on my father's shoulders. He's got a firm grip on my little hands so I won't fall.

After Mom's funeral, my daughters, my husband and I went back to her apartment, and the first thing I looked for was my beloved album. The ten or so that had been stacked underneath the coffee table were there, and I found others in her wall unit. But no shiny brown leather book. The grief from Mom's passing coupled with the possibility of never seeing my album again overcame me. I found the couch, sat down heavily and began to cry. My daughters assured me they'd find it. They disappeared into the bedroom, and I heard, "I think we have it!"

They emerged with a small leather book bound with a brown ribbon. The cover read, "Our Honeymoon," and it had a beautiful hand-painted rose on it. I'd never seen this album before. When I opened it, my mother's dried corsage fell to the floor. Out of curiosity I flipped through the first few pages and promised myself I'd give it a thorough look-through after I found my book. If she saved this one, I thought, she had to have saved mine.

But a second trip and a thorough sweep of closets and drawers turned up nothing. All I found were loose photos piled into shoeboxes and stuffed into envelopes. Hundreds were still in their old-fashioned photo-processing packages. I collected all the albums and photos in bigger boxes that sat in my study for several weeks, until one day I was ready.

I took a seat in the center of the floor and pulled out the first shoebox. I found old photos, some that I'd seen before, others that I hadn't. I even found a few that I recognized from my album. But none of me.

I proceeded to sort through each and every one. They went into stacks, arranged loosely by chronology, location and subject matter. Sprinkled among them were some of my favorites, and they went into a separate pile right in front of my crossed legs.

When I got to the envelopes, I discovered that my mother had deliberately categorized them. Many were labeled in Polish. Maybe she was planning some sort of project, and that's where I'd find the bulk of my childhood photos.

It took days and much sorting to finish. When my stacks were complete, I sat in the middle of them, on my big pink pillow with an ornate flower embroidered into it. I woefully but carefully placed the piles back in their boxes, leaving my special pile in front of me. It was paltry compared to the others; it barely filled a large Ziploc bag. Some of the photos I loved were among them, but where were all the others? Where were all my birthday parties? The ones with my mother standing nearby as I blew out the candles? Where were our outings to Weequaic Park? The only picture of me feeding the deer was out of focus. There was just one photo left of our sleigh rides in South Mountain Reservation, and it wasn't the one I adored. Where were all those pictures?

Some time passed before I could bring myself to view the other albums I'd found. Many were filled with shots from Mom's vacations. But one was different. It was large and heavy. On the first page were three photos of my mother at different ages. In the lower lefthand corner she'd written, in all caps: "THREE STAGES OF IRENE." Hope returned.

All the subsequent pages were meticulously laid out and lovingly labeled with handwritten captions. Below beautiful black-and-white and sepia shots she wrote: "MY PARENTS AND I (ON SKATES)," "ON VACATION IN KRYNICA," "AT A FAIR," "IN FRONT OF THE FIRST STORE," "NEIGHBORS' WEDDING." Lots of group photos identifying cousins, aunts, uncles and friends. I was especially touched by all the shots of her father and the way she referred to him: "MY DADDY," or "DADDY WITH FRIENDS."

When I was a little girl, whenever Mom and I looked through my special album, she'd stop at one particular shot. In it, she was around nine years old, dressed all in white, sitting on a donkey. She'd tell me, "When my father and I looked at this photo together, he loved to say, 'A little ass on a big ass.'" And now here it was, five pages in, with his humorous quote in all caps handwritten underneath.

While scrolling through the pages of the book, I came upon a spread of only two pictures. The first was of Mom and her father. The caption read, "LAST PICTURE WITH MY FATHER." In the other she was in a large group of young people. Above the shot she wrote, "1939," and below, in two lines: "SUMMER CAMP" and "LAST PICTURE BEFORE THE WAR." My mother rarely spoke about the war. These shots and her inscriptions were heartbreaking. The way she wrote the word "LAST" screamed of the pain she must have been feeling as she adhered these pictures in their places.

I had more than half of the book to go through; there was still a chance that my dear shots were a page away. But when I flipped to the next spread, it was empty, and so was the remainder of the book. As I sadly laid the back cover over the last blank page, I marked the moment as the end of my quest for my precious album. It was gone forever.

What I'd found instead was my mother's attempt to curate an archive of her life. She must have deconstructed my album. And considering how many of my photos were missing, it seemed unlikely that she was planning to include me in her chronicle. She had not collected and carefully protected my photos for future placement. She was not going to lovingly arrange my pictures and handwrite endearing captions underneath them. No, they were scattered, damaged and forgotten.

I thought about the thousands of photos I had of my own daughters and how sacred they were to me. There would be no documentation of my life without them. And perhaps if I had felt love from my mother in other ways, the loss of my pictures would have been inconsequential. But they were the only tangible link I had to my past, and their disappearance felt monumental.

My special album had been a staple throughout my childhood. It was a hub around which my young life had turned. I sought it out regularly, and I poured over its photos out of a deep need. When the chaos and confusion of my actual life overwhelmed me, those pictures told me a different story. I saw a little girl who belonged to a normal, happy and loving family. I remember staring at certain pictures, incredulous that I was cute—not ugly, fat or miserable. The album glued me back together when I felt ripped to shreds. It was the gravity that pulled me back to a reality that told me I existed.

The absence of my album symbolized and confirmed for me that I had indeed been missing from my mother's life.

53

I DIDN'T MISS YOU

Memory: I've just turned 30, and I'm in my studio apartment on 23rd Street. My mother has recently returned from one of her many vacations, and I'm waiting for her to call. When my wall phone rings, I pick up the receiver, greet her and stretch the long coiled wire so I can sit at my butcher block table.

"How was your trip?" I ask.

I listen as she gushes about the beautiful hotels, the fascinating sights and the wonderful time she had with her travel-mates. All the male tour guides "liked" her, and the female guides became her "friends." As she describes all the iconic landmarks, I drift off into my own reverie. I've never seen these places other than in books or on TV.

When she finally pauses, I say, "I missed you!"

Her immediate response: "I didn't miss you." It's not followed by a chuckle or a "just joking." It lands like the elephant that it is, and I instantly convince myself that she did not utter those words.

I was still reeling from the loss of my treasured book, but I was ready to review the hundreds and hundreds of pictures my mother had saved from her vacations. It did not escape me that, unlike my childhood photos, these were organized in boxes, and she'd thoughtfully arranged many into albums. I began flipping through the pages of the first album. She had dated and labeled every sheet, again handwritten in all caps. "SAN JUAN PUERTO RICO 1974:" picture after picture of Mom with Phyllis and my grandmother. "PARADISE BEACH HOTEL BARBADOS:" Mom sitting on the ledge of a balcony with palm trees and the ocean in the background. "OUR BEACH:" Mom, one foot strategically placed in front of the other, her hands clasped behind her back, wearing my pink and white bikini. On the next page she's at "SAM LORDE CASTLE," wearing my polka-dot dress. I don't recall her asking me if she could borrow either of these garments.

Onto "CALIFORNIA, 1976." My mother with Phyllis, their friend Iris and her daughter hitting the hot spots: "UNIVERSAL CITY," "DISNEYLAND," "GRAUMAN'S CHINESE THEATRE," "SAN SIMEON, HEARST CASTLE."

"SPAIN," "ITALY," "ENGLAND," "SWITZERLAND," "HAWAII," "ISRAEL." With Wanda and Sue, with Aunt Roslyn, with other people I didn't know.

Before each vacation I'd tease her, "Now where are you going?"

After each trip, Mom would visit me and pull out the envelopes of her newly processed photos. While I obediently viewed them and listened to her rhapsodic tales, undercurrent rumblings and bitterness stirred. At the time I had no idea where these feeling were coming from.

Now here I was, nearly five decades later, sitting on the floor of my study, looking at the same pictures and feeling equally as frazzled. But I was different. I had gained an understanding that the enigmatic forces within me were there to protect me. So rather than turn away from the activity, I welcomed it. The endless shots of Mom being happy, effervescent and silly, arm in arm with fellow travelers and total strangers, made me jealous. I would have given anything to be one of her companions. Why wasn't she cavorting with me? Why wasn't I sharing those joyful moments with her? Why, in her 40 years of traveling, had she never once invited me?

Although symbolic, the absence of my photo album, Mom's curation of her own childhood, her seeming disinterest in mine and the story told by her travel photos felt like the final knot in the tassel. The mother that I was realizing I'd had and the one I was coming to terms with would definitely have wanted to filter out any adverse chapters in her narrative. There was only one way for me to interpret my absence. And with that came the answer to the nagging question of where I fit into her life. I didn't.

"I didn't miss you," the words that she'd uttered all those years ago, returned as prickly and raw as the day she'd said them. There was a reason they had reverberated for weeks, months and years. Back then I told myself she hadn't meant them. Now I knew she had.

Some of the recovered pictures
from my beloved photo album

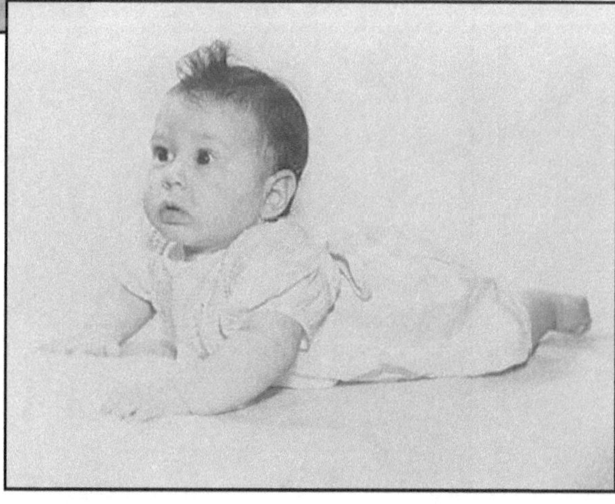

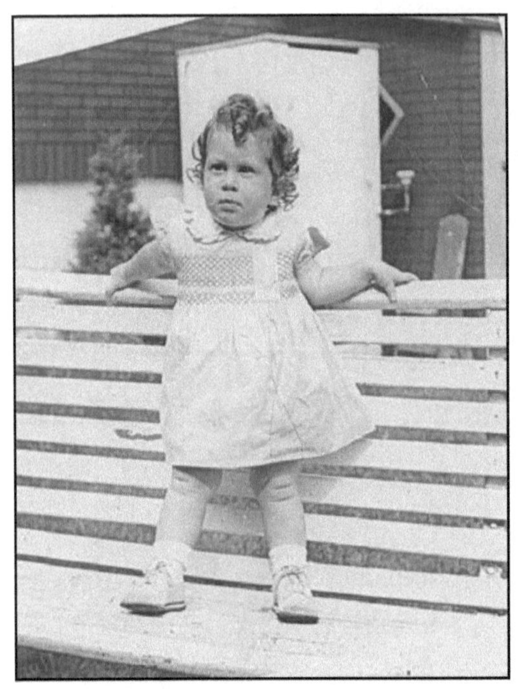

54
KNOWING

I didn't know then but I do know now: I stand firmly planted on my path. My eyes, my heart, my solar plexus and my feet are fully turned to face my past, my real childhood. Through a clear lens I can see that both my parents were damaged people who had their own demons. I wish I could justify that the burdens they bore were responsible for their misdeeds. And perhaps they were. But I cannot forgive the impact on me: From the day I was born, I twisted, negated, dismembered and censured myself to accommodate their needs. And what they needed was for me to be inferior, defenseless, discredited and invisible.

As a result, I lived seven decades with the pervasive undercurrent that I was flawed and defective. It was an invisible foe, constantly humming in the background. I was crippled by doubt. I woke up with it and went to sleep with it almost daily. A cloud of doom cloaked my every move. It checked and blocked me at each turn. It stopped me and it scared me.

What I see now—what I had never imagined—is that my mother was the true source of it all. It was her absence that permitted Phyllis to torment me and my father to abuse me. Her silence erased any tracks left by the perpetrators. And her complicity kept the abusive cycle spinning. What I see now is that my mother was the cog of that wheel.

Her unyielding disavowal of my experience wrapped a permanent seal around my memories. Her indifference sentenced me to suffer alone. Her invalidation caused me to dismiss and devalue big swaths of my life. Her denial of everything that happened to me was the seed of my own denial, which is the epitome of self-betrayal. Neutralizing or normalizing trauma does not make it go away. It lives and breathes behind everything. It alters reality, which is the most formidable impairment of all.

As my story has come into focus, so has another undertow: a deep and aching sense of loss. So much was stolen from me. Looking back, I can see that my competence, my confidence—even my speech—had been exiled, my innate creative expression locked in a vault. Anything that managed to leak out had squeezed through a pinhole.

I've often wondered how different my life would have been had I had the full love and support of my parents. Then I'm reminded of what I accomplished in spite of it. And I ask myself: How did that happen? It's taken me 74 years to grasp that I've been blessed with an indomitable spirit that functioned as a separate enterprise—it clinked and clanged, day and night, in order to keep me operational.

That spirit is responsible for the fact that I am entirely self-taught, which is a recent revelation. I've always felt undereducated, inadequate and inferior to those who were more academically skilled than I. Had I had an inkling of how pernicious my upbringing was, I would have valued my tenaciousness. Now, in hindsight and with clarity, I'm awed by the seven-year-old girl who copied the pirate on the matchbook. By the high-schooler who practiced day after day to learn how to dance to a different beat and to master cheerleading. It was I who ultimately taught *myself how to drive a stick shift. My entrepreneurial aspirations led me to start my own businesses in graphic design, Pilates and equestrian supplies. Thirty years ago I jumped in without any formal training and began teaching yoga. I turned a part-time endeavor into my own yoga studio, which has endured for the past two decades.*

What I didn't know, most of my life, but I do know now is that my soul, my essence, depends on my ability to create. In my early 40s I became a stay-at-home mom. The conditions were right for me to teach myself to paint in oils. When my youngest daughter entered elementary school, I found a studio space on the second floor of a one-car-garage-size building on a main street in town. This was my dream—but it was complicated. I was a representational artist—I relished painting what I saw—yet my passion for realism felt like a willful act of defiance against my father, and I paid a price. I could not override his pervasive condemnations, still vivid from my childhood. I remember standing at my easel with my father's excoriating words ringing in my ears as though he were in the studio with me. When I look at those paintings now, I liken each tortured brushstroke to a cut into my flesh.

In spite of that, I persevered. When a space downstairs became available, I turned it into an art gallery. The Celia Hirsch Gallery opened its doors with an exhibition of those oil paintings, and it practically sold out. Concurrently, I'd resumed classes in figure drawing, which I did on a large scale with handmade pastels, using Mr. Novack's technique from my days at UB. That was my second show, and it, too, was a success. What played out in the confines of that tiny building encapsulates the pure power of my spirit.

I'll never know why my parents lived as they did or why they treated me so badly. But now, finally, I understand that it had nothing to do with me. I've been softened by that notion, and different air has entered my lungs. The tightness and disharmony I carried within me has thawed. The accusatory voices have been silenced. With all the strands untangled, the tassel swings freely, and its binding suppression has disappeared. White noise does not sweep in because I know the truth. And the bond with my mother that I so desperately longed for, the bond that put me on this path, turned out to be the bond I've found with myself.

EPILOGUE

"How excited are you?" my husband asked when I picked up the
first hardcopy manuscript of this book. Holding it in my hand felt surreal. I had written a book, with a beginning, a middle and an end. Excited did not sum it up. For the first few days I couldn't find the right
word. Finally it struck me that what I was feeling, or, more accurately,
what I was doing, was assimilating and integrating a whole new account of my life.

When trying to articulate what has happened since then, it comes
in clichés: Dots have been connected, puzzle pieces have found their
places, holes have been filled, and there are no more dangling wires
concerning my childhood.

What lingers are questions about my mother's and father's real
childhoods. I have to assume that my mother's dire need to paint her
life with such a rosy brush was to mask what she could not face. Since
clearing away my own fog, I recall looking through my special album
with my mother and seeing many photographs of my grandfather with
another woman by his side. When I was old enough to notice it as an

oddity, I asked my mother who the woman was. "Oh, that's my father's mistress!" She even knew her name. Then she told me that when he fled the Nazis, he took her to Russia with him, which is where he perished. All of this was delivered with such complacency that I paid it no mind. "Daddy was a great father, but he was a lousy husband," is how she tied up that package. I guess my grandfather was not as perfect as my mother made him out to be.

The data regarding my father's childhood experience is sparse. Here is what I know.

He was the second of three sons, the middle child. He described himself as a troublemaker who was always being punished He'd brag about doing poorly in school. At the same time he boasted about being such a good-looking child that people would stop him on the street.

Information about his family dynamics was equally lacking. Tzilah, my paternal grandmother, was the dominant parent, a strong woman who was a talented milliner and the sole provider for the household. Abraham, my paternal grandfather, did not work. The impression I was left with was that he was ineffectual—essentially a failure. According to my dad, his older brother, Joseph, was a child prodigy in music and art; my mother claimed that she knew about him before the war. My father exhibited no ambivalence when declaring that Joseph was the favored child. I think it was my mother who divulged that my grandmother was abusive to my father. If that were true, perhaps it is the origin of my father's mistreatment of me.

My father's losses during the war were great. Not only did he suffer his own horrors, but three members of his family were murdered. I never saw him display an ounce of emotion when speaking of losing his parents. The only grief I witnessed was for his baby brother. And his assessments of his surviving sibling, Joseph, confused me.

After the war, Joseph and his wife migrated to Israel, where they were raising their two daughters. From the bits and pieces I was able to pick up, my father wanted nothing to do with his brother. He refused to correspond with him and showed no interest in either inviting him to America or going to visit him in his chosen country. "They are poor in Israel, and they think that because we're in America, we are rich," he explained. I don't know if Joseph and his family actually thought that, but my father did. It was my mother who communicated with them and sent them care packages because, she'd say, "Life in Israel is difficult." It never made any sense to me.

Upon reflection, I see that my father's animosity toward his brother colored my own feelings. I've always had a total lack of curiosity regarding my ancestry, and as a result, I never got to know my closest family members.

My connection to extended family ended up in the same dissociated bucket as all the other traumatic losses. I viewed my disinterest as another example of how flawed I was. I know now that the fear that had stopped me from asking my parents questions would not stop me today.

It needs to be noted that since I wrote this book I have connected with my cousins from Israel. Through a series of miraculous events I now know that most of what I was told by my parents is not true.

Well into the writing of this book, my beloved Sharon passed away. It is the saddest and most poignant part of my story. Ours was the most genuine and fulfilling friendship of my life. She was my sister, my kindred spirit and my champion. Without her on my shoulder, I would not have been able to complete this book.

Sharon and I, on occasion, did speak about our abusive parents— her mother, my father. But we never spoke of that incident in South

Mountain Reservation. I've often wondered if she eventually did yield to my father's amorous overtures and if that had anything to do with her early demise.

Over the years I took it for granted that we had it all in perspective. I never doubted that we would grow old together. But partway into our fifth decade, I started to notice changes in Sharon. Whenever I asked, she denied that anything was wrong. It took her ten years until, in 2012, she admitted that she'd been diagnosed with multiple sclerosis. I knew several people with the same illness, and they were able to manage it. I assumed Sharon would as well. However, she began a slow decline and was gone by January 2023, at the age of 72.

As it turned out, Sharon kept other secrets from me. From her oldest daughter I was to learn many things. I knew she'd sought out psychiatric help before I did, but I was unaware of the depth of her depression. It began before her first pregnancy and apparently only grew worse as time went on.

But the most shocking and devastating disclosure was that Sharon had tried to take her own life multiple times. No matter how overwhelmed I've gotten by my own dark forces, I could never have seriously entertained suicide. The more I've pondered Sharon's pain, her isolation and despondence, the more I understand that her life experience was no different from mine. And I wonder why I survived and she did not. I'm sure there are many explanations, but my question is: If Sharon had understood that her father was as much of an enabler as my mother, would she still be alive? Or would that have been too much for her to bear, as it almost was for me? In Sharon's case, what remained hidden became lethal.

Lastly, the matter of abuse is still unresolved. As with so much in my life, the topic was never discussed. Even though as a society we talk about it more freely, and there is far greater awareness about it, for me a lot is ambiguous. What line has to be crossed in order for a behavior or comment to count as abuse? And the criteria for sexual abuse are even vaguer. In my case, where do a lifetime of sexualization, inappropriate verbal sexual assaults and my father's three clear sexual advances toward me fall on the spectrum? I know that my father did not rape me, but what do I do with the strong sense that he molested me while I slept? Are those visceral memories trustworthy? And because I don't "remember" them, does that diminish what I do know happened?

I believe the answers lie in the fallout that impacted the quality of my life. In addition to the pervasive sense that something was wrong, I always felt that my creative dreams were unfulfilled. Each endeavor fell short of what I knew was my potential. Dissociation along with the judgmental voices interrupted and stole my confidence and, therefore, my incentive. Each project was aborted in order to escape the assaults.

In the course of writing this memoir, I was threatened with the same disruption. I could not let that happen. I had to search for and find a new form of courage. My perseverance resulted in a true breakthrough, and I ultimately superseded the blocks that have stood in my way. The monumental feat of finishing this book represents a final slaying of those dragons.